9.95

MW01269267

Property,
Profits,
and
Economic Justice

•

Virginia Held
City University of New York

Wadsworth Publishing Company
Belmont, California
A Division of Wadsworth, Inc.

"Get off this estate."
"What for?"
"Because it's mine."
"Where did you get it?"
"From my father."
"Where did he get it?"
"From his father."
"And where did he get it?"
"He fought for it."
"Well, I'll fight you for it."
—Carl Sandburg*

*From *The People, Yes* by Carl Sandburg, copyright 1936 by Harcourt Brace Jovanovich, Inc.; copyright 1964 by Carl Sandburg. Reprinted by permission of the publisher.

Philosophy Editor: Kenneth King
Production Editor: Brian K. Williams
Copy Editor: Suzanne Pfeiffer Williams
Cover: Robert Bausch

Printed in the United States of America   2 3 4 5 6 7 8 9 10—84 83 82 81

Library of Congress Cataloging in Publication Data
Main entry under title:

Held, Virginia
    Property, profits, and economic justice.

    Bibliography: p.
        1. Property—Addresses, essays, lectures.
    2. Profit—Addresses, essays, lectures.   3. Distributive justice—Addresses, essays, lectures.   I. Held, Virginia.
    HB701.P755   330.1   79–25056
    ISBN 0-534-00819-4

Contents

3 Economic Justice   177

Should the state redistribute wealth and income? What would economic justice require? What economic rights should citizens in a democracy have?

Appendix   231

Suggestions for Further Reading

Preface

This collection of readings is designed for students of business, economics, and philosophy, and for the general reader. I try to present in one brief volume some of the most important questions about how a society ought to arrange its economic affairs and about the appropriate goals of economic activity. The book considers our rights and interests in acquiring and holding property and in increasing or limiting profits; it explores some basic and urgent issues concerning economic justice.

I am indebted for some initial suggestions on readings in the area of political economy to Alexander Erlich and Sidney Morgenbesser of Columbia University. I am grateful to the members of the Graduate School Colloquium in Philosophy, Politics, and Economics of the City University of New York for their comments on an earlier version of my introduction; to Robert Heilbroner, James Nickel, and especially Richard Wasserstrom for comments and suggestions on a later version; and to Carol Gould and Suzanne and Brian Williams for advice at a final stage.

I first began to gather these readings while teaching a course called "Capitalism, Socialism, and Morality" at the Graduate School of CUNY in 1977, and I became aware of the pressing need for a collection such as this when I planned to teach an undergraduate course along similar lines. I thank my students in that graduate course for their enthusiasm and their arguments, and among them especially Joel Goldstein and Elaine Weber for further research and editorial assistance. Kenneth King of Wadsworth has been a considerate editor. My daughter Julia has generously helped with proofreading.

Finally, my son Philip's interest in spending money has contributed to my eagerness to complete this book and to exchange the unpaid leave during which I worked on it for the rewards of teaching.

1

Introduction
●
Virginia Held

I

The image that is evoked by the word 'property' is apt to be a physical object: a car, a house, a plot of ground, a Ping-Pong paddle. The image is misleading, for as soon as one begins to look into the meaning of the word, it is apparent that property is not a set of things but a set of rights and interests.

Most writers on property have recognized it as a set of rights. In the seventeenth century, John Locke defined 'property' so widely as to mean by it rights to "life, liberty, and estate." Most usage since has narrowed the meaning of the term to what Locke meant by 'estate.' Standard interpretations see property as consisting of rights to possess, use, manage, dispose of, and keep others away from things.[1]

Property is also a set of interests, for if the things we own become worthless we no longer have property. A person who owns a car has an interest in its resale price. A person who owns a house has an interest in having the value of the property increase, though he or she may have no right to have its value thus increase.

Property rights and interests often give us rights and interests in relation to physical objects. But many property rights and interests, especially in developed societies, are more complicated. We have rights to pay our debts with the balances in our accounts and interests that the paper they represent not be devalued. We have rights to the dividends that our shares in a corporation accord and interests in the corporation paying as high a dividend as possible. We have rights to a pension from the plan we have joined and interests in the plan not going bankrupt. We have rights to unemployment insurance when we lose our jobs or rights to a license to practice a profession if we meet the qualifications, and we have interests in increasing our wages or sales and interests in having the kind of economic system within which we can make economic gains. These rights and interests are aspects of property.

[1] For an account of these rights, see especially A. M. Honoré, "Ownership," in *Oxford Essays in Jurisprudence*, ed. A. G. Guest (Oxford: Clarendon Press, 1961), pp. 107–147.

In advanced economies, with governments that seek to curb the deficiencies and abuses of the economic systems with which they are joined, property is increasingly composed of what Charles Reich calls government "largesse" (see pp. 46–59). This may, however, be a misnomer, since, as Reich acknowledges, *all* property has always been, in a sense, government largesse. It is law that allows a given physical object to be legally acquired or owned by one person and not another, and it is the police and other protection that government provides which allows those who have what the law designates as property to hold on to it or get more of it. It is the social stability and order that government makes possible which allows economic activity to flourish when it does and economic interests to be served or thwarted. But the misconception that new forms of property depend on government, while traditional forms do not, persists (see pp. 6, 57, and 157).

Also misleading is the traditional division between the public and the private, between the political and the economic, between "sovereignty" and "property." The myth beneath the division is that political power coerces us but that economic power does not. As Morris Cohen made clear in exploring this contrast, property is power compelling service and obedience, as is political sovereignty (see pp. 39–45). We can be restricted by an employer we cannot defy as we can be restricted by a government official we cannot ignore; we can be forced to do what we do not wish to do by the demands of a landlord for payment as we can be forced by the nightstick of that landlord's protector. And because we can be compelled by economic necessity as well as by threats of legal penalties, we can demand for citizens of states with morally justifiable social arrangements that, where the economic development of the society is sufficient to do so, all citizens have the right to enough economic sustenance to allow them the liberty we deem a fundamental right.

For property to achieve its traditional purpose—to guard the citizen's freedom against the tyranny with which concentrations of power may threaten him—property must include guarantees that each citizen can acquire the necessities of life, and not only protection in holding on to existing possessions (see especially pp. 58 and 59). Such rights of citizens to a measure of economic self-sufficiency should be secured against governments and the wielders of economic power, just as the rights of citizens to a fair trial or to free speech are assured against both.

A society that fails to provide ways for persons to acquire food, shelter, and so on, through honest employment or payments to which they are entitled may force them into a surrender of their liberty unworthy of citizens in a free and decent society. Contemporary advocates of economic freedom could more persuasively represent the tradition of Western liberalism if they recognized the facts of economic coercion in industrial society more adequately than they often do.

We must distinguish between, on the one hand, rights to have or do something and, on the other, rights to merely try to have or do something. An often used example is that of two persons who see a ten-dollar bill on the street between them. Both have rights to try to be the first to pick it up—they have no obligations not to. Neither has rights to *have* the bill (before they win the contest to be first), though they have rights not to be prevented from trying. This situation exemplifies many situations of economic competition. Some writers on rights suggest that rights to try to do or have things should be called 'liberties' rather than 'rights,'[2] but if we keep in mind what rights are rights *to*, we can continue to use the term for both kinds. Even the most conservative champions of property rights will agree that the poor and the unemployed should have rights to *try* to obtain what they need to live. The issues in dispute will be whether they should have legal rights not merely to try to have but actually to possess food, shelter, employment, and so on.

As soon as we understand that property is a set of rights and interests, we can consider questions about whether those rights and interests composing a given or proposed system of property are morally justified. What a society decides to make into legal rights and its policy decisions concerning interests may or may not reflect what morality requires. As A. M. Honoré makes clear, we could come to a moral view that would specify a very different set of legal property rights than those familiar to us (see pp. 84–92). We might hold, for instance, that people have rights to use property, but not to dispose of it as they please. Or we might build into our scheme of property rights a moral requirement that people share their surplus property with those in need. We might think people hold property "in trust" for everyone in the society.

A separate but fundamental question is whether property can "exist" without government or law. If there are moral rights to property, we might assert that property claims can be valid even if none of the mechanisms of enforcement which a legal system provides are available. If we could establish what moral rights to property we have, we then could ask that our laws reflect and uphold these rights. And if we could establish what property interests of ours are morally justifiable, we could ask for political and economic institutions that would promote these interests.

Some writers assert that in the absence of an enforceable system of law to make moral rights into legal rights, no such rights really exist.[3] In other words, rights that are "merely" moral rights—or, as certain of them may be called, "human rights," or, as some of them have been known in a large segment of traditional political philosophy, "natural rights"—are not really *rights* at all.

If, however, we explore the issues surrounding this controversy, we may come to hold that rights can exist independently of whether they are enforced. Because we can assert claims about rights we can argue about what legal systems ought to do even when they are not doing it. It is not a necessary feature of our concept of "a right" that force *is* used to uphold it, nor, as will be seen below, is it even a necessary feature of all rights that force *ought* to be used to uphold them. But let us consider further what rights are.

Although there is no clear consensus of what rights are, I shall take the position that rights are central or stringent entitlements yielded by justifiable rules

[2] See especially Wesley Hohfeld, *Fundamental Legal Conceptions as Applied to Judicial Reasoning* (New Haven, Conn.: Yale University Press, 1919 and 1964), and H. L. A. Hart, "Are There Any Natural Rights?" *The Philosophical Review* 64 (1955):175–91.

[3] An outstanding example of this view is pressed by Jeremy Bentham in *Anarchical Fallacies*, thought to be written about 1791.

or principles. The rights of one person impose obligations on other persons, as the right of a person not to be assaulted imposes obligations on other persons not to assault that person. The obligations that rights impose may be both obligations not to interfere and obligations to enable, as when the right of a child to live imposes obligations on others to provide the child with food and shelter. In some circumstances we respect the rights of persons by leaving them alone, in other circumstances by assisting them. Part of what we mean by a right is that it ought to be respected for its own sake and need not be defended by an estimate of its consequences. For instance, a right to equal opportunities for employment ought to be respected whether or not this contributes to feelings of satisfaction. The major grounds on which claims to rights can be asserted are those of freedom, justice, equality, and dignity. Moral rights are yielded by moral principles or rules, legal rights by legal rules or principles.[4]

Rights are not absolute, whether they are moral rights or legal rights. *Prima facie* rights, or what appear to be rights "at first sight," may have to yield to other rights with greater stringency. When rights conflict, we need additional principles or rules to determine priorities between rights, as when we might hold that in a conflict between a person's right to have a promise made to him kept and another person's right not to be killed, the latter would generally have priority. Thus, we would decide that we ought not to cause the likely death of a bedridden occupant of a house in wintertime, even though we have promised our employer to shut off the heat by noon. We can adopt principles that will always give some rights high priority—our rights to life and liberty, for instance. But even these are not absolute, and their interpretation will require the working out of meanings and priorities and the specification of aspects and requirements.

Rights should be respected for their own sake, because they are yielded by valid principles; they need no further justification. We ought to respect the rights of persons to be free in specifiable ways not because of some further use to which we think they will put this freedom, such as to produce more industrial products or to bring about pleasurable feelings, but just because, as human beings, they are entitled to freedom within such limits as are required to respect the freedom and rights of others. Again, we have a moral right to have another person tell us the truth just because it is the truth, not because of some further benefit this may bring about, such as that telling the truth will make us, or the other person, or both of us, happy. Rights should be respected in themselves, on grounds of the moral principles or rules that yield them, which we can also accept because they are valid in themselves; we need not argue that rights are useful for some further interest. An appeal to consequences, to the effects of such rights, is out of place.

We can understand this as an aspect of what we mean by the concept "rights" and also as an aspect of the moral theories we find acceptable. A utilitarian

[4]For further discussion of the concept of a right, see Ronald Dworkin, *Taking Rights Seriously* (Cambridge, Mass.: Harvard University Press, 1977); Rex Martin and James W. Nickel, "Recent Work on the Concept of Rights," *American Philosophical Quarterly*, in press; Joel Feinberg, *Social Philosophy* (Englewood Cliffs, N.J.: Prentice-Hall, 1973); and John Plamenatz, "Rights," *Aristotelian Society Supplementary Volume* 24 (1950).

moral theory, limited as it is to judging moral issues exclusively in terms of consequences, is thus, in my view and in that of many moral theorists, inherently unable to provide an adequate interpretation of rights, though it may be quite appropriate for moral decisions concerning interests. Utilitarians characteristically interpret rights as protections of certain central or especially important interests. Reasons to reject this interpretation are considered below (see pp. 6–8).

That force may justifiably be used to uphold a right has often been thought to be part of the meaning of "rights"; this is the view of H. L. A. Hart.[5] But there are strong reasons to consider it a separate question.[6] We might hold, for instance, that we have moral rights to have our friends tell us the truth in our private conversations, but we would not thereby maintain that such a right ought to be turned into an enforceable legal right. That such a right is not and should not be enforceable does not imply that it is not a moral *right*.

I shall take it as given, then, that we do have moral rights; the question to get back to is whether, among our moral rights, we have rights to property. A very significant range of moral rights ought to be spelled out and assured by a legal system that requires and brings about actual compliance with its rules. Our moral rights not to be assaulted or killed and our moral rights to speak freely are of this kind. If we can establish that we have moral rights to acquire and hold property, we can ask of a legal system that it enforce compliance with rules upholding these rights as well.

What are the grounds for moral rights to property? One answer, developed by Locke, is that we are morally entitled to the products of our labor (see pp. 22–38). Locke and others have argued that when we mix our labor with the natural world we are entitled to the resulting product. For instance, we may have the fish we bring in from the sea which belong to no one; or we may have the fruit we gather from the forest, which belongs to everyone in common. But Locke added the important proviso that when a resource was not in unlimited supply we should take only as much as would leave "enough and as good for others." He also argued that to take more of a limited natural resource than one needs and can put to good use is contrary to the requirements of morality.

Locke's assumptions concerning the justifiable acquisition of property are, however, seldom plausible in the contemporary world. The unowned wilderness waiting to be appropriated, so central to Locke's argument, no longer exists. Rarely do we simply mix our labor with nature. Nearly always we mix our labor with an economic system, an industrial economy, and it makes little sense to think of the result as the outcome of *our* labor. A person's labor cannot be distinguished from

[5] Hart, "Natural Rights."

[6] See David Lyons, ed., *Rights* (Belmont, Calif.: Wadsworth Publishing Company, 1979).

[7] Locke maneuvered around his own suggested principles by holding that the introduction of money changed the applicability of the principles: since money does not "spoil," a person who has more of it than he needs is not "wasting" it. Locke argued as well that the bequeathing of property from fathers to sons could lead to acceptable accumulations far beyond what a person needed or could make good use of. But Locke's principles, if they would be applicable, were more persuasive than his evasions of them.

the other labor it is mixed with in producing a product or contributing to production. Furthermore, the service sector of the economy does not fit the depiction, nor does the labor involved in raising the next generation of workers.

An even more serious difficulty with this attempt to justify moral rights to property is that the Lockean proviso, in the contemporary world of overpopulation and scarce resources, can almost never be met. Instead, more property for some will almost always result in less for others. The problem, as Lawrence Becker indicates, is even more troublesome if the loss of a position of equality relative to others counts as a "loss," as some persons move ahead and accumulate more property and some thus fall relatively behind (see pp. 60–83). In a developed economy, the argument from "I made it" to "It's mine" thus loses almost all the plausibility it may have had for an imagined Lockean man husbanding sheep on the commons or an imagined American pioneer putting uninhabited territory to the plow. The argument is defective for more reasons than that it ignores advances in agribusiness and overlooks the American Indians.

We can still ask, "What am I entitled to as a result of my labor?" But the answer should now depend on moral justifications for using, managing, disposing of, keeping others away from, and having access to things. It should not depend on the illusion that a self-sufficient man creates a product from an inexhaustible supply in such a way that a pure gain for him brings no loss to anyone else, or on the illusion that all persons have an equal chance to be creators of products to which they are entitled.

Lawrence Becker suggests a complex formulation of what can be justifiably asserted as a moral principle giving those who labor rewards for their labor under certain conditions (see p. 81). The question of what economic rights ought to be recognized by the law will be discussed further in the last section. It should be remembered, however, that whatever scheme of property rights a society has, it is a scheme the society has adopted and could decide to change. As John Stuart Mill put it clearly:

> Even what a person has produced by his individual toil, unaided by anyone, he cannot keep, unless by permission of society. Not only can society take it from him, but individuals could and would take it from him, if society only remained passive; if it didn't interfere en masse, or employ and pay people for the purpose of preventing him from being disturbed in the possession.[8]

II

Let us turn now to a further consideration of property interests, since property includes both rights and interests. Rights and interests are not the same. We may have rights to do things that are contrary to our interests, such as a right to

[8] John Stuart Mill, *Principles of Political Economy*, bk. II, chap. 1.

make a bet that we will surely lose, and we may have interests in things to which we have no right, such as that the price of the gold we hold will skyrocket. We may even have rights to what will never be in our interests, such as to give away all our assets or to endanger ourselves in useless ways.

In my view, which not all philosophers share, rights and interests are so significantly different that they belong to distinct domains of morality and should be judged on different grounds.[9] The claim of Charles Fried that "there is an interest behind every right"[10] seems mistaken, since we may have rights to do what will be harmful to our interests, in both the short and the long run.

Interests, in contrast to rights, need not necessarily be respected for their own sake but are usually to be judged in terms of the further consequences of pursuing them. Interests are needs or desires or claims for some state of affairs to be effected, which state of affairs may be good in itself. We may have an interest in health for the sake of health, but our interests in all those things we desire for the sake of health will be judged in terms of whether they actually are conducive to health or not. Justifiable interests are what would be good for us in the long run if we were fully enlightened. They are what we would want if we were fully informed and wanted what would be good for us.

Rights are entitlements to something we can either do or have or not do or not have done to us. Interests, in contrast, are matters of more and less. The relevant questions will concern the degree of a person's interest, or how much one interest is greater than another.

When interests conflict, as they often do, for any given individual—and especially between individuals, and between individuals and groups, and between groups—we can seek moral solutions. The solution should be in terms of maximizing something judged to be good: utility, happiness, efficiency, satisfaction. This is different from respecting rights; rights are not subject to maximizing. We cannot speak of a right to vote more for a candidate or less for a candidate, but our interests in his victory will be greater or less. If we have a right to equal education, we do not have a right to an education that is more equal, but to an education that is equal, though what this implies requires interpretation. We may have interests in more and more education, or in more equal education. We often have interests in having moral rights—to nondiscriminatory treatment, say—recognized as legal rights when this is not yet the case. Or, if we are unfairly privileged, we may have interests in preventing some of the moral rights of others from becoming legal rights, though these interests are morally unjustifiable.

The most plausible moral grounds on which to base judgments about interests are those that promote the greatest good to be brought about by any given decision or arrangement. In the case of property interests, questions of who made the product, how hard it was to hire the workers, or whether a certain risk was taken might be relevant, but would not be decisive. The decisive questions would be whether furthering the property interests of entrepreneurs in a certain way

---

[9]See Virginia Held, "Justification: Legal and Political," *Ethics* 86, no. 1 (October 1975):1–16.

[10]Charles Fried, *Right and Wrong* (Cambridge, Mass.: Harvard University Press, 1978), p. 85. The interests are those of the person having the right.

would have better consequences in terms of efficiency, growth, or pollution than not doing so; whether paying workers one wage or another would lead to greater happiness or to greater discontent for more persons; whether changing from a labor-intensive to a more mechanized form of production would increase general satisfaction through increased productivity or decrease general satisfaction by increasing unemployment; and so on.

Various interests can be protected as legal rights in any given legal system. But we must judge interests on moral grounds to decide which interests should be protected in which ways and to what extent by legal rights. Legal rights of this kind are then *merely* legal rights, not moral rights reflected in law. They can, where moral rights cannot, appropriately be changed to promote maximization of interests. Moral rights should be upheld even *against* considerations of the general interest—in Ronald Dworkin's phrase, rights "trump" such interests. But rights that are merely legal rather than both legal and moral need not do so.

Some of the most important questions about property interests have to do with accumulating property. What should we say about using property to create more property? What should we think about the role and justifiability of holding capital and making profits? Is it morally legitimate for an individual or a firm to try to *maximize* profits?

The eighteenth century philosopher Adam Smith argued that, in the area of economic activity, each person pursuing his own individual interests produces, without even intending it, the greatest good for all (pp. 94–113). To Adam Smith, acquisitiveness has a better outcome than generosity. Thus, the farmer, acting in his own interest, works harder and produces more than if the economy would depend on the motive of benevolence, a motive that, though not absent, is weak. Similarly for "the butcher, the brewer, or the baker," who, through the natural human propensity for trading, develop economies in which all can work for themselves in ways useful to all others.

In this framework, persons who sell their labor to someone else for a wage are not thought to be doing anything very different from persons who sell their extra wheat or loaves of bread. Likewise, the accumulated stock of machines and buildings, products and money that is capital is thought to play a role that is not notably different from the one played by persons who use their labor to produce things and sell their surplus.

All such transactions are assumed to be made voluntarily, as in the case of an even exchange or barter between equals where both parties gain and no one loses. Labor is assumed to be an item to be bought and sold like any other, and capital is assumed to be a collection of some such items or their equivalents in terms of money. And everyone is applauded for making as large a profit as possible.

Thus, Adam Smith can be thought to have offered a moral justification for what has been taken to be capitalism. The moral theory appealed to in this judgment is utilitarian. According to such a theory, we ought to perform those actions and adopt those policies and procedures that will bring about the greatest happiness or satisfaction or "utility" of the greatest number of people. There are many controversies about how to interpret this formula, but they are controversies within utilitarianism.[11]

Those defending various current economic practices still often claim that capitalism operates along the lines imagined by Adam Smith and can be justified on utilitarian grounds.

But very different assessments have been made. According to Ricardo and Marx, the results of all pursuing their own economic interests in a system allowing capital accumulation and unlimited profits are not at all the results claimed by Adam Smith. Ricardo, writing in England in the early nineteenth century, thought that it is landowners, not everyone, who gain under such a scheme. And later in the century Marx, as everyone who has been a classroom member may know, thought that it is the capitalist class that gains at the expense of the working class (see pp. 114–37). One way of interpreting Marx's claims is to see him as holding that the capitalist extracts for himself a part of what the work done by the worker would be worth in an exchange that really was what Adam Smith assumed such exchanges to be. It is only by paying workers less than the value their work would have in an even exchange that the entrepreneur makes a profit and acquires capital. Then the entrepreneur can use this capital to make more profits and to acquire more capital. Though capitalist economists scoff at this conception of what labor is "worth," from the point of view of what it would be morally justifiable to pay someone who would freely sell his or her labor from a position of equality, the conception makes perfectly good sense.

Capitalists, Marx thought, are able to exploit workers because workers have nothing to sell but their labor, and economic necessity forces them to sell it for less than it would be worth if the transaction were an even exchange between equals. Thus, the more capital the bourgeoisie accumulates, and the more the working class contributes to this by its labor, the greater becomes the power of the bourgeoisie to exploit the working class. Capitalists institute governments and legal systems that serve and protect their interests, and, the Marxist venture into prediction suggests, the oppression of workers will become ever more severe. According to Marx, capitalism can thus be expected to produce its own demise, as workers becoming more and more exploited will rise up, overpower their oppressors, and institute an economic system that really will benefit all.

Marx's vision of socialism sees human beings as having progressed beyond the self-interested pursuit of individual satisfactions that conflict with the satisfactions of others. Socialism as defended by British socialist thinkers and those they influence, however, has often been defended on utilitarian grounds, in terms of its ability to satisfy individual interests. Socialism is then seen as an economic system that can, while capitalism cannot, bring about the greatest happiness of the greatest number. For both kinds of socialism, the basic means of production are to be owned collectively by all members of society and run as the society, not just its

[11]For a helpful summary of recent versions of these controversies, see Dan Brock, "Recent Work in Utilitarianism," *American Philosophical Quarterly* 10, no. 4 (October 1973):241–76.

bourgeois class, decides. Industry is to be developed and products produced and distributed for the purpose of serving human needs and human betterment, not for the purpose of increasing the profits of capitalists.

It has been recognized that the power of workers to organize and to assert their interests through political as well as economic channels can modify the disaster for capitalism predicted by Marx. The state can intervene in a capitalist economy sufficiently to lessen its downswings, to cushion the pains of unemployment through insurance, and of deprivation through welfare payments. And government can regulate business to avoid the worst excesses that the pursuit of profits for the sake of profits allows. Workers can press for increasing wages, and even though the rich may get richer at a faster rate or the relative gap between rich and poor may remain about the same, the lot of workers under capitalism can improve significantly. Much of their opposition can thus be bought off, to the dismay of those who have hoped that the discontent of the working class would lead to a transformation of bourgeois society into more humanly admirable and decent forms of social interaction than the generalized scramble after economic self-advancement.

Still, it can be shown, as Joan Robinson (see pp. 138–52) and, more recently, John Kenneth Galbraith, Robert Heilbroner, and Michael Harrington have—in their different ways—made clear, that for many economic activities capitalist mechanisms are highly deficient ways of reaching the best outcome. Much that is useful to society is not profitable, and much that is profitable is not useful to society. Thus, capitalism may fail to supply adequate public transportation, parks, and child-care facilities and may overproduce advertising and pollution.

When many try to use various resources to maximize their own interests, the results may be a depletion of the resource and an outcome exactly the opposite of the one predicted by Adam Smith. For example, it is estimated that there were between thirty and sixty million American buffalo (bison) roaming the West in the mid–nineteenth century. Whereas the Indians had killed only enough to meet their needs for meat and hides, white hunters slaughtered them indiscriminately for all the hides they could sell and even for sport. By 1903 there were only thirty-four buffalo left.

More recently, the pursuit of profits by oil corporations, auto manufacturers, and power companies has led to an enormously wasteful expansion of energy use. The political system has reflected these interests—as in its vast subsidies to highway construction and home mortgage financing—rather than restrained them. Now, as it becomes apparent that the world's oil may before very long run out and that it will become more and more socially costly and environmentally dangerous to use nuclear and synthetic substitutes, we confront the effects of following capitalism's advice.

The problem is a general one. Perhaps it is only within a very restricted area of activity that each pursuing his or her own economic interests and a market determining the outcome can possibly produce the greatest good for the greatest number. Moreover, the problems are greatly magnified when seen on a global scale, with impoverished countries struggling for survival in a world dominated by economic Leviathans.

Many persons who raise moral questions about economic activity believe that at least a significant range of the major choices about the direction of investment, the provision of employment, and the allocation of economic gains ought to be made in terms of what will best serve society, not most increase the profits of corporations. This point is so obvious it is remarkable that it remains obscure to so many. But even if we agree with the judgment, it is not clear how it ought to be carried out.

Clearly, state ownership of the means of production need not in itself lead to serving the interests of everyone. State economic power and tyrannical government bureaucracies can oppress people more effectively than capitalist economic power. The joining of political and economic power in the same hands that has occurred in Communist states has not served the interests of most citizens and often has led to a disregard of not only any property rights citizens may or may not have, but of their political and civil rights as well.

Such regressive developments have, however, often been due to a lack of democratic political forms. Where strong democratic government has been joined with various socialist economic and social programs, as in many countries of Western Europe and Scandinavia, where social democratic parties have won power through democratic elections, the result has been a variety of mixed economies and an enlargement rather than curbing of political freedom. Social ownership of some industries has proceeded along with continued capitalist control of many others. Some governmental planning and especially coordination has taken place, but governments have not tried to force their economic plans on all segments of society. Substantial growth of the social services that protect those less fortunate in the capitalist marketplace has taken place. National health insurance, family support payments, and generous unemployment insurance are standard features in most Western European countries. The United States, in contrast, remains far more unrelievedly capitalistic.

Whether the United States will develop along similar lines remains to be seen. Robert Dahl notes the lack of a socialist tradition in America (see pp. 153–60). Perhaps subjecting the giant corporation to some measure of democratic control, and developing more responsible forms of economic activity along highly individualistic lines—such as in the local development of appropriate technology and of decentralized, benign processes for production and service—will be a more promising route toward economic decency in the United States than trying to import the social democratic tendencies Americans lack.

The modern corporation does not bear the faintest resemblance to Adam Smith's self-sufficient farmer or tradesman. The modern corporation is an almost feudal institution in its hierarchical structure and lack of democratic organization. Arguments similar to those that led to the development of democratic political institutions replacing feudal ones can be applied to economic institutions, though the road from argument to action may be dense with obstructions. Modern corporations are no more "private" in their ability to control people's lives than are state governments. In addition, contrary to what most Americans believe, the United States is *not* becoming more egalitarian; the vast disparities between rich and poor, and between the few in the former category and the many in the latter, have hardly changed at all in many decades. Large corporations have the power to assure themselves profits in good economic times and in bad, while those at the lower end of the economic hierarchy may find no way to sell their labor. Minorities, women, children, the sick, and the aged are especially ill-served by American capitalism in its present forms. [12]

Robert Dahl suggests that the modern corporation be democratized by having its workers share in the making of its decisions. However, since the workers of a large corporation may, like its managers, pursue their own interests at the expense of the wider society, Gar Alperovitz suggests a "decentralist" approach in which local entities join in a "commonwealth" where all would pursue their own interests only within a framework of concern and consideration for the interests of others (see pp. 161–67).

Women and minorities have been disadvantaged by both big business and big labor. Even the most reluctant egalitarians profess support for equality of opportunity, but it has been blatantly denied to women and minorities. Through segregation into lower-paying ("pink collar") kinds of work as well as through outright failure to accord equal pay and advancement for equal work, the median income of women working year round and full time in 1977 was still only 59 percent of that of men working year round and full time;[13] in 1956 it was 63 percent. The median earnings of minority males working full time was only 78 percent of that of white males doing so in 1977,[14] and unemployment rates among blacks are routinely more than twice as high as those among whites. [15]

Feminists, to make an at least temporarily valid point, sometimes apply the individualistic and contractual perspectives of political liberalism to relations within the family, asking how much the work of the unpaid housewife and mother is worth and what her economic rights should be. But feminists also suggest a different approach: we should extend to the wider society some of the traditionally feminine and feminist values of concern, caring, nurturing, and the meeting of needs that are characteristic of the relations that ought to exist within the family. The work place would be a good place to start. Why should not organizations for work, whether for service or production, be places where members care about one another, provide satisfying work, and produce useful products in ways that will reflect concern for each person's development and freedom? The corporation might then model itself on the nonprofit service or educational institution or on the economic collective, rather than on the profit-greedy industrial firm whose lines of command resemble those of a military unit.

[12] For a discussion of such facts as these and their causes, see Ira Katznelson and Mark Kesselman, *The Politics of Power* (New York: Harcourt Brace Jovanovich, 1975).

[13] U.S., Department of Commerce, Bureau of the Census, *Statistical Abstract of the U.S. 1978*, (Washington, D.C.: Government Printing Office, 1978), p. 464.

[14] Ibid., p. 423.

[15] See U.S., Department of Labor, Bureau of Labor Statistics, *Employment and Earnings* for periodic reports.

Nancy Hartsock looks at the way work itself might be restructured to reflect the feminist goal of overcoming the domination and control now exercised by some over others in the work place (see pp. 168–76). These objectives are shared by many young people eager to engage in economic activity but distressed at the authoritarian forms into which almost all of it is now structured.

No basic arrangements for the conduct of economic activity can be morally justifiable unless the interests of others are taken into account along with the pursuit of economic self-interest. This does not mean we need to turn into a nation of altruists, sacrificing our interests on some utopian altar. Because the raw pursuit of self-interest is ultimately self-defeating for most people, except in a narrow range of allowable egoistic pursuits, we need to develop forms of cooperation in which all *can* benefit. Under such arrangements, the gain for some individuals will have to be more modest than it would have been if a few lucky winners would continue to triumph over many losers. But the general good will be served.[16]

While we are still groping for the best ways of achieving such cooperation, it is clear that the myth of Adam Smith should be overcome. The delusion that all pursuing their own economic interests unrestrained can yield an outcome that will be good for everyone is still prevalent in the ideologies of many, especially neoconservatives and those who think they have no ideologies but are pragmatic businessmen and value-neutral social scientists. It is a delusion that should give way to a greater measure of reasonable cooperation between the members of national societies, and between the fortunate nations and all the rest.

III

If we express our moral demands in terms of justice, a question we must ask is: What does economic justice require? In answering it we will have to consider what the relation between government and economic activity ought to be, and we will have to decide what moral rights persons have to property, to the economic goods needed for a decent life, to a share of the output, or a share in the satisfying work of an economy. Again, how should our rights and interests be reflected in our economic arrangements?

John Stuart Mill, a nineteenth-century advocate of minimal government control over or intervention into economic activity, recognized that there were valid reasons for some departures from the laissez-faire principle he recommended (see pp. 178–87). He thought the case for governmental provision of services was especially clear in the case of education, which not even those who proclaimed that government should do no more than protect persons and property against force and fraud would really want left to market forces alone to provide. He thought basic necessities for the poor also should be provided by government rather than by

---

[16]I have discussed some problems of egoism, altruism, competition, and cooperation in "Rationality and Reasonable Cooperation," *Social Research* 44, no. 4 (Winter 1977):708–744.

private charity, because citizens should be as certain of being able to obtain relief against destitution as of anything society can assure.

Mill understood the difficulties that have in recent years received much discussion under the formulation of the "free-rider problem."[17] There are many activities that will be advantageous to all if all participate in them; however, it will be still more advantageous to any given individual to freeload, while others bear the burden of acting. For instance, if most *other* motorists install antipollution devices while a given individual does not, the air will get cleaner and the individual will benefit without paying the cost. But if most people behave this way, only a few naïve citizens will install devices, the air will not get cleaner, and the naïve citizens will pay the cost without even enjoying any benefit. Government may be needed to ensure that all share in a fair way in supporting activities that will benefit everyone or many. The argument may apply to any number of collective goods, such as parks, libraries, and subways, that are underdeveloped by capitalists pursuing high returns on their investments.

John Hospers and others who call themselves "libertarians" suggest another picture. As they depict it, economic activity takes place quite independently of government, and government, to fund its activities, *takes away* part of the output of useful, independent, economic activity (see pp. 188–97). In this interpretation, government is seen as a kind of thief, taking from people something belonging to them that it should, instead, stay away from.[18]

The picture overlooks the reality that the legal rights of people to have *any* property protected, or to be able to consider anything to be *their* holdings—their possessions, products, income, capital, or whatever—depends on government. As we saw in section I, *any* given scheme of property rights protected by law and assured by the enforcement powers of government is the result of a social decision to enact or maintain *that* scheme rather than some other. For any such scheme to be justifiable, it must be judged on moral grounds.

The orthodox Western scheme of property rights and interests, as A. M. Honoré made clear, is by no means the most plausible that could be maintained on moral grounds. It lacks a requirement that those with a surfeit help those unable to obtain what they need. This fundamental moral concern, recognized by such forerunners of conservative economic thought as Locke and Mill and by almost all developed schemes of morality, should certainly find reflection in *any* legal and political arrangements concerning the acquisition and holding of economic goods, if such arrangements lay claim to moral justifiability. This concern, however, would be no more than a minimal requirement of decency. Morality might be even more demanding.

What are the fundamental principles by which we should judge whether any proposed scheme of economic arrangements is morally justifiable or not? Can they be made explicit and adequate?

[17] See especially Mancur Olsen, *The Logic of Collective Action* (Cambridge, Mass.: Harvard University Press, 1965).
[18] Robert Nozick, in *Anarchy, State, and Utopia* (New York: Basic Books, 1974), begins with similar assumptions and reaches, by long and clever routes, similar conclusions.

John Rawls has presented one of the most powerful and widely discussed formulations of such principles in many years.[19] In his view, the fundamental principles of justice are those principles for the regulation of society to which we could all, unanimously, agree, if we chose them impartially from a standpoint outside any actual society, without knowing in which positions—rich or poor, male or female, white, tan, or black, untalented or talented, and so on—we would actually find ourselves. A society's basic social institutions, and their arrangement into a structure, should accord with such principles of justice. The principles would, Rawls holds, require first of all as extensive a scheme of equal basic liberties for each of us as would be compatible with the similar liberties of others. Once such liberties are assured, we should apply what Rawls calls "the difference principle" to the basic structure of society. The difference principle would require that *all* inequalities of social primary goods—rights, opportunities, income, wealth, and so on—could only be justified if such inequalities would contribute to raising the position in these respects of the least advantaged groups in the society. Thus, high rewards for entrepreneurs could only be justified if their effect was to improve the lot of the least advantaged members of the society, who might benefit from new economic activity that otherwise would not take place.

Government should, in Rawls's view, continually adjust the rewards allowed to various groups by its scheme of property rights and economic policies so that the results will accord with this principle. Government should tax those whose economic benefits would exceed those allowed by this principle, and government should redistribute these funds, in some form, to those least advantaged in the society, such as those who cannot work because of illness (within a normal range), those unable to find work, or those working for the most meager wages.

In Rawls's view, we would certainly choose, from his equivalent of the "state of nature" of traditional social contract theory, to insure ourselves against the worst outcome that could befall us in organized society: being among the "least advantaged." If we did not know where we ourselves would wind up, we would choose principles of economic justice that would raise us from the bottom, and we would want those at the top to be taxed up to the point at which it would decrease their contribution to our well-being to be taxed further.

C. B. Macpherson also thinks that our economic and social rights extend across the whole range of economic activity, and that on moral grounds we all have rights to a share of the total fruits of that activity sufficient for full self-development (see pp. 209–220). He interprets the concept of "property" in as wide a sense as possible, admittedly to bring some of the support now given by society to the protection of property to bear on achieving new rights that ought to be recognized. In his view, every citizen should have assured rights of access to the means of labor and the means to live a fully human life. Instead of providing only rights to exclude people from what one owns, property should provide persons with rights not to be

---

[19]John Rawls, *A Theory of Justice* (Cambridge, Mass.: Harvard University Press, 1971). One of the best short expositions of Rawls's theory is his article "A Kantian Conception of Equality," reprinted here on pp. 198–208.

excluded from employment and a share in the society's whole material output. And property should include even more: rights to a share of political power and to participation in a satisfying set of social relations. Property, Macpherson holds with Locke, should provide rights to life and liberty as well as to material revenue, but to an even fuller and freer life than Locke could have imagined.

A more moderate view would be to recognize that persons have economic and social rights as well as political and civil rights, but that these economic and social rights are to an adequate minimum, or enough for basic necessities or a decent life, but not to a certain share in the whole of the economic product of a society. It can well be argued on the basis of *any* plausible structure of moral principles that just as citizens are entitled to certain political rights, such as the right to vote, to a fair trial, to be free from assault, and to speak freely, so they ought to be entitled, by law, to enough economic and social goods—food, housing, medical care, and so on—to enable them to live a decent life. "Welfare" payments would then cease to be seen as charity, or benefits, that the fortunate members of an economic system bestow through collective generosity on the unfortunate, expecting the recipients to feel gratitude and shame. Our rights to adequate well-being would be recognized as *rights*.

Article 25 of the United Nations Universal Declaration of Human Rights (pp. 232–36) states that "everyone has the right to a standard of living adequate for the health and well-being of himself and his family, including food, clothing, housing and medical care and necessary social services. . . ." Although it is a document not free of sexism, it does proclaim a commendable standard for basic political and economic rights to which many countries subscribe, at least in principle. The United States has not ratified *any* of the conventions or covenants[20] designed to implement the declaration, despite its professed commitment to human rights. And, although local and federal programs help the poor in various ways, no such rights as in Article 25 have been found by the Supreme Court to be required by the Constitution, though lower courts have come closer to doing so. In *Wyman* v. *James* (see pp. 237–40), in 1971, a majority on the Supreme Court treated welfare payments as "charity" that persons might be accorded only if they are willing to waive their Fourth Amendment guarantees of the privacy of a person's home. In *Rodriguez* (pp. 241–48), in 1973, the Supreme Court considered whether basing educational funding on property taxes, which yield seriously disparate budget amounts for rich and poor school districts, was in conflict with the Equal Protection Clause of the Fourteenth Amendment of the Constitution. A majority of the Court decided it was not. They noted that although education is necessary for the exercise of such other rights as free speech and the intelligent use of the right to vote, this is even more true for "the basics of decent food and shelter." As the Court observed, "empirical examination might well buttress an assumption that the ill-fed, ill-clothed, and ill-housed are among the most ineffective participants in the political process, and that they derive the least enjoyment from the benefits of the First Amendment." But instead of seeing this as an argument *for* substantive rights to food, shelter, and

[20]For the texts, see *Basic Documents on Human Rights,* ed. Ian Brownlie (Oxford: Clarendon Press, 1967), pp. 138–74.

so on, which, in addition to even better arguments it is, the Court took it as an argument *against* a right to equal education.

Many advocates of economic and social rights hope for more progressive legislation from Congress or more enlightened Supreme Court decisions to provide, as matters of right, enough economic goods for a decent life for all citizens. When this may take place in the United States is problematic; the mood of the country at the start of the 1980s does not appear favorable.

Arthur Okun discusses the way our political and civil rights are off-bounds to market determination (see pp. 221–30). We nearly all agree that rights to a fair trial, to vote, and to hold political office should not be bought and sold but protected alike for those who have and those who lack economic power. Similarly, he argues, rights to those basic economic goods necessary for a modest level of dignity should not be subject to determination by a market that will enrich some while depriving others of these rights. These rights should also be treated as off-bounds to the market.

Clearly, there will be some difficulties in establishing the level up to which persons are entitled to economic support by a society. One person's necessity is another's luxury to some extent. And a "decent life" is a vague notion. Still, we would have no difficulty in judging that a person who is seriously malnourished because of poverty is below this level in a rich society. If we admit that a line should be drawn, we can get on with questions of where to draw it.

To draw such a line is to take a more limited view of rights to economic goods than does Rawls's difference principle. The latter entitles persons to a share of a society's total economic product. It would subject the *entire* range of property relations to decisions on grounds of justice and of the rights it requires. No one would be morally entitled to any property above what would be yielded by arrangements benefiting the least advantaged. Similarly, in Macpherson's conception of the property rights we ought to have, we would not be excluded from *any* of the total production and economic activity of a society.

Rights to enough for a decent life would, in contrast, be rights to economic goods up to a certain level only. Such rights should be respected because they are moral *rights,* whether or not any calculation of utility or efficiency would recommend them. Above the level of the requirements for meeting these rights, however, economic activity *should* then be judged on utilitarian grounds rather than on grounds of rights. It might, on these grounds, be quite appropriate to leave considerable room for egoism in those restricted spheres where Adam Smith's pursuit of individual gain can increase the satisfaction of all. In this view, once the claims of rights have been met, economic activity ought to maximize the satisfaction of the property interests of as many as possible.

Against Rawls it may be argued that even from an "original position of equality" we might choose to allow some room for gambling on success, rather than choosing only to insure against failure.[21] If we were to be at the bottom of the society we would want our rights to a decent life to be guaranteed—rights of access

[21] See especially John C. Harsanyi, "Can the Maximin Principle Serve as a Basis for Morality?" *American Political Science Review* 69, no. 2 (June 1975):594–606.

to what we require to meet our basic needs as well as rights to be left alone and not attacked. This much of the argument against the economic conservatives and neo-conservatives such as Milton Friedman and Robert Nozick is clear. We might, however, also want to be able to take a chance on being more fortunate. In doing so we would risk being less well off than otherwise, if we did not succeed, but we could look forward to being *better* off than otherwise if we did succeed. If the difference principle were applied, any earnings of movie stars and fast-food moguls which did not contribute to economic activity benefitting the least advantaged would be taxed and redistributed to do so. But in this alternative view, *once* the rights to a decent life to which *all* are entitled had been assured, winners could retain as much of their earnings as would maximize the general happiness.

Many economists and businessmen depict the sphere of economic activity as a kind of game, where winners and losers compete on friendly terms as if engaged in a sporting event. They argue that just as the winners of a fair game of basketball can be awarded trophies without violating the rights of the losers, so the winners of a fair game of economic competition should be permitted to enjoy the rewards of doing so. Even losers may prefer having had a chance to play the game, and especially having a chance to play again and win, rather than to have been and to be assured all along of an even share of all proceeds.

Morally serious persons will question such game playing as a major life activity, considering the rights of human beings throughout the world to what they need for a decent life. They will question the squandering of resources involved in the process, as the United States, with 5 percent of the world's population, consumes 40 percent of the world's resources. If, on the other hand, we could justifiably isolate a given group of persons and consider the issues of economic justice within that group only, then on moral grounds we might agree that *if* all could be assured their rights to a decent life and to adequate self development, then economic game playing beyond this level might justifiably result in winners and losers, as players pursue their economic interests. While the players would have no *moral* rights to such winnings, society might allow, on utilitarian grounds, legal rights to them.

In my view, every person has moral rights. These derive from the moral principles and considerations to which we can commit ourselves here and now, without presupposing a social contract. I believe these principles can stand up to the tests to which we should all subject our moral theories.[22] Among these moral rights are, where it is possible to assure them, rights to enough material goods for a decent life; rights to adequate self-development, as through education and leisure; and rights to useful employment. Of course there will be difficulties in deciding how much is adequate and what is decent and useful, but so is there difficulty in deciding how much police protection is adequate and whether a right to free speech must include rights to equal time on the airwaves or not. If we concede that the all or nothing views—that persons have no rights to any level of even the most basic necessities, or that persons have rights to a share of the total of all economic

---

[22] I have discussed these matters in two papers, "The Pursuit of Morality" and "On the Testing of Moral Theories," not yet published.

production and activity—are not persuasive, we must look for ways to draw lines designating levels of adequacy. Such lines will always be subject to discussion and revision along with all our legal and political decisions, but we will have made progress if we decide that the domain of rights must include rights of access to some level of economic goods, and yet leave some room for self-interested economic endeavor.

We could then see that to the extent that property rights are moral rights, they extend only to the satisfaction of needs and of the requirements for adequate self-development. Above that level, property "rights" should be seen *not* as moral rights, but as legal fictions that should be based on political decisions aimed at maximizing interests. Thus, allowing successful entertainers legal property rights to spend lavishly would have to be weighed against the possibly greater interests of others in other forms of spending. If, however, enough persons gain enough enjoyment from being able to watch and aspire to the expensive expressions of the successful, entertainers might be permitted to retain substantial amounts of their winnings.

Whether we call the relevant *moral* rights "property rights," or "basic economic rights" or "rights to the economic goods necessary for life and adequate self-development" is somewhat arbitrary. The important point is that moral rights to property include rights to what is needed for a decent life, and do not include rights beyond what is needed and needed equally by all members of a community of rights holders. Beyond this there are not moral rights to property, there are instead property interests. Political and legal decisions about them should be made responsibly, but not in terms of moral rights or economic justice.

Economic justice is a serious matter. While those with moral rights to decent lives are deprived of these rights, playing games is not only frivolous but immoral. However, if such rights *were* respected along with the political and civil rights we take for granted, and if, on utilitarian grounds, playing economic games could be justified in terms of the maximization of interests, there might then be nothing wrong with capitalist games between consenting gamblers—for recreation. But first, the children ought to be fed.

Property

What is property?

What do property rights give us rights to do?

On what grounds ought people to have property rights?

Rights to Property
•
John Locke

The First Treatise

40. I find the Apostle seems to have as little notion of any such *Private Dominion of Adam* as I, when he says, God *gives us all things richly to enjoy,* which he could not do, if it were all given away already, to Monarch *Adam,* and the Monarchs his Heirs and Successors. To conclude, this Text is so far from proving *Adam* Sole Proprietor, that on the contrary, it is a Confirmation of the Original Community of all things amongst the Sons of Men, which appearing from this Donation of God, as well as other places of Scripture; the Soveraignty of *Adam,* built upon his *Private Dominion,* must fall, not having any Foundation to support it.

41. But yet, if after all, any one will needs have it so, that by this Donation of God, *Adam* was made sole Proprietor of the whole Earth, what will this be to his Soveraignty? And how will it appear, that *Property* in Land gives a Man Power over the Life of another? Or how will the Possession even of the whole Earth, give any one a Soveraign Arbitrary Authority over the Persons of Men? The most specious thing to be said, is, that he that is Proprietor of the whole World, may deny all the

From John Locke, *Two Treatises of Government* (1764 edition). Selections from the First and Second Treatises.

The thinking of the Englishman John Locke (1632–1704) had a profound influence on the development of parliamentary government in England, on revolutionary thought in America and France, and in the writing of the American Declaration of Independence. His *Two Treatises* were first published in 1690. His other most important work is *An Essay Concerning Human Understanding*.

In the *First Treatise*, Locke attacked the argument of Robert Filmer, influential at the time, that political power should be based on original title (God gave the earth to Adam) and correct transferral (from the patriarchs to the kings of nations). In the *Second Treatise*, Locke developed his views concerning the natural rights of human beings and argued that government ought to be based on the consent of the governed.

rest of Mankind Food, and so at his pleasure starve them, if they will not acknowledge his Soveraignty, and Obey his Will. If this were true, it would be a good Argument to prove, that there was never any such *Property*, that God never gave any such *Private Dominion;* since it is more reasonable to think, that God who bid Mankind increase and multiply, should rather himself give them all a Right, to make use of the Food and Rayment, and other Conveniencies of Life, the Materials whereof he had so plentifully provided for them; than to make them depend upon the Will of a Man for their Subsistence, who should have Power to destroy them all when he pleased, and who being no better than other Men, was in Succession likelier by want and the dependance of a scanty Fortune, to tye them to hard Service, than by liberal Allowance of the Conveniencies of Life, to promote the great Design of God, *Increase* and *Multiply:* He that doubts this, let him look into the Absolute Monarchies of the World, and see what becomes of the Conveniencies of Life, and the Multitudes of People.

42. But we know God hath not left one Man so to the Mercy of another, that he may starve him if he please: God the Lord and Father of all, has given no one of his Children such a Property, in his peculiar Portion of the things of this World, but that he has given his needy Brother a Right to the Surplusage of his Goods; so that it cannot justly be denied him, when his pressing Wants call for it. And therefore no Man could ever have a just Power over the Life of another, by Right of property in Land or Possessions; since 'twould always be a Sin in any Man of Estate, to let his Brother perish for want of affording him Relief out of his Plenty. As *Justice* gives every Man a Title to the product of his honest Industry, and the fair Acquisitions of his Ancestors descended to him; so *Charity* gives every Man a Title to so much out of another's Plenty, as will keep him from extream want, where he has no means to subsist otherwise; and a Man can no more justly make use of another's necessity, to force him to become his Vassal, by with-holding that Relief, God requires him to afford to the wants of his Brother, than he that has more strength can seize upon a weaker, master him to his Obedience, and with a Dagger at his Throat offer him Death or Slavery. . . .

The Second Treatise

Chap. II

Of the State of Nature

4. To understand Political Power right, and derive it from its Original, we must consider what State all Men are naturally in, and that is, a *State of perfect Freedom* to order their Actions, and dispose of their Possessions, and Persons as they think fit, within the bounds of the Law of Nature, without asking leave, or depending upon the Will of any other Man.

A *State* also *of Equality,* wherein all the Power and Jurisdiction is reciprocal, no one having more than another: there being nothing more evident, than that Creatures of the same species and rank promiscuously born to all the same advantages of Nature, and the use of the same faculties, should also be equal one amongst another without Subordination or Subjection, unless the Lord and Master of them all, should by any manifest Declaration of his Will set one above another, and confer on him by an evident and clear appointment an undoubted Right to Dominion and Sovereignty.

5. This *equality* of Men by Nature, the Judicious *Hooker* looks upon as so evident in it self, and beyond all question, that he makes it the Foundation of that Obligation to mutual Love amongst Men, on which he Builds the Duties they owe one another, and from whence he derives the great Maxims *of Justice* and *Charity.* His words are;

> *The like natural inducement, hath brought Men to know that it is no less their Duty, to Love others than themselves, for seeing those things which are equal, must needs all have one measure; If I cannot but wish to receive good, even as much at every Man's hands, as any Man can wish unto his own Soul, how should I look to have any part of my desire herein satisfied, unless my self be careful to satisfie the like desire, which is undoubtedly in other Men, being of one and the same nature? to have any thing offered them repugnant to this desire, must needs in all respects grieve them as much as me, so that if I do harm, I must look to suffer, there being no reason that others should shew greater measure of love to me, than they have by me, shewed unto them; my desire therefore to be lov'd of my equals in nature, as much as possible may be, imposeth upon me a natural Duty of bearing to themward, fully the like affection; From which relation of equality between our selves and them, that are as our selves, what several Rules and Canons, natural reason hath drawn for direction of Life, no Man is ignorant. Eccl. Pol. Lib. 1.*

6. But though this be a *State of Liberty,* yet it is *not a State of Licence,* though Man in that State have an uncontroleable Liberty, to dispose of his Person or Possessions, yet he has not Liberty to destroy himself, or so much as any Creature in his Possession, but where some nobler use, than its bare Preservation calls for it. The *State of Nature* has a Law of Nature to govern it, which obliges every one: And Reason, which is that Law, teaches all Mankind, who will but consult it, that being all equal and independent, no one ought to harm another in his Life, Health, Liberty, or Possessions. For Men being all the Workmanship of one Omnipotent, and infinitely wise Maker; All the Servants of one Sovereign Master, sent into the World by his order and about his business, they are his Property, whose Workmanship they are, made to last during his, not one anothers Pleasure. And being furnished with like Faculties, sharing all in one Community of Nature, there cannot be supposed any such *Subordination* among us, that may Authorize us to destroy

one another, as if we were made for one anothers uses, as the inferior ranks of Creatures are for ours. Every one as he is *bound to preserve himself,* and not to quit his Station wilfully; so by the like reason when his own Preservation comes not in competition, ought he, as much as he can, *to preserve the rest of Mankind,* and may not unless it be to do Justice on an Offender, take away, or impair the life, or what tends to the Preservation of the Life, Liberty, Health, Limb or Goods of another.

7. And that all Men may be restrained from invading others Rights, and from doing hurt to one another, and the Law of Nature be observed, which willeth the Peace and *Preservation of all Mankind,* the *Execution* of the Law of Nature is in that State, put into every Mans hands, whereby every one has a right to punish the transgressors of that Law to such a Degree, as may hinder its Violation. For the *Law of Nature* would, as all other Laws that concern Men in this World, be in vain, if there were no body that in the State of Nature, had a *Power to Execute* that Law, and thereby preserve the innocent and restrain offenders, and if any one in the State of Nature may punish another, for any evil he has done, every one may do so. For in that *State of perfect Equality,* where naturally there is no superiority or jurisdiction of one, over another, what any may do in Prosecution of that Law, every one must needs have a Right to do.

8. And thus in the State of Nature, *one Man comes by a Power over another;* but yet no Absolute or Arbitrary Power, to use a Criminal when he has got him in his hands, according to the passionate heats, or boundless extravagancy of his own Will, but only to retribute to him, so far as calm reason and conscience dictates, what is proportionate to his Transgression, which is so much as may serve for *Reparation* and *Restraint.* For these two are the only reasons, why one Man may lawfully do harm to another, which is that we call *punishment.* In transgressing the Law of Nature, the Offender declares himself to live by another Rule, than that of *reason* and common Equity, which is that measure God has set to the actions of Men, for their mutual security: and so he becomes dangerous to Mankind, the tye, which is to secure them from injury and violence, being slighted and broken by him. Which being a trespass against the whole Species, and the Peace and Safety of it, provided for by the Law of Nature, every man upon this score, by the Right he hath to preserve Mankind in general, may restrain, or where it is necessary, destroy things noxious to them, and so may bring such evil on any one, who hath transgressed that Law, as may make him repent the doing of it, and thereby deter him, and by his Example others, from doing the like mischief. And in this case, and upon this ground, every *Man hath a Right to punish the Offender, and be Executioner of the Law of Nature.* . . .

10. Besides the Crime which consists in violating the Law, and varying from the right Rule of Reason, whereby a Man so far becomes degenerate, and declares himself to quit the Principles of Human Nature, and to be a noxious Creature, there is commonly *injury* done to some Person or other, and some other Man receives damage by his Transgression, in which Case he who hath received

any damage, has besides the right of punishment common to him with other Men, a particular Right to seek *Reparation* from him that has done it. And any other Person who finds it just, may also joyn with him that is injur'd, and assist him in recovering from the Offender, so much as may make satisfaction for the harm he has suffer'd.

11. From these *two distinct Rights*, the one of *Punishing* the Crime *for restraint*, and preventing the like Offence, which right of punishing is in every body; the other of taking *reparation*, which belongs only to the injured party, comes it to pass that the Magistrate, who by being Magistrate, hath the common right of punishing put into his hands, can often, where the publick good demands not the execution of the Law, *remit* the punishment of Criminal Offences by his own Authority, but yet cannot *remit* the satisfaction due to any private Man, for the damage he has received. That, he who has suffered the damage has a Right to demand in his own name, and he alone can *remit:* The damnified Person has this Power of appropriating to himself, the Goods or Service of the Offender, by *Right of Self-preservation*, as every Man has a Power to punish the Crime, to prevent its being committed again, *by the Right he has of Preserving all Mankind*, and doing all reasonable things he can in order to that end: And thus it is, that every Man in the State of Nature, has a Power to kill a Murderer, both to deter others from doing the like Injury, which no Reparation can compensate, by the Example of the punishment that attends it from every body, and also *to secure* Men from the attempts of a Criminal, who having renounced Reason, the common Rule and Measure, God hath given to Mankind, hath by the unjust Violence and Slaughter he hath committed upon one, declared War against all Mankind, and therefore may be destroyed as a *Lyon* or a *Tyger*, one of those wild Savage Beasts, with whom Men can have no Society nor Security: And upon this is grounded the great Law of Nature, *Who so sheddeth Mans Blood, by Man shall his Blood be shed.* And *Cain* was so fully convinced, that every one had a Right to destroy such a Criminal, that after the Murther of his Brother, he cries out, *Every one that findeth me, shall slay me;* so plain was it writ in the Hearts of all Mankind.

12. By the same reason, may a Man in the State of Nature *punish the lesser breaches* of that Law. It will perhaps be demanded, with death? I answer, Each Transgression may be *punished* to that *degree*, and with so much *Severity* as will suffice to make it an ill bargain to the Offender, give him cause to repent, and terrifie others from doing the like. Every Offence that can be committed in the State of Nature, may in the State of Nature be also punished, equally, and as far forth as it may, in a Common-wealth; for though it would be besides my present purpose, to enter here into the particulars of the Law of Nature, or its *measures of punishment*; yet, it is certain there is such a Law, and that too, as intelligible and plain to a rational Creature, and a Studier of that Law, as the positive Laws of Common-wealths, nay possibly plainer; As much as Reason is easier to be understood, than the Phansies and intricate Contrivances of Men, following contrary and hidden interests put into Words; For so truly are a great part of the *Municipal Laws* of

Countries, which are only so far right, as they are founded on the Law of Nature, by which they are to be regulated and interpreted.

13. To this strange Doctrine, *viz.* That *in the State of Nature, every one has the Executive Power* of the Law of Nature, I doubt not but it will be objected, That it is unreasonable for Men to be Judges in their own Cases, that Self-love will make Men partial to themselves and their Friends. And on the other side, that Ill Nature, Passion and Revenge will carry them too far in punishing others. And hence nothing but Confusion and Disorder will follow, and that therefore God hath certainly appointed Government to restrain the partiality and violence of Men. I easily grant, that *Civil Government* is the proper Remedy for the Inconveniences of the State of Nature, which must certainly be Great, where Men may be Judges in their own Case, since 'tis easily to be imagined, that he who was so unjust as to do his Brother an Injury, will scarce be so just as to condemn himself for it: But I shall desire those who make this Objection, to remember that *Absolute Monarchs* are but Men, and if Government is to be the Remedy of those Evils, which necessarily follow from Mens being Judges in their own Cases, and the State of Nature is therefore not to be endured, I desire to know what kind of Government that is, and how much better it is than the State of Nature, where one Man commanding a multitude, has the Liberty to be Judge in his own Case, and may do to all his Subjects whatever he pleases, without the least liberty to any one to question or controle those who Execute his Pleasure? And in whatsoever he doth, whether led by Reason, Mistake or Passion, must be submitted to? Much better it is in the State of Nature wherein Men are not bound to submit to the unjust will of another: And if he that judges, judges amiss in his own, or any other Case, he is answerable for it to the rest of Mankind.

14. 'Tis often asked as a mighty Objection, *Where are,* or ever were, there any *Men in such a State of Nature?* To which it may suffice as an answer at present; That since all *Princes* and Rulers of *Independent* Governments all through the World, are in a State of Nature, 'tis plain the World never was, nor ever will be, without Numbers of Men in that State. I have named all Governors of *Independent* Communities, whether they are, or are not, in League with others: For 'tis not every Compact that puts an end to the State of Nature between Men, but only this one of agreeing together mutually to enter into one Community, and make one Body Politick; other Promises and Compacts, Men may make one with another, and yet still be in the State of Nature. The Promises and Bargains for Truck, &c. between the two Men in the Desert Island, mentioned by *Garcilasso De la vega*, in his History of *Peru*, or between a *Swiss* and an *Indian*, in the Woods of *America*, are binding to them, though they are perfectly in a State of Nature, in reference to one another. For Truth and keeping of Faith belongs to Men, as Men, and not as Members of Society.

15. To those that say, There were never any Men in the State of Nature; I will not only oppose the Authority of the Judicious *Hooker, Eccl. Pol. Lib. I. Sect.* 10.

where he says, *The Laws which have been hitherto mentioned*, i.e. the Laws of Nature, *do bind Men, although they have never any settled fellowship, never any Solemn Agreement amongst themselves what to do or not to do, but for as much as we are not by our selves sufficient to furnish our selves with competent store of things, needful for such a Life, as our Nature doth desire, a Life, fit for the Dignity of Man; therefore to supply those Defects and Imperfections which are in us, as living singly and solely by our selves, we are naturally induced to seek Communion and Fellowship with others, this was the Cause of Mens uniting themselves, at first in Politick Societies.* But I moreover affirm, That all Men are naturally in that State, and remain so, till by their own Consents they make themselves Members of some Politick Society; And I doubt not in the Sequel of this Discourse, to make it very clear. . . .

Chap. V

Of Property

25. Whether we consider natural *Reason*, which tells us, that Men, being once born, have a right to their Preservation, and consequently to Meat and Drink, and such other things, as Nature affords for their Subsistence: Or *Revelation*, which gives us an account of those Grants God made of the World to *Adam*, and to *Noah*, and his Sons, 'tis very clear, that God, as King *David* says, *Psal.* CXV. xvi. *has given the Earth to the Children of Men*, given it to Mankind in common. But this being supposed, it seems to some a very great difficulty, how any one should ever come to have a *Property* in any thing: I will not content my self to answer, That if it be difficult to make out *Property*, upon a supposition, that God gave the World to *Adam* and his Posterity in common; it is impossible that any Man, but one universal Monarch, should have any *Property*, upon a supposition, that God gave the World to *Adam*, and his Heirs in Succession, exclusive of all the rest of his Posterity. But I shall endeavour to shew, how Men might come to have a *property* in several parts of that which God gave to Mankind in common, and that without any express Compact of all the Commoners.

26. God, who hath given the World to Men in common, hath also given them reason to make use of it to the best advantage of Life, and convenience. The Earth, and all that is therein, is given to Men for the Support and Comfort of their being. And though all the Fruits it naturally produces, and Beasts it feeds, belong to Mankind in common, as they are produced by the spontaneous hand of Nature; and no body has originally a private Dominion, exclusive of the rest of Mankind, in any of them, as they are thus in their natural state: yet being given for the use of Men, there must of necessity be a means *to appropriate* them some way or other before they can be of any use, or at all beneficial to any particular Man. The Fruit, or Venison, which nourishes the wild *Indian*, who knows no Inclosure, and is still a Tenant in common, must be his, and so his, *i.e.* a part of him, that another can no longer have any right to it, before it can do him any good for the support of his Life.

27. Though the Earth, and all inferior Creatures be common to all Men, yet every Man has a *Property* in his own *Person*. This no Body has any Right to but himself. The *Labour* of his Body, and the *Work* of his Hands, we may say, are properly his. Whatsoever then he removes out of the State that Nature hath provided, and left it in, he hath mixed his *Labour* with, and joyned to it something that is his own, and thereby makes it his *Property*. It being by him removed from the common state Nature placed it in, hath by this *labour* something annexed to it, that excludes the common right of other Men. For this *Labour* being the unquestionable Property of the Labourer, no Man but he can have a right to what that is once joyned to, at least where there is enough, and as good left in common for others.

28. He that is nourished by the Acorns he pickt up under an Oak, or the Apples he gathered from the Trees in the Wood, has certainly appropriated them to himself. No Body can deny but the nourishment is his. I ask then, When did they begin to be his? When he digested? Or when he eat? Or when he boiled? Or when he brought them home? Or when he pickt them up? And 'tis plain, if the first gathering made them not his, nothing else could. That *labour* put a distinction between them and common. That added something to them more than Nature, the common Mother of all, had done; and so they became his private right. And will any one say he had no right to those Acorns or Apples he thus appropriated, because he had not the consent of all Mankind to make them his? Was it a Robbery thus to assume to himself what belonged to all in Common? If such a consent as that was necessary, Man had starved, notwithstanding the Plenty God had given him. We see in *Commons*, which remain so by Compact, that 'tis the taking any part of what is common, and removing it out of the state Nature leaves it in, which *begins the Property*; without which the Common is of no use. And the taking of this or that part, does not depend on the express consent of all the Commoners. Thus the Grass my Horse has bit; the Turfs my Servant has cut; and the Ore I have digg'd in any place where I have a right to them in common with others, become my *Property*, without the assignation or consent of any body. The *labour* that was mine, removing them out of that common state they were in, hath *fixed* my *Property* in them.

29. By making an explicit consent of every Commoner, necessary to any ones appropriating to himself any part of what is given in common, Children or Servants could not cut the Meat which their Father or Master had provided for them in common, without assigning to every one his peculiar part. Though the Water running in the Fountain be every ones, yet who can doubt, but that in the Pitcher is his only who drew it out? His *labour* hath taken it out of the hands of Nature, where it was common, and belong'd equally to all her Children, and *hath* thereby *appropriated* it to himself.

30. Thus this Law of reason makes the Deer, that *Indian's* who hath killed it; 'tis allowed to be his goods who hath bestowed his labour upon it, though before, it was the common right of every one. And amongst those who are counted

the Civiliz'd part of Mankind, who have made and multiplied positive Laws to determine Property, this original Law of Nature for the *beginning of Property*, in what was before common, still takes place; and by vertue thereof, what Fish any one catches in the Ocean, that great and still remaining Common of Mankind; or what Ambergriese any one takes up here, is *by* the *Labour* that removes it out of that common state Nature left it in, *made* his *Property* who takes that pains about it. And even amongst us the Hare that any one is Hunting, is thought his who pursues her during the Chase. For being a Beast that is still looked upon as common, and no Man's private Possession; whoever has imploy'd so much *labour* about any of that kind, as to find and pursue her, has thereby removed her from the state of Nature, wherein she was common, and hath *begun a Property.*

31. It will perhaps be objected to this, That if gathering the Acorns, or other Fruits of the Earth, *&c.* makes a right to them, then any one may *ingross* as much as he will. To which I Answer, Not so. The same Law of Nature, that does by this means give us Property, does also *bound* that *Property* too. *God has given us all things richly,* 1 Tim. vi. 17. is the Voice of Reason confirmed by Inspiration. But how far has he given it us? *To enjoy.* As much as any one can make use of to any advantage of life before it spoils; so much he may by his labour fix a Property in. Whatever is beyond this, is more than his share, and belongs to others. Nothing was made by God for Man to spoil or destroy. And thus considering the plenty of natural Provisions there was a long time in the World, and the few spenders, and to how small a part of that provision the industry of one Man could extend it self, and ingross it to the prejudice of others; especially keeping within the *bounds,* set by reason of what might serve for his *use;* there could be then little room for Quarrels or Contentions about Property so establish'd.

32. But the *chief matter of Property* being now not the Fruits of the Earth, and the Beasts that subsist on it, but the *Earth it self;* as that which takes in and carries with it all the rest: I think it is plain, that *Property* in that too is acquired as the former. *As much Land* as a Man Tills, Plants, Improves, Cultivates, and can use the Product of, so much is his *Property.* He by his Labour does, as it were, inclose it from the Common. Nor will it invalidate his right to say, Every body else has an equal Title to it; and therefore he cannot appropriate, he cannot inclose, without the Consent of all his Fellow-Commoners, all Mankind. God, when he gave the World in common to all Mankind, commanded Man also to labour, and the penury of his Condition required it of him. God and his Reason commanded him to subdue the Earth, *i.e.* improve it for the benefit of Life, and therein lay out something upon it that was his own, his labour. He that in Obedience to this Command of God, subdued, tilled and sowed any part of it, thereby annexed to it something that was his *Property,* which another had no Title to, nor could without injury take from him.

33. Nor was this *appropriation* of any parcel of *Land,* by improving it, any prejudice to any other Man, since there was still enough, and as good left; and more than the yet unprovided could use. So that in effect, there was never the less

another can make use of, does as good as take nothing at all. No Body could think himself injur'd by the drinking of another Man, though he took a good Draught, who had a whole River of the same Water left him to quench his thirst. And the Case of Land and Water, where there is enough of both, is perfectly the same.

34. God gave the World to Men in Common; but since he gave it them for their benefit, and the greatest Conveniencies of Life they were capable to draw from it, it cannot be supposed he meant it should always remain common and uncultivated. He gave it to the use of the Industrious and Rational, (and *Labour* was to be *his Title* to it;) not to the Fancy or Covetousness of the Quarrelsom and Contentious. He that had as good left for his Improvement, as was already taken up, needed not complain, ought not to meddle with what was already improved by another's Labour: If he did, 'tis plain he desired the benefit of another's Pains, which he had no right to, and not the Ground which God had given him in common with others to labour on, and whereof there was as good left, as that already possessed, and more than he knew what to do with, or his Industry could reach to.

35. 'Tis true, in *Land* that is *common* in *England*, or any other Country, where there is Plenty of People under Government, who have Money and Commerce, no one can inclose or appropriate any part, without the consent of all his Fellow-Commoners: Because this is left common by Compact, *i.e.* by the Law of the Land, which is not to be violated. And though it be Common, in respect of some Men, it is not so to all Mankind; but is the joint property of this Countrey, or this Parish. Besides, the remainder, after such inclosure, would not be as good to the rest of the Commoners as the whole was, when they could all make use of the whole: whereas in the beginning and first peopling of the great Common of the World, it was quite otherwise. The Law Man was under, was rather for *appropriating*. God Commanded, and his Wants forced him to *labour*. That was his *Property* which could not be taken from him where-ever he had fixed it. And hence subduing or cultivating the Earth, and having Dominion, we see are joyned together. The one gave Title to the other. So that God, by commanding to subdue, gave Authority so far to *appropriate*. And the Condition of Humane Life, which requires Labour and Materials to work on, necessarily introduces *private Possessions*.

36. The measure of Property, Nature has well set, by the Extent of Mens *Labour, and the Conveniency of Life:* No Mans Labour could subdue, or appropriate all: nor could his Enjoyment consume more than a small part; so that it was impossible for any Man, this way, to intrench upon the right of another, or acquire, to himself, a Property, to the Prejudice of his Neighbour, who would still have room, for as good, and as large a Possession (after the other had taken out his) as before it was appropriated. This *measure* did confine every Man's *Possession*, to a very moderate Proportion, and such as he might appropriate to himself, without Injury to any Body in the first Ages of the World, when Men were more in danger to be lost, by wandering from their Company, in the then vast Wilderness of the Earth, than to be

without prejudice to any Body, as full as the World seems. For supposing a Man, or Family, in the state they were, at first peopling of the World by the Children of *Adam*, or *Noah;* let him plant in some in-land, vacant places of *America*, we shall find that the *Possessions* he could make himself upon the *measures* we have given, would not be very large, nor, even to this day, prejudice the rest of Mankind, or give them reason to complain, or think themselves injured by this Man's Incroachment, though the Race of Men have now spread themselves to all the corners of the World, and do infinitely exceed the small number [which] was at the beginning. Nay, the extent of *Ground* is of so little value, *without labour,* that I have heard it affirmed, that in *Spain* it self, a Man may be permitted to plough, sow, and reap, without being disturbed, upon Land he has no other Title to, but only his making use of it. But, on the contrary, the Inhabitants think themselves beholden to him, who, by his Industry on neglected, and consequently waste Land, has increased the stock of Corn, which they wanted. But be this as it will, which I lay no stress on; This I dare boldly affirm, That the same *Rule of Propriety, (viz.)* that every Man should have as much as he could make use of, would hold still in the World, without straitning any body, since there is Land enough in the World to suffice double the Inhabitants had not the *Invention of Money,* and the tacit Agreement of Men to put a value on it, introduced (by Consent) larger Possessions, and a Right to them; which, how it has done, I shall, by and by, shew more at large.

37. This is certain, That in the beginning, before the desire of having more than Men needed, had altered the intrinsick value of things, which depends only on their usefulness to the Life of Man; or had *agreed, that a little piece of yellow Metal,* which would keep without wasting or decay, should be worth a great piece of Flesh, or a whole heap of Corn; though Men had a Right to appropriate, by their Labour, each one to himself, as much of the things of Nature, as he could use: Yet this could not be much, nor to the Prejudice of others, where the same plenty was still left, to those who would use the same Industry. To which let me add, that he who appropriates land to himself by his labour, does not lessen but increase the common stock of mankind. For the provisions serving to the support of humane life, produced by one acre of inclosed and cultivated land, are (to speak much within compasse) ten times more, than those, which are yeilded by an acre of Land, of an equal richnesse, lyeing wast in common. And therefor he, that incloses Land and has a greater plenty of the conveniencys of life from ten acres, than he could have from an hundred left to Nature, may truly be said, to give ninety acres to Mankind. For his labour now supplys him with provisions out of ten acres, which were but the product of an hundred lying in common. I have here rated the improved land very low in making its product but as ten to one, when it is much nearer an hundred to one. For I aske whether in the wild woods and uncultivated wast of America left to Nature, without any improvement, tillage or husbandry, a thousand acres will yeild the needy and wretched inhabitants of many conveniencies of life as ten acres of equally fertile land doe in Devonshire when they are well cultivated?

Before the Appropriation of Land, he who gathered as much of the wild Fruit, killed, caught, or tamed, as many of the Beasts as he could; he that so employed his Pains about any of the spontaneous Products of Nature, as any way to alter them, from the state which Nature put them in, *by* placing any of his *Labour* on them, did thereby *acquire a Property in them:* But if they perished, in his Possession, without their due use; if the Fruits rotted, or the Venison putrified, before he could spend it, he offended against the common Law of Nature, and was liable to be punished; he invaded his Neighbour's share, for he had *no Right, farther than his Use* called for any of them, and they might serve to afford him Conveniencies of Life.

38. The same *measures* governed the *Possession of Land* too: Whatsoever he tilled and reaped, laid up and made use of, before it spoiled, that was his peculiar Right; whatsoever he enclosed, and could feed, and make use of, the Cattle and Product was also his. But if either the Grass of his Inclosure rotted on the Ground, or the Fruit of his planting perished without gathering, and laying up, this part of the Earth, notwithstanding his Inclosure, was still to be looked on as Waste, and might be the Possession of any other. Thus, at the beginning, *Cain* might take as much Ground as he could till, and make it his own Land, and yet leave enough to *Abel's* Sheep to feed on; a few Acres would serve for both their Possessions. But as Families increased, and Industry inlarged their Stocks, their *Possessions inlarged* with the need of them; but yet it was commonly *without any fixed property in the ground* they made use of, till they incorporated, settled themselves together, and built Cities, and then, by consent, they came in time, to set out the *bounds of their distinct Territories,* and agree on limits between them and their Neighbours, and by Laws within themselves, settled the *Properties* of those of the same Society. For we see, that in that part of the World which was first inhabited, and therefore like to be best peopled, even as low down as *Abraham's* time, they wandred with their Flocks, and their Herds, which was their substance, freely up and down; and this *Abraham* did, in a Country where he was a Stranger. Whence it is plain, that at least, a great part of the *Land lay in common;* that the Inhabitants valued it not, nor claimed Property in any more than they made use of. But when there was not room enough in the same place, for their Herds to feed together, they, by consent, as *Abraham* and *Lot* did, *Gen.* xiii. 5. separated and inlarged their pasture, where it best liked them. And for the same Reason *Esau* went from his Father, and his Brother, and planted in *Mount Seir,* Gen. xxxvi. 6.

39. And thus, without supposing any private Dominion, and property in *Adam,* over all the World, exclusive of all other Men, which can no way be proved, nor any ones Property be made out from it; but supposing the *World* given as it was to the Children of Men *in common,* we see how *labour* could make Men distinct titles to several parcels of it, for their private uses; wherein there could be no doubt of Right, no room for quarrel.

40. Nor is it so strange, as perhaps before consideration it may appear, that the *Property of labour* should be able to over-ballance the Community of Land. For 'tis *Labour* indeed that *puts the difference of value* on every thing; and let any one consider, what the difference is between an Acre of Land planted with Tobacco, or

Sugar, sown with Wheat or Barley; and an Acre of the same Land lying in common, without any Husbandry upon it, and he will find, that the improvement of *labour makes* the far greater part of *the value*. I think it will be but a very modest Computation to say, that of the *Products* of the Earth useful to the Life of Man $^9/_{10}$ are the *effects of labour:* nay, if we will rightly estimate things as they come to our use, and cast up the several Expenses about them, what in them is purely owing to *Nature*, and what to *labour*, we shall find, that in most of them $^{99}/_{100}$ are wholly to be put on the account of *labour*.

41. There cannot be a clearer demonstration of any thing, than several Nations of the *Americans* are of this, who are rich in Land, and poor in all the Comforts of Life; whom Nature having furnished as liberally as any other people, with the materials of Plenty, *i.e.* a fruitful Soil, apt to produce in abundance, what might serve for food, rayment, and delight; yet for want of improving it by labour, have not one hundredth part of the Conveniencies we enjoy: And a King of a Large fruitful Territory there feeds, lodges, and is clad worse than a day Labourer in *England.*

42. To make this a little clearer, let us but trace some of the ordinary provisions of Life, through their several progresses, before they come to our use, and see how much they receive of their *value from Humane Industry.* Bread, Wine and Cloth, are things of daily use, and great plenty, yet notwithstanding, Acorns, Water, and Leaves, or Skins, must be our Bread, Drink and Clothing, did not *labour* furnish us with these more useful Commodities. For whatever *Bread* is more worth than Acorns, *Wine* than Water, and *Cloth* or *Silk* than Leaves, Skins, or Moss, that is wholly *owing to labour* and industry. The one of these being the Food and Rayment which unassisted Nature furnishes us with; and other provisions which our industry and pains prepare for us, which how much they exceed the other in value, when any one hath computed, he will then see, how much *labour makes the far greatest part of the value* of things, we enjoy in this World: And the ground which produces the materials, is scarce to be reckon'd in, as any, or at most, but a very small, part of it; So little, that even amongst us, Land that is left wholly to Nature, that hath no improvement of Pasturage, Tillage, or Planting, is called, as indeed it is, *wast*; and we shall find the benefit of it amount to little more than nothing. This shews, how much numbers of men are to be preferd to largenesse of dominions, and that the increase of lands and the right imploying of them is the great art of government. And that Prince who shall be so wise and godlike as by established laws of liberty to secure protection and incouragement to the honest industry of Mankind against the oppression of power and narrownesse of Party will quickly be too hard for his neighbors. But this bye the bye. To return to the argument in hand.

43. An Acre of Land that bears here Twenty Bushels of Wheat, and another in *America*, which, with the same Husbandry, would do the like, are without doubt, of the same natural, intrinsick Value. But yet the Benefit Mankind receives from the one, in a Year, is worth 5 *l.* and from the other possibly not worth a Penny, if all the Profit an *Indian* received from it were to be valued, and sold here;

at least, I may truly say, not $\frac{1}{1000}$. 'Tis *Labour* then which *puts the greatest part of Value upon Land,* without which it would scarcely be worth any thing: 'tis to that we owe the greatest part of all its useful Products: for all that the Straw, Bran, Bread, of that Acre of Wheat, is more worth than the Product of an Acre of as good Land, which lies wast, is all the Effect of Labour. For 'tis not barely the Plough-man's Pains, the Reaper's and Thresher's Toil, and the Bakers Sweat, is to be counted into the *Bread* we eat; the Labour of those who broke the Oxen, who digged and wrought the Iron and Stones, who felled and framed the Timber imployed about the Plough, Mill, Oven, or any other Utensils, which are a vast Number, requisite to this Corn, from its being seed to be sown to its being made Bread, must all be *charged on* the account of *Labour,* and received as an effect of that: Nature and the Earth furnished only the almost worthless Materials, as in themselves. 'Twould be a strange *Catalogue of things, that Industry provided and made use of, about every Loaf of Bread,* before it came to our use, if we could trace them; Iron, Wood, Leather, Bark, Timber, Stone, Bricks, Coals, Lime, Cloth, Dying-Drugs, Pitch, Tar, Masts, Ropes, and all the Materials made use of in the Ship, that brought any of the Commodities made use of by any of the Workmen, to any part of the Work, all which, 'twould be almost impossible, at least too long, to reckon up.

44. From all which it is evident, that though the things of Nature are given in common, yet Man (by being Master of himself, and *Proprietor of his own Person,* and the actions of *Labour* of it) had still in himself *the great Foundation of Property;* and that which made up the great part of what he applied to the Support or Comfort of his being, when Invention and Arts had improved the conveniencies of Life, was perfectly his own, and did not belong in common to others.

45. Thus *Labour,* in the Beginning, *gave a Right of Property,* where-ever any one was pleased to imploy it, upon what was common, which remained, a long while, the far greater part, and is yet more than Mankind makes use of. Men, at first, for the most part, contented themselves with what un-assisted Nature Offered to their Necessities: and though afterwards, in some parts of the World, (where the Increase of People and Stock, with the *Use of Money*) had made Land scarce, and so of some Value, the several *Communities* settled the Bounds of their distinct Territories, and by Laws within themselves, regulated the Properties of the private Men of their Society, and so, *by Compact* and Agreement, *settled the Property* which Labour and Industry began; and the Leagues that have been made between several States and Kingdoms, either expressly or tacitly disowning all Claim and Right to the Land in the others Possession, have, by common Consent, given up their Pretences to their natural common Right, which originally they had to those Countries, and so have, by *positive agreement, settled a Property* amongst themselves, in distinct Parts and parcels of the Earth: yet there are still *great Tracts of Ground* to be found, which (the Inhabitants thereof not having joyned with the rest of Mankind, in the consent of the Use of their common Money) *lie waste,* and are more than the People, who dwell on it, do, or can make use of, and so still lie in common. Tho' this can scarce happen amongst that part of Mankind, that have consented to the use of Money.

46. The greatest part of *things really useful* to the Life of Man, and such as the necessity of subsisting made the first Commoners of the World look after, as it doth the *Americans* now, *are* generally things *of short duration;* such as, if they are not consumed by use, will decay and perish of themselves: Gold, Silver, and Diamonds, are things, that Fancy or Agreement hath put the Value on, more then real Use, and the necessary Support of Life. Now of those good things which Nature hath provided in common, every one had a Right (as hath been said) to as much as he could use, and had a Property in all that he could affect with his Labour: all that his Industry could extend to, to alter from the State Nature had put it in, was his. He that *gathered* a Hundred Bushels of Acorns or Apples, had thereby a *Property* in them; they were his Goods as soon as gathered. He was only to look that he used them before they spoiled; else he took more than his share, and robb'd others. And indeed it was a foolish thing, as well as dishonest, to hoard up more than he could make use of. If he gave away a part to any body else, so that it perished not uselesly in his Possession, these he also made use of. And if he also bartered away Plumbs that would have rotted in a Week, for Nuts that would last good for his eating a whole Year, he did no injury; he wasted not the common Stock; destroyed no part of the portion of Goods that belonged to others, so long as nothing perished uselesly in his hands. Again, if he would give us Nuts for a piece of Metal, pleased with its colour; or exchanged his Sheep for Shells, or Wool for a sparkling Pebble or a Diamond, and keep those by him all his Life, he invaded not the Right of others, he might heap up as much of these durable things as he pleased; the *exceeding of the bounds of his* just *Property* not lying in the largeness of his Possession, but the perishing of any thing uselesly in it.

47. And thus *came in the use of Money,* some lasting thing that Men might keep without spoiling, and that by mutual consent Men would take in exchange for the truly useful, but perishable Supports of Life.

48. And as different degrees of Industry were apt to give Men Possessions in different Proportions, so this *Invention of Money* gave them the opportunity to continue to enlarge them. For supposing an Island, separated from all possible Commerce with the rest of the World, wherein there were but a hundred Families, but there were Sheep, Horses and Cows, with other useful Animals, wholsome Fruits, and Land enough for Corn for a hundred thousand times as many, but nothing in the Island, either because of its Commonness, or Perishableness, fit to supply the place of *Money:* What reason could any one have there to enlarge his Possessions beyond the use of his Family, and a plentiful supply to its Consumption, either in what their own Industry produced, or they could barter for like perishable, useful Commodities, with others? Where there is not something both lasting and scarce, and so valuable to be hoarded up, there Men will not be apt to enlarge their *Possessions of Land,* were it never so rich, never so free for them to take. For I ask, What would a Man value Ten Thousand, or an Hundred Thousand Acres of excellent *Land,* ready cultivated, and well stocked too with Cattle, in the middle of the in-land Parts of *America,* where he had no hopes of Commerce with other

Parts of the World, to draw *Money* to him by the Sale of the Product? It would not be worth the inclosing, and we should see him give up again to the wild Common of Nature, whatever was more than would supply the Conveniencies of Life to be had there for him and his Family.

49. Thus in the beginning all the World was *America,* and more so than that is now; for no such thing as *Money* was any where known. Find out something that hath the *Use and Value of Money* amongst his Neighbours, you shall see the same Man will begin presently to *enlarge* his *Possessions.*

50. But since Gold and Silver, being little useful to the Life of Man in proportion to Food, Rayment, and Carriage, has its *value* only from the consent of Men, whereof Labour yet makes, in great part, *the measure,* it is plain, that Men have agreed to disproportionate and unequal Possession of the Earth, they having by a tacit and voluntary consent found out a way, how a man may fairly possess more land than he himself can use the product of, by receiving in exchange for the overplus, Gold and Silver, which may be hoarded up without injury to any one, these metalls not spoileing or decaying in the hands of the possessor. This partage of things, in an inequality of private possessions, men have made practicable out of the bounds of Societie, and without compact, only by putting a value on gold and silver and tacitly agreeing in the use of Money. For in Governments the Laws regulate the right of property, and the possession of land is determined by positive constitutions.

51. And thus, I think it is very easie to conceive without any difficulty, *how Labour could at first begin a title of Property* in the common things of Nature, and how the spending it upon our uses bounded it. So that there could then be no reason of quarrelling about Title, nor any doubt about the largeness of Possession it gave. Right and conveniency went together; for as a Man had a Right to all he could imploy his Labour upon, so he had no temptation to labour for more than he could make use of. This left no room for Controversie about the Title, nor for Incroach-ment on the Right of others; what Portion a Man carved to himself, was easily seen; and it was useless as well as dishonest to carve himself too much, or take more than he needed. . . .

Chap. IX

Of the Ends of Political Society and Government

123. If Man in the State of Nature be so free, as has been said; If he be absolute Lord of his own Person and Possessions, equal to the greatest, and subject to no Body, why will he part with his Freedom? Why will he give up this Empire, and subject himself to the Dominion and Controul of any other Power? To which 'tis obvious to Answer, that though in the state of Nature he hath such a right, yet

the Enjoyment of it is very uncertain, and constantly exposed to the Invasion of others. For all being Kings as much as he, every Man his Equal, and the greater part no strict Observers of Equity and Justice, the enjoyment of the property he has in this state is very unsafe, very unsecure. This makes him willing to quit a Condition, which however free, is full of fears and continual dangers: And 'tis not without reason, that he seeks out, and is willing to joyn in Society with others who are already united, or have a mind to unite for the mutual *Preservation* of their Lives, Liberties and Estates, which I call by the general Name, *Property*.

124. The great and *chief end* therefore, of Mens uniting into Common-wealths, and putting themselves under Government, *is the Preservation of their Property*. To which in the state of Nature there are many things wanting.

First, There wants an *establish'd*, settled, known *Law*, received and allowed by common consent to be the Standard of Right and Wrong, and the common measure to decide all Controversies between them. For though the Law of Nature be plain and intelligible to all rational Creatures; yet Men being biassed by their Interest, as well as ignorant for want of study of it, are not apt to allow of it as a Law binding to them in the application of it to their particular Cases.

125. *Secondly,* In the State of Nature there wants a *known and indifferent Judge,* with Authority to determine all differences according to the established Law. For every one in that state being both Judge and Executioner of the Law of Nature, Men being partial to themselves, Passion and Revenge is very apt to carry them too far, and with too much heat, in their own Cases; as well as negligence, and unconcernedness, to make them too remiss, in other Mens.

126. *Thirdly,* In the state of Nature there often wants *Power* to back and support the Sentence when right, and to *give* it due *Execution*. They who by any Injustice offended, will seldom fail, where they are able, by force to make good their Injustice: such resistance many times makes the punishment dangerous, and frequently destructive, to those who attempt it.

127. Thus Mankind, notwithstanding all the Priviledges of the state of Nature, being but in an ill condition, while they remain in it, are quickly driven into Society. Hence it comes to pass, that we seldom find any number of Men live any time together in this State. The inconveniencies, that they are therein exposed to, by the irregular and uncertain exercise of the Power every Man has of punishing the transgressions of others, make them take Sanctuary under the establish'd Laws of Government, and therein seek *the preservation of their Property*. 'Tis this makes them so willingly give up every one his single power of punishing to be exercised by such alone as shall be appointed to it amongst them; and by such Rules as the Community, or those authorised by them to that purpose, shall agree on. And in this we have the original *right and rise* of both *the Legislative and Executive Power,* as well as of the Governments and Societies themselves. . . .

Property and Sovereignty [1]
•
Morris R. Cohen

Property and sovereignty, as every student knows, belong to entirely different branches of the law. Sovereignty is a concept of political or public law and property belongs to civil or private law. This distinction between public and private law is a fixed feature of our law-school curriculum. It was expressed with characteristic eighteenth-century neatness and clarity by Montesquieu, when he said that by political laws we acquire liberty and by civil law property, and that we must not apply the principles of one to the other.[2] Montesquieu's view that political laws must in no way retrench on private property, because no public good is greater than the maintenance of private property, was echoed by Blackstone and became the basis of legal thought in America. Though Austin, with his usual prolix and near-sighted sincerity, managed to throw some serious doubts on this classical distinction,[3] it has continued to be regarded as one of the fixed divisions of the jural field. In the second volume of his *Genossenschaftrecht* the learned Gierke treated us to some very interesting speculations as to how the Teutons became the founders of public law just as the Romans were the founders of private law. But in later years he somewhat softened this sharp distinction;[4] and common-law lawyers are inclined rather to regard the Roman system as giving more weight to public than to private law.

[1] This lecture, originally delivered at the Cornell Law School as the Irvine Lecture for 1927, is reprinted here, with slight changes, from *Cornell Law Quarterly,* Vol. XIII (1927), p. 8.

[2] *L'Esprit des lois,* Book XXVI, Chap. 15, 1748.

[3] Austin, *Lectures on Jurisprudence,* 5th ed., 1911, Vol. I, p. 457.

[4] Holtzendorff-Kohler, *Enzyklopädie,* 1913–15, Vol. I, pp. 179–80. . . .

From Morris R. Cohen, "Property and Sovereignty," in *Law and the Social Order* (New York: Harcourt, Brace and Co., 1933), pp. 41–49, 64. Copyright 1961 Leonora Cohen Rosenfield. Reprinted by permission.

Morris R. Cohen (1880–1947) was Professor of Philosophy at the City College of New York for many years. He was the author of *Reason and Nature, A Preface to Logic,* and other books.

The distinction between property and sovereignty is generally identified with the Roman discrimination between *dominium*, the rule over things by the individual, and *imperium*, the rule over all individuals by the prince. Like other Roman distinctions, this has been regarded as absolutely fixed in the nature of things. But early Teutonic law—the law of the Anglo-Saxons, Franks, Visigoths, Lombards, and other tribes—makes no such distinction; and the state long continued to be the prince's estate, so that even in the eighteenth century the Prince of Hesse could sell his subjects as soldiers to the King of England. The essence of feudal law—a system not confined to medieval Europe—is the inseparable connection between land tenure and personal homage involving often rather menial services on the part of the tenant and always genuine sovereignty over the tenant by the landlord.

The feudal baron had, for instance, the right to determine the marriage of the ward, as well as the right to nominate the priest; and the great importance of the former as a real property right is amply attested in Magna Carta and in the Statute Quia Emptores. Likewise was the administration of justice in the baron's court an incident of landownership; and if, unlike the French up to the Revolution, the English did not regard the office of judge as a revenue-producing incident of seigniorage to be sold in the open market (as army commissions were up to the time of Gladstone), the local squire did in fact continue to act as justice of the peace. Ownership of the land and local political sovereignty were inseparable.

Can we dismiss all this with the simple exclamation that all this is medieval and we have long outgrown it?

Well, right before our eyes the Law of Property Act of 1925 is sweeping away substantial remains of the complicated feudal land laws of England, by abolishing the difference between the descent of real and that of personal property, and by abolishing all legal (though not equitable) estates intermediate between leaseholds and fees simple absolute. These remains of feudalism have not been mere vestiges. They have played an important part in the national life of England. Their absurdities and indefensible abuses were pilloried with characteristic wit and learning by the peerless Maitland. The same thing had been done most judiciously by Joshua Williams, the teacher of several generations of English lawyers brought up on the seventeen editions of his great text-book on real property law. Yet these and similar efforts made no impression on the actual law. What these great men did not see with sufficient clearness was that back of the complicated law of settlement, fee-tail, copyhold estates, of the heir-at-law, of the postponement of women, and other feudal incidents, there was a great and well-founded fear that by simplifying and modernizing the real property law of England the land might become more marketable. Once land becomes fully marketable it can no longer be counted on to remain in the hands of the landed aristocratic families; and this means the passing of their political power and the end of their control over the destinies of the British Empire. For if American experience has demonstrated anything, it is that the continued leadership by great families cannot be as well founded on a money as on a land economy. The same kind of talent that enables Jay Gould to acquire dominion over certain railroads enables Mr. Harriman to take it away from his sons. From the point of view of an established land economy, a money economy thus seems a state of perpetual war instead of a social order where son succeeds father. The motto that a career should be open to talent thus seems a justification of anarchy, just as the election of rulers (kings or priests) seems an anarchic procedure to those used to the regular succession of father by son.

That which was hidden from Maitland, Joshua Williams, and the other great ones, was revealed to a Welsh solicitor who in the budget of 1910 proposed to tax the land so as to force it on the market. The radically revolutionary character of this proposal was at once recognized in England. It was bitterly fought by all those who treasured what had remained of the old English aristocratic rule. When this budget finally passed, the basis of the old real property law and the effective power of the House of Lords was gone. The legislation of 1925–26 was thus a final completion in the realm of private law of the revolution that was fought in 1910 in the forum of public law, i.e., in the field of taxation and the power of the House of Lords.

As the terms "medievalism" and "feudalism" have become with us terms of opprobrium, we are apt to think that only unenlightened selfishness has until recently prevented English land law from cutting its medieval moorings and embarking on the sea of purely money or commercial economy. This light-hearted judgment, however, may be somewhat sobered by reflection on a second recent event—the Supreme Court decision on the Minimum Wage Law.[5] Without passing judgment at this point on the soundness of the reasoning whereby the majority reached its decision, the result may still fairly be characterized as a high-water mark of law in a purely money or commercial economy. For by that decision private monetary interests receive precedence over the sovereign duty of the state to maintain decent standards of living.

The state, which has an undisputed right to prohibit contracts against public morals or public policy, is here declared to have no right to prohibit contracts under which many receive wages less than the minimum of subsistence, so that if they are not the objects of humiliating public or private charity, they become centres of the physical and moral evils that result from systematic underfeeding and degraded standards of life. Now I do not wish here to argue the merits or demerits of the minimum wage decision. Much less am I concerned with any quixotic attempt to urge England to go back to medievalism. But the two events together show in strong relief how recent and in the main exceptional is the extreme position of the laissez faire doctrine, which, according to the insinuation of Justice Holmes, has led the Supreme Court to read Herbert Spencer's extreme individualism into the Fourteenth Amendment, and according to others, has enacted Cain's motto, "Am I my brother's keeper?" as the supreme law of industry. Dean Pound has shown[6] that in making a property right out of the freedom to contract, the Supreme Court has stretched the meaning of the term "property" to include what it has never before signified in the law or jurisprudence of any civilized country. But whether this

---

[5] Adkins v. Children's Hospital, U.S. 261, 525; Supr. Ct. 43, 394 (1923).
[6] "Liberty of Contract," *Yale Law Journal*, Vol. XVIII (1909), pp. 454, 482.

extension is justified or not, it certainly means the passing of a certain domain of sovereignty from the state to the private employer of labour, who now has the absolute right to discharge and threaten to discharge any employee who wants to join a trade-union, and the absolute right to pay a wage that is injurious to a basic social interest.

It may be that economic forces will themselves correct the abuse which the Supreme Court does not allow the state to remove directly, that economic forces will eliminate parasitic industries which do not pay the minimum of subsistence, because such industries are not as economically efficient and profitable as those which pay higher wages. It was similarly argued that slavery was bound to disappear on account of its economic inefficiency. Meanwhile, however, the sovereignty of the state is limited by the manner in which the courts interpret the term "property" in the Fifth and Fourteenth Amendments to the Federal Constitution and in the bills of rights in our state constitutions. This makes it imperative for us to consider the nature of private property with reference to the sovereign power of the state to look after the general welfare. A dispassionate scientific study of this requires an examination of the nature of property, its justification, and the ultimate meaning of the policies based on it.

Property as Power

Any one who frees himself from the crudest materialism readily recognizes that as a legal term "property" denotes not material things but certain rights. In the world of nature apart from more or less organized society, there are things but clearly no property rights.

Further reflection shows that a property right is not to be identified with the fact of physical possession. Whatever technical definition of property we may prefer, we must recognize that a property right is a relation not between an owner and a thing, but between the owner and other individuals in reference to things. A right is always against one or more individuals. This becomes unmistakably clear if we take specifically modern forms of property such as franchises, patents, goodwill, etc., which constitute such a large part of the capitalized assets of our industrial and commercial enterprises.

The classical view of property as a right over things resolves it into component rights such as the *jus utendi, jus disponendi,* etc. But the essence of private property is always the right to exclude others. The law does not guarantee me the physical or social ability of actually using what it calls mine. By public regulations it may indirectly aid me by removing certain general hindrances to the enjoyment of property. But the law of property helps me directly only to exclude others from using the things that it assigns to me. If, then, somebody else wants to use the food, the house, the land, or the plough that the law calls mine, he has to get my consent. To the extent that these things are necessary to the life of my neighbour, the law thus confers on me a power, limited but real, to make him do what I want. If Laban has the sole disposal of his daughters and his cattle, Jacob must serve him if he desires to possess them. In a régime where land is the principal source of obtaining a livelihood, he who has the legal right over the land receives homage and service from those who wish to live on it.

The character of property as sovereign power compelling service and obedience may be obscured for us in a commercial economy by the fiction of the so-called labour contract as a free bargain and by the frequency with which service is rendered indirectly through a money payment. But not only is there actually little freedom to bargain on the part of the steel-worker or miner who needs a job, but in some cases the medieval subject had as much power to bargain when he accepted the sovereignty of his lord. Today I do not directly serve my landlord if I wish to live in the city with a roof over my head, but I must work for others to pay him rent with which he obtains the personal services of others. The money needed for purchasing things must for the vast majority be acquired by hard labour and disagreeable service to those to whom the law has accorded dominion over the things necessary for subsistence.

To a philosopher this is of course not at all an argument against private property. It may well be that compulsion in the economic as well as the political realm is necessary for civilized life. But we must not overlook the actual fact that dominion over things is also *imperium* over our fellow human beings.

The extent of the power over the life of others which the legal order confers on those called owners is not fully appreciated by those who think of the law as merely protecting men in their possession. Property law does more. It determines what men shall acquire. Thus, protecting the property rights of a land-lord means giving him the right to collect rent, protecting the property of a railroad or a public-service corporation means giving it the right to make certain charges. Hence the ownership of land and machinery, with the rights of drawing rent, interest, etc., determines the future distribution of the goods that will come into being—determines what share of such goods various individuals shall acquire. The average life of goods that are either consumable or used for production of other goods is very short. Hence a law that merely protected men in their possession and did not also regulate the acquisition of new goods would be of little use.

From this point of view it can readily be seen that when a court rules that a gas company is entitled to a return of 6 per cent on its investment, it is not merely protecting property already possessed, it is also determining that a portion of the future social produce shall under certain conditions go to that company. Thus not only medieval landlords but the owners of all revenue-producing property are in fact granted by the law certain powers to tax the future social product. When to this power of taxation there is added the power to command the services of large numbers who are not economically independent, we have the essence of what historically has constituted political sovereignty.

Though the sovereign power possessed by the modern large property owners assumes a somewhat different form from that formerly possessed by the lord of the land, they are not less real and no less extensive. Thus the ancient lord had a limited power to control the modes of expenditure of his subjects by direct sumptuary legislation. The modern captain of industry and of finance has no such direct power himself, though his direct or indirect influence with the legislature may in that respect be considerable. But those who have the power to standardize and advertise certain products do determine what we may buy and use. We cannot well wear clothes except within lines decreed by their manufacturers, and our food is becoming more and more restricted to the kinds that are branded and standardized.

This power of the modern owner of capital to make us feel the necessity of buying more and more of his material goods (that may be more profitable to produce than economical to use) is a phenomenon of the utmost significance to the moral philosopher. The moral philosopher must also note that the modern captain of industry or finance exercises great influence in setting the fashion of expenditure by his personal example. Between a landed aristocracy and the tenantry, the difference is sharp and fixed, so that imitation of the former's mode of life by the latter is regarded as absurd and even immoral. In a money or commercial economy differences of income and mode of life are more gradual and readily hidden, so that there is great pressure to engage in lavish expenditure in order to appear in a higher class than one's income really allows. Such expenditure may even advance one's business credit. This puts pressure not merely on ever greater expenditure but more specifically on expenditure for ostentation rather than for comfort. Though a landed aristocracy may be wasteful in keeping large tracts of land for hunting purposes, the need for discipline to keep in power compels the cultivation of a certain hardihood that the modern wealthy man can ignore. An aristocracy assured of its recognized superiority need not engage in the race of lavish expenditure regardless of enjoyment.

In addition to these indirect ways in which the wealthy few determine the mode of life of the many, there is the somewhat more direct mode that bankers and financiers exercise when they determine the flow of investment, e.g., when they influence building operations by the amount that they will lend on mortgages. This power becomes explicit and obvious when a needy country has to borrow foreign capital to develop its resources.

I have already mentioned that the recognition of private property as a form of sovereignty is not itself an argument against it. Some form of government we must always have. For the most part men prefer to obey and let others take the trouble to think out rules, regulations, and orders. That is why we are always setting up authorities; and when we cannot find any we write to the newspaper as the final arbiter. But although government is a necessity, not all forms of it are of equal value. At any rate it is necessary to apply to the law of property all those considerations of social ethics and enlightened public policy which ought to be brought to the discussion of any just form of government. . . .

Political vs. Economic Sovereignty

If the discussion of property by those interested in private law has suffered from a lack of realism and from too great a reliance on vague *a priori* plausibilities, much the same can be said about political discussion as to the proper limits of state action in regard to property and economic enterprise. Utterly unreal is all talk of men's being robbed of their power of initiative because the state undertakes some service, e.g., the building of a bridge across a river. Men are not deprived of opportunities for real self-reliance if the state lights their streets at night, fills up holes in the pavements, and removes other dangers to life and limb, or provides opportunities for education to all. The conditions of modern life are complex and distracting enough so that if we can ease the strain by simplifying some things through state action we are all the gainers by it. Certain things have to be done in a community and the question whether they should be left to private enterprise dominated by the profit motive, or to the government dominated by political considerations, is not a question of man versus the state, but simply a question of which organization and motive can best do the work.

The New Property
●
Charles A. Reich

The institution called property guards the troubled boundary between individual man and the state. It is not the only guardian; many other institutions, laws, and practices serve as well. But in a society that chiefly values material well-being, the power to control a particular portion of that well-being is the very foundation of individuality.

One of the most important developments in the United States during the past decade has been the emergence of government as a major source of wealth. Government is a gigantic syphon. It draws in revenue and power, and pours forth wealth: money, benefits, services, contracts, franchises, and licenses. Government has always had this function. But while in early times it was minor, today's distribution of largess is on a vast, imperial scale.

The valuables dispensed by government take many forms, but they all share one characteristic. They are steadily taking the place of traditional forms of wealth—forms which are held as private property. Social insurance substitutes for savings; a government contract replaces a businessman's customers and goodwill. The wealth of more and more Americans depends upon a relationship to government. Increasingly, Americans live on government largess—allocated by government on its own terms, and held by recipients subject to conditions which express "the public interest." . . .

The Largess of Government

The Forms of Government-created Wealth

The valuables which derive from relationships to government are of many kinds. Some primarily concern individuals; others flow to businesses and organizations. Some are obvious forms of wealth, such as direct payments of money, while others, like licenses and franchises, are indirectly valuable.

Income and Benefits. For a large number of people, government is a direct source of income although they hold no public job. Their eligibility arises from legal status. Examples are Social Security benefits, unemployment compensation, aid to dependent children, veterans benefits, and the whole scheme of state and local welfare. These represent a principal source of income to a substantial segment of the community.

Jobs. Millions |of| persons receive income from public funds because they are directly employed by federal, state, or local government. The size of the publicly employed working force has increased steadily since the founding of the United States, and seems likely to keep on increasing. If the . . . persons employed in defense industries, which exist mainly on government funds, are added to |those| directly employed, it may be estimated that fifteen to twenty percent of the labor force receives its primary income from government.

Occupational Licenses. Licenses are required before one may engage in many kinds of work, from practicing medicine to guiding hunters through the woods. Even occupations which require little education or training, like that of longshoremen, often are subject to strict licensing. Such licenses, which are dispensed by government, make it possible for their holders to receive what is ordinarily their chief source of income.

Franchises. A franchise, which may be held by an individual or by a company, is a partial monopoly created and handed out by government. Its value depends largely upon governmental power; by limiting the number of franchises, government can make them extremely remunerative. A New York City taxi medallion, which costs very little when originally obtained from the city, can be sold for over twenty thousand dollars. The reason for this high price is that the city has not issued new transferable medallions despite the rise in population and traffic. A television channel, handed out free, can often be sold for many millions. Government distributes wealth when it dispenses route permits to truckers, charters to bus lines, routes to air carriers, certificates to oil and gas pipelines, licenses to liquor stores, allotments to growers of cotton or wheat, and concessions in national parks.

Contracts. Many individuals and many more businesses enjoy public generosity in the form of government contracts. Fifty billion dollars annually flows from the federal government in the form of defense spending. These contracts often resemble subsidies; it is virtually impossible to lose money on them. Businesses sometimes make the government their principal source of income, and many "free enterprises" are set up primarily to do business with the government.

From Charles Reich, "The New Property," *The Yale Law Journal* 73, no. 5 (April 1964): 733–87. Reprinted by permission of the author and publisher.
    Charles Reich was formerly a professor of law at Yale University. He now lives and writes in the San Francisco Bay area.

Subsidies. Analogous to welfare payments for individuals who cannot manage independently in the economy are subsidies to business. Agriculture is subsidized to help it survive against better organized (and less competitive) sectors of the economy, and the shipping industry is given a dole because of its inability to compete with foreign lines. Local airlines are also on the dole. So are other major industries, notably housing. Still others, such as the railroads, are eagerly seeking help. Government also supports many non-business activities, in such areas as scientific research, health, and education. . . .

Use of Public Resources. A very large part of the American economy is publicly owned. Government owns or controls hundreds of millions of acres of public lands valuable for mining, grazing, lumbering, and recreation; sources of energy such as the hydroelectric power of all major rivers, the tidelands reservoirs of oil, and the infant giant of nuclear power; routes of travel and commerce such as the airways, highways, and rivers; the radio-television spectrum which is the avenue for all broadcasting; hoards of surplus crops and materials; public buildings and facilities; and much more. These resources are available for utilization by private businesses and individuals; such use is often equivalent to a subsidy. The radio-television industry uses the scarce channels of the air, free of charge; electric companies use publicly-owned water power; stockmen graze sheep and cattle on public lands at nominal cost; ships and airplanes arrive and depart from publicly-owned docks and airports; the atomic energy industry uses government materials, facilities, and know-how, and all are entitled to make a profit.

Services. Like resources, government services are a source of wealth. Some of these are plainly of commercial value: postal service for periodicals, newspapers, advertisers, and mail-order houses; insurance for home builders and savings banks; technical information for agriculture. Other services dispensed by government include sewage, sanitation, police and fire protection, and public transportation. The Communications Satellite represents an unusual type of subsidy through service: the turning over of government research and know-how to a quasi-private organization. The most important public service of all, education, is one of the greatest sources of value to the individual. . . .

Largess and the Changing Forms of Wealth

The significance of government largess is increased by certain underlying changes in the forms of private wealth in the United States. Changes in the forms of wealth are not remarkable in themselves; the forms are constantly changing and differ in every culture. But today more and more of our wealth takes the form of rights or status rather than of tangible goods. An individual's profession or occupation is a prime example. To many others, a job with a particular employer is the principal form of wealth. A profession or a job is frequently far more valuable than a house or bank account, for a new house can be bought, and a new bank account created, once a profession or job is secure. For the jobless, their status as governmentally assisted or insured persons may be the main source of subsistence.

The automobile dealer's chief wealth is his franchise from the manufacturer which gives him exclusive sales rights within a certain territory, for it is his guarantee of income. His building, his stock of cars, his organization, and his goodwill may all be less valuable than his franchise. Franchises represent the principal asset of many businesses: the gasoline station, chain restaurant, motel or drug store, and many other retail suppliers. To the large manufacturer, contracts, business arrangements, and organization may be the most valuable assets. The steel company's relationships with coal and iron producers and automobile manufacturers and construction companies may be worth more than all its plant and equipment.

The kinds of wealth dispensed by government consist almost entirely of those forms which are in the ascendancy today. To the individual, these new forms, such as a profession, job, or right to receive income, are the basis of his various statuses in society, and may therefore be the most meaningful and distinctive wealth he possesses.

The Emerging System of Law

Wealth or value is created by culture and by society; it is culture that makes a diamond valuable and a pebble worthless. Property, on the other hand, is the creation of law. A man who has property has certain legal rights with respect to an item of wealth; property represents a relationship between wealth and its "owner." Government largess is plainly "wealth," but it is not necessarily "property."

Government largess has given rise to a distinctive system of law. This system can be viewed from at least three perspectives; the rights of holders of largess, the powers of government over largess, and the procedure by which holders' rights and governmental power are adjusted. At this point, analysis will not be aided by attempting to apply or to reject the label "property." What is important is to survey—without the use of labels—the unique legal system that is emerging.

Individual Rights in Largess

As government largess has grown in importance, quite naturally there has been pressure for the protection of individual interests in it. The holder of a broadcast license or a motor carrier permit or a grazing permit for the public lands tends to consider this wealth his "own," and to seek legal protection against interference with his enjoyment. The development of individual interests has been substantial, but it has not come easily.

From the beginning, individual rights in largess have been greatly affected by several traditional legal concepts, each of which has had lasting significance:

Rights vs. privilege. The early law is marked by courts' attempts to distinguish which forms of largess were "rights" and which were "privileges." Legal protection of the former was by far the greater. If the holder of a license had a "right," he might be entitled to a hearing before the license could be revoked; a "mere privilege" might be revoked without notice or hearing.

The gratuity principle. Government largess has often been considered a "gratuity" furnished by the state. Hence it is said that the state can withhold, grant, or revoke the largess at its pleasure. Under this theory, government is considered to be in somewhat the same position as a private giver.

The whole and the parts. Related to the gratuity theory is the idea that, since government may completely withhold a benefit, it may grant it subject to any terms or conditions whatever. This theory is essentially an exercise in logic: the whole power must include all of its parts.

Internal management. Particularly in relation to its own contracts, government has been permitted extensive power on the theory that it should have control over its own housekeeping or internal management functions. Under this theory, government is treated like a private business. In its dealings with outsiders it is permitted much of the freedom to grant contracts and licenses that a private business would have.

Quite often these four theories are blurred in a single statement of judicial attitude. . . . One court put the idea in . . . pithy form: ". . . in accepting charity, the appellant has consented to the provisions of the law under which the charity is bestowed." . . .

The most common forms of protection are procedural, coupled with an insistence that government action be based on standards that are not "arbitrary" or unauthorized. Development has varied mainly according to the particular type of wealth involved. The courts have most readily granted protection to those types which are intimately bound up with the individual's freedom to earn a living. They have been reluctant to grant individual rights in those types of largess which seem to be exercises of the managerial functions of government, such as subsidies and government contracts. . . .

. . . In general, courts tend to afford the greatest measure of protection in revocation or suspension cases. The theory seems to be that here some sort of rights have "vested" which may not be taken away without proper procedure. On the other hand, an applicant for largess is thought to have less at stake, and is therefore entitled to less protection. The mere fact that a particular form of largess is protected in one context does not mean that it will be protected in all others.

While individual interests in largess have developed along the lines of procedural protection and restraint upon arbitrary official action, substantive rights to possess and use largess have remained very limited. . . .

Largess and the Power of Government

Affirmative Powers. When government—national, state, or local—hands out something of value, whether a relief check or a television license, government's power grows forthwith; it automatically gains such power as is necessary and proper to supervise its largess. It obtains new rights to investigate, to regulate, and to punish. . . .

Political activities thought to be subversive or communistic have been the chief area of concern. One of the earliest illustrations is the Emergency Relief Appropriation Act, which sought to prevent any member of the Communist Party or Nazi Bund from getting work under the act. Another example is the effort—ultimately frustrated by the courts—to bar communists or subversives from occupying public housing. Attempts to justify such restrictions followed these lines:

> . . . since low-rent housing projects are subsidized by taxpayers' money, the special benefits thereof shall be available only to loyal tenants, and not to those who elect to join and support organizations whose purposes are inimical to the public welfare.

Membership in the Communist Party or subversive organizations has been considered relevant to the right to pursue a number of important occupations and professions, including that of the lawyer, the radio-telegraph operator, and the port worker. . . . Nor does the list stop at occupations. Ohio required a loyalty oath to receive unemployment compensation. For a time a loyalty oath was required under the National Defense Education Act. New York has provided for the mandatory revocation of the driver's license of any motorist convicted under the Smith Act of advocating the overthrow of the government. . . .

. . . Objections to regulation fade, whether in the minds of the general public or legal scholars, before the argument that government should make sure that its bounty is used in the public interest. Benefits, subsidies, and privileges are seen as "gifts" to be given on conditions, and thus the political and legal sources of government power merge into one. . . .

Broad as is the power derived from largess, it is magnified by many administrative factors when it is brought to bear on a recipient. First, the agency granting government largess generally has a wide measure of discretion to interpret its own power. Second, the nature of administrative agencies, the functions they combine, and the sanctions they possess, give them additional power. Third, the circumstances in which the recipients find themselves sometimes makes them abettors, rather than resisters of the further growth of power.

The legislature generally delegates to an administrative agency its authority with respect to a given form of largess. In this very process of delegation there can be an enlargement of power. The courts allow the agencies a wide measure of discretion to make policy and to interpret legislative policy. Sometimes a legislature gives the agency several different, possibly conflicting policies, allowing it (perhaps unintentionally) to enforce now one and now another. There is little if any requirement of consistency or adherence to precedent, and the agency may, instead of promulgating rules of general application, make and change its policies in the process of case-to-case adjudication. For example, New Jersey's Waterfront Commission has power "in its discretion" to deny the right to work to any longshoreman if he is a person "whose presence at the piers or other waterfront terminals in the Port of New York is found by the commission on the basis of the facts and evidence before it, to constitute a danger to the public peace or safety." The discretion of an agency is even broader, and even less reviewable, when the subject matter is highly technical. . . .

Most dispensing agencies possess the power of delay. They also possess the power of investigation and harassment; they can initiate inquiries which will prove expensive and embarrassing to an applicant. Surveillance alone can make a recipient of largess uncomfortable. And agencies have so many criteria to use, so many available grounds of decision, and so much discretion, that they, like the FCC, can usually find other grounds to accomplish what they cannot do directly. This is a temptation to the honest but zealous administrator, and an invitation to the official who is less than scrupulous. In addition, the broader the regulation, the greater the chance that everyone violates the law in some way, and the greater the discretion to forgive or to punish. . . .

The recipients of largess themselves add to the powers of government by their uncertainty over their rights, and their efforts to please. . . . Instead of contesting, recipients are likely to be overzealous in their acceptance of government authority so that a government contractor may be so anxious to root out "disloyal" employees that he dismisses men who could probably be retained consistently with government policy. Likewise a "think institute" existing primarily on government contracts, may be more eager to "think" along accepted lines because it has its next month's bills to "think" about. . . .

From Governmental Power to
Private Power

The preceding description has pictured two fundamentally opposite forces: government versus the private sector of society. Emphasis on a sharp dichotomy highlights some of the relationships created by government largess. But to a considerable extent this picture distorts reality. First, the impact of governmental power falls unequally on different components of the private sector, so that some gain while others lose. Second, government largess often creates a partnership with some sectors of the private economy, which aids rather than limits the objectives of those private sectors. Third, the apparatus of governmental power may be utilized by private interests in their conflicts with other interests, and thus the tools of government become private rather than public instrumentalities.

Inequalities lie deep in the administrative structure of government largess. The whole process of acquiring it and keeping it favors some applicants and recipients over others. The administrative process is characterized by uncertainty, delay, and inordinate expense; to operate within it requires considerable know-how. All of these factors strongly favor larger, richer, more experienced companies or individuals over smaller ones. Only the most secure can weather delay or seemingly endless uncertainty. A company accused of misusing a license can engage counsel to fight the action without being ruined by the expenses of the defense; an individual may find revocation proceedings are enough to send him to the poorhouse regardless of the outcome. And the large and the small are not always treated alike. For example, small firms which deal with the government are sometimes placed on a blacklist because of delinquencies in performance, thus losing out on all government contracts. But giant contractors who are guilty of similar delinquencies are apparently not subject to this drastic punishment. Similarly, regulation of taxicabs tends to be harder on the individual owner or driver, who may lose his driver's license, while little harm comes to the company controlling a fleet, which may lose drivers but not its precious franchises.

Beside this unacknowledged double standard there is also the fact that sometimes the government quite openly favors one class of applicants—frequently the large and successful. Atomic energy benefits have generally gone to industry giants. Television channels seem to be in the hands of large corporate applicants, often those which control newspapers or other stations. Another illustration of this tendency is in the award of franchises for turnpike restaurants; the business seems to go to large established chains, although they can hardly be said to provide service of outstanding culinary distinction.

All these inequalities modify somewhat the simple picture of a government-private dichotomy. But a second modification is required: government and the private sector (or a favored part of that sector) are often partners rather than opposing interests. The concept of partnership covers many quite different situations. Sometimes government largess serves to aid the private objectives of an industry, as when government supplies grazing land to stockmen, timber to the lumber industry, and scientific know-how to the private investors in Telstar. A second type of partnership exists where governmental action protects the recipient of largess from adverse forces with which he would otherwise have to contend; this is illustrated by the defense contract, with its virtual guarantee against losses due to most economic or management factors. The Atomic Energy Commission provides insurance against public liability due to negligence. Just as frequently, government largess offers protection against the disadvantages of competition. ICC motor carrier regulation provides partial monopolies for each trucker. CAB routes give partial monopolies to airlines. Professional or occupational licensing limits competition and adds a tone of respectability and reliability as well. Often the leaders in seeking regulation have been the persons affected, and not government or the general community; the professional and occupational groups want government protection just as the property owner wants zoning. Sometimes licensing is a particularly obvious cover for monopoly. An ordinance in Seattle limited to a handful the number of persons or firms who could be licensed to operate juke boxes, but allowed each licensee to have a large number of juke boxes in different establishments; this effectively restricted the business to a small but highly privileged group. The partnership of government and private may give further protection—not merely from the consequences of competition, but also from the legal consequences of eliminating competition. Some privilege-dispensing agencies can exempt their clients from the antitrust laws, and, like the Maritime Board, use this power in connection with the grant of franchises to make lawful all sort of anticompetitive practices that otherwise would violate the Sherman Act.

The federal government's role in defense and research and development has created new forms of partnership. Substantial sectors of the economy become committed to a system of government contracting in which both the contractors and the politicians have a tremendous stake in the continuance of the system. . . . The so-called "think institute," a product of the fashion for group research and development, raises partnership to a new level. In effect the government hires a private enterprise to do its thinking. The government directs a steady flow of largess to the enterprise, and in return is told what it should think on a variety of subjects; what it is told very likely will have an impact on the future flow of largess. Thus a significant governmental power is actually placed in private hands, and the private group is supported in its power by public funds. . . .

In any society with powerful or dominant private groups, it is not unexpected that governmental systems of power will be utilized by private groups. Hence the frequency with which regulatory agencies are taken over by those they are supposed to regulate. Significantly, most of these agencies are also the chief federal dispensers of largess. They quarrel with the industries they regulate, but seen in a larger perspective these quarrels are all in the family. In sum, the great system of power created by government largess is a ready means to further some private groups, and not merely an advance in the position of government over that which is "private" in society as a whole. . . .

Property and the Public Interest:
An Old Debate Revisited

. . . Property is a legal institution the essence of which is the creation and protection of certain private rights in wealth of any kind. The institution performs many different functions. One of these functions is to draw a boundary between public and private power. Property draws a circle around the activities of each private individual or organization. Within that circle, the owner has a greater degree of freedom than without. Outside, he must justify or explain his actions, and show his authority. Within, he is master, and the state must explain and justify any interference. It is as if property shifted the burden of proof; outside, the individual has the burden; inside, the burden is on government to demonstrate that something the owner wishes to do should not be done.

Thus, property performs the function of maintaining independence, dignity and pluralism in society by creating zones within which the majority has to yield to the owner. Whim, caprice, irrationality and "antisocial" activities are given the protection of law; the owner may do what all or most of his neighbors decry. The Bill of Rights also serves this function, but while the Bill of Rights comes into play only at extraordinary moments of conflict or crisis, property affords day-to-day protection in the ordinary affairs of life. Indeed, in the final analysis the Bill of Rights depends upon the existence of private property. Political rights presuppose that individuals and private groups have the will and the means to act independently. But so long as individuals are motivated largely by self-interest, their well-being must first be independent. Civil liberties must have a basis in property, or bills of rights will not preserve them.

Property is not a natural right but a deliberate construction by society. If such an institution did not exist, it would be necessary to create it, in order to have the kind of society we wish. The majority cannot be expected, on specific issues, to yield its power to a minority. Only if the minority's will is established as a general principle can it keep the majority at bay in a given instance. Like the Bill of Rights, property represents a general, long range protection of individual and private interests, created by the majority for the ultimate good of all.

Today, however, it is widely thought that property and liberty are separable things; that there may, in fact, be conflicts between "property rights" and "personal rights." Why has this view been accepted? The explanation is found at least partly in the transformations which have taken place in property.

During the industrial revolution, when property was liberated from feudal restraints, philosophers hailed property as the basis of liberty, and argued that it must be free from the demands of government or society. But as private property grew, so did abuses resulting from its use. In a crowded world, a man's use of his property increasingly affected his neighbor, and one man's exercise of a right might seriously impair the rights of others. Property became power over others; the farm landowner, the city landlord, and the working man's boss were able to oppress their tenants or employees. Great aggregations of property resulted in private control of entire industries and basic services capable of affecting a whole area or even a nation. At the same time, much private property lost its individuality and in effect became socialized. Multiple ownership of corporations helped to separate personality from property, and property from power. When the corporations began to stop competing, to merge, agree, and make mutual plans, they became private governments. Finally, they sought the aid and partnership of the state, and thus by their own volition became part of public government.

These changes led to a movement for reform, which sought to limit arbitrary private power and protect the common man. Property rights were considered more the enemy than the friend of liberty. The reformers argued that property must be separated from personality. Walton Hamilton wrote:

> As late as the turn of the last century justices were not yet distinguishing between liberty and property; in the universes beneath their hats liberty was still the opportunity to acquire property.
>
> . . . the property of the Reports is not a proprietary thing; it is rather a shibboleth in whose name the domain of business enterprises has enjoyed a limited immunity from the supervision of the state.
>
> In the annals of the law property is still a vestigial expression of personality and owes its current constitutional position to its former association with liberty.

During the first half of the twentieth century, the reformers enacted into law their conviction that private power was a chief enemy of society and of individual liberty. Property was subjected to "reasonable" limitations in the interests of society. The regulatory agencies, federal and state, were born of the reform. In sustaining these major inroads on private property, the Supreme Court rejected the older idea that property and liberty were one, and wrote a series of classic opinions upholding the power of the people to regulate and limit private rights.

The struggle between abuse and reform made it easy to forget the basic importance of individual private property. The defense of private property was almost entirely a defense of its abuses—an attempt to defend not individual property but arbitrary private power over other human beings. Since this defense was cloaked in a defense of private property, it was natural for the reformers to attack too broadly. Walter Lippmann saw this in 1934:

> But the issue between the giant corporation and the public should not be allowed to obscure the truth that the only dependable foundation of personal liberty is the economic security of private property.
>
> For we must not expect to find in ordinary men the stuff of martyrs, and we must, therefore, secure their freedom by their normal motives. There is no surer way to give men the courage to be free than to insure them a competence upon which they can rely.

The reform took away some of the power of the corporations and transferred it to government. In this transfer there was much good, for power was made responsive to the majority rather than to the arbitrary and selfish few. But the reform did not restore the individual to his domain. What the corporation had taken from him, the reform simply handed on to government. And government carried further the powers formerly exercised by the corporation. Government as an employer, or as a dispenser of wealth, has used the theory that it was handing out gratuities to claim a managerial power as great as that which the capitalists claimed. Moreover, the corporations allied themselves with, or actually took over, part of government's system of power. Today it is the combined power of government and the corporations that presses against the individual.

From the individual's point of view, it is not any particular kind of power, but all kinds of power, that are to be feared. This is the lesson of the public interest state. The mere fact that power is derived from the majority does not necessarily make it less oppressive. Liberty is more than the right to do what the majority wants, or to do what is "reasonable." Liberty is the right to defy the majority, and to do what is unreasonable. The great error of the public interest state is that it assumes an identity between the public interest and the interest of the majority.

The reform, then, has not done away with the importance of private property. More than ever the individual needs to possess, in whatever form, a small but sovereign island of his own. . . .

Toward Individual Stakes in the
Commonwealth

Ahead there stretches—to the farthest horizon—the joyless landscape of the public interest state. The life it promises will be comfortable and comforting. It will be well planned—with suitable areas for work and play. But there will be no precincts sacred to the spirit of individual man.

There can be no retreat from the public interest state. It is the inevitable outgrowth of an interdependent world. An effort to return to an earlier economic order would merely transfer power to giant private governments which would rule not in the public interest, but in their own interest. If individualism and pluralism are to be preserved, this must be done not by marching backwards, but by building these values into today's society. If public and private are now blurred, it will be necessary to draw a new zone of privacy. If private property can no longer perform its protective functions, it will be necessary to establish institutions to carry on the work that private property once did but can no longer do.

In these efforts government largess must play a major role. As we move toward a welfare state, largess will be an ever more important form of wealth. And largess is a vital link in the relationship between the government and private sides of society. It is necessary, then, that largess begin to do the work of property.

The chief obstacle to the creation of private rights in largess has been the fact that it is originally public property, comes from the state, and may be withheld completely. But this need not be an obstacle. Traditional property also comes from the state, and in much the same way. Land, for example, traces back to grants from the sovereign. In the United States, some was the gift of the King of England, some that of the King of Spain. The sovereign extinguished Indian title by conquest, became the new owner, and then granted title to a private individual or group. Some land was the gift of the sovereign under laws such as the Homestead and Preemption Acts. Many other natural resources—water, minerals and timber, passed into private ownership under similar grants. In America, land and resources all were originally government largess. In a less obvious sense, personal property also stems from government. Personal property is created by law; it owes its origin and continuance to laws supported by the people as a whole. These laws "give" the property to one who performs certain actions. Even the man who catches a wild animal "owns" the animal only as a gift from the sovereign, having fulfilled the terms of an offer to transfer ownership.

Like largess, real and personal property were also originally dispensed on conditions, and were subject to forfeiture if the conditions failed. The conditions in the sovereign grants, such as colonization, were generally made explicit, and so was the forfeiture resulting from failure to fulfill them. In the case of the Preemption and Homestead Acts, there were also specific conditions. Even now land is subject to forfeiture for neglect; if it is unused it may be deemed abandoned to the state or forfeited to an adverse possessor. In a very similar way, personal property may be forfeited by abandonment or loss. Hence, all property might be described as government largess, given on condition and subject to loss.

If all property is government largess, why is it not regulated to the same degree as present-day largess? Regulation of property has been limited, not because society had no interest in property, but because it was in the interest of society that property be free. Once property is seen not as a natural right but as a construction designed to serve certain functions, then its origin ceases to be decisive in determining how much regulation should be imposed. The conditions that can be attached to receipt, ownership, and use depend not on where property came from, but on what job it should be expected to perform. Thus in the case of government largess, nothing turns on the fact that it originated in government. The real issue is how it functions and how it should function. . . .

. . . To assure the status of individual man with respect to largess: . . . First, the growth of government power based on the dispensing of wealth must be kept within bounds. Second, there must be a zone of privacy for each individual beyond which neither government nor private power can push—a hiding place from the all-pervasive system of regulation and control. Finally, it must be recognized that we are becoming a society based upon relationship and status—status deriving primarily from source of livelihood. Status is so closely linked to personality that destruction of one may well destroy the other. Status must therefore be surrounded with the kind of safeguards once reserved for personality.

Eventually those forms of largess which are closely linked to status must be deemed to be held as of right. Like property, such largess could be governed by a system of regulation plus civil or criminal sanctions, rather than a system based upon denial, suspension and revocation. As things now stand, violations lead to forfeitures—outright confiscation of wealth and status. But there is surely no need for these drastic results. Confiscation, if used at all, should be the ultimate, not the most common and convenient penalty. The presumption should be that the professional man will keep his license, and the welfare recipient his pension. These interests should be "vested." If revocation is necessary, not by reason of the fault of the individual holder, but by reason of overriding demands of public policy, perhaps payment of just compensation would be appropriate. The individual should not bear the entire loss for a remedy primarily intended to benefit the community.

The concept of right is most urgently needed with respect to benefits like unemployment compensation, public assistance, and old age insurance. These benefits are based upon a recognition that misfortune and deprivation are often caused by forces far beyond the control of the individual, such as technological change, variations in demand for goods, depressions, or wars. The aim of these benefits is to preserve the self-sufficiency of the individual, to rehabilitate him where necessary, and to allow him to be a valuable member of a family and a community; in theory they represent part of the individual's rightful share in the commonwealth.[1] Only by making such benefits into rights can the welfare state

[1] The phrase is adapted from Hamilton and Till's definition of the word "property": "a general term for the miscellany of equities that persons hold in the commonwealth." Hamilton & Till, *Property*, 12 Encyc. Soc. Sci.

achieve its goal of providing a secure minimum basis for individual well-being and dignity in a society where each man cannot be wholly the master of his own destiny.[2] . . .

Government largess is only one small corner of a far vaster problem. There are many other new forms of wealth: franchises in private businesses, equities in corporations, the right to receive privately furnished utilities and services, status in private organizations. These too may need added safeguards in the future. Similarly, there are many sources of expanded governmental power aside from largess. By themselves, proposals concerning government largess would be far from accomplishing any fundamental reforms. But, somehow, we must begin. . . .

The time has come for us to remember what the framers of the Constitution knew so well—that "a power over a man's subsistence amounts to a power over his will." We cannot safely entrust our livelihoods and our rights to the discretion of authorities, examiners, boards of control, character committees, regents, or license commissioners. We cannot permit any official or agency to pretend to sole knowledge of the public good. We cannot put the independence of any man . . . wholly in the power of other men.

If the individual is to survive in a collective society, he must have protection against its ruthless pressures. There must be sanctuaries or enclaves where no majority can reach. To shelter the solitary human spirit does not merely make possible the fulfillment of individuals; it also gives society the power to change, to grow, and to regenerate, and hence to endure. These were the objects which property sought to achieve, and can no longer achieve. The challenge of the future will be to construct, for the society that is coming, institutions and laws to carry on this work. Just as the Homestead Act was a deliberate effort to foster individual values at an earlier time, so we must try to build an economic basis for liberty today—a Homestead Act for rootless twentieth century man. We must create a new property.

[2] Experts in the field of social welfare have often argued that benefits should rest on a more secure basis, and that individuals in need should be deemed "entitled" to benefits. See Ten Broek & Wilson, *Public Assistance and Social Insurance—A Normative Evaluation*, 1 U.C.L.A.L. Rev. 237 (1954); Kieth-Lucas, *Decisions About People in Need* (1957). The latter author speaks of a "right to assistance" which is a corollary of the "right to self-determination" (*id.* at 251) and urges public assistance workers to pledge to respect the rights and dignity of welfare clients (*id.* at 263). See also Wynn, *Fatherless Families* 78–83, 162–63 (1964). The author proposes a "fatherless child allowance," to which every fatherless child would be entitled.

Starting from a quite different frame of reference—the problem of the rule of law in the welfare state—Professor Harry Jones has similarly argued that the welfare state must be regarded as a source of new rights, and that such rights as Social Security must be surrounded by substantial and procedural safeguards comparable to those enjoyed by traditional rights of property. Jones, *The Rule of Law and the Welfare State*, 58 Colum. L. Rev. 143, 154–55 (1958). See also Note, *Charity Versus Social Insurance in Unemployment Compensation Laws*, 73 Yale L.J. 357 (1963).

A group called the Ad Hoc Committee on the Triple Revolution recently urged that, in view of the conditions created by the "cybernation revolution" in the United States, every American should be guaranteed an adequate income as a matter of right whether or not he works. *N.Y. Times*, March 23, 1964, p. 1, cols. 2–3.

The Labor Theory of Property Acquisition
•
Lawrence C. Becker

The Root Idea

The root idea of the labor theory is that people are entitled to hold, as property, whatever they produce by their own initiative, intelligence, and industry. It is an idea which, once enunciated in the context of natural rights theories of the seventeenth century, has seemed nearly inescapable and self-evident. Yet it is worth remembering that it only emerges "naturally" from a very particular theoretical context—specifically, the attempt to build up an account of the just society from an (imaginary) state of nature in which there were no rules, no obligations, no political relations of superior to inferior, and in which all things were held in common. Outside the confines of state-of-nature theory (as, for example, in ancient Greek political theory), the right to the product of one's labor is hardly mentioned at all, and never made a cornerstone of the theory of property. Indeed, it is barely mentioned even in state-of-nature theorists as late as Grotius and Pufendorf.[1] But once the idea had clearly emerged, it became virtually unchallengeable. One might

Lawrence C. Becker, *Property Rights,* Chapter Four (London: Routledge & Kegan Paul Ltd., 1977), pp. 32–56. Reprinted by permission of the author and the publisher.

Lawrence C. Becker is Professor of Philosophy at Hollins College, Virginia, and the author of *On Justifying Moral Judgments* (1973).

[1]For a review of the relevant history, see Richard Schlatter, *Private Property: The History of an Idea* (New Brunswick, N.J., Rutgers University Press, 1951). I do not mean to say, of course, that the idea was unknown outside state-of-nature theory. The Romans, who gave it no legal force at all, did in practice sometimes recognize it in the case of sons who could not formally own property at all; what they produced on their own was occasionally treated by the *paterfamilias* as their (the sons') own. See Barry Nicholas, *An Introduction to Roman Law* (Oxford, Clarendon Press, 1962), p. 68.

ignore it (as Hume did), but would not deny it, even if one were attacking the whole notion of "primitive acquisition."[2]

Oddly, proponents of the labor theory rarely discuss the warrant for its root idea. That is, they rarely argue for it as a general justification of property rights. (It is, of course, *used* as a general justification, but that is quite another matter.) There are intricate arguments about the *specific sorts* of property rights labor can produce (whether it can give title to land, or only to produce from land, and whether it can yield the right of transmission, for example). But there is scant evidence, outside of Locke, of any serious thinking about how it is that labor can entitle anyone to anything. Time and again writers profess their inability to think of any alternative to it (short of a social compact) which could produce property rights. But the absence of a valid alternative proves nothing about the validity of the case at hand, and previous "alternatives" (such as one of the strands which runs through Christian property theory to the effect that the land belongs to the righteous, or what presumably would have been Aristotle's view, that property ought to be held by people who can use it properly) are not considered. Locke, however, made the effort, and so I shall organize my account (loosely) around his arguments.

Locke's Theory

There are several distinct arguments in Locke[3] for a labor theory of primitive acquisition, and they involve two distinct conceptions of the root idea that labor entitles one to property. The standardly quoted line is this:

(1a) Everyone "has a property in his own person; this nobody has a right to but himself." (27)*

(1b) "[T]he labour of his body and the work of his hands we may say are properly his." (27)

(1c) Whenever someone, by his labor, changes a thing from its natural state (to make it more useful or beneficial to him [26, 28, 34]), he has "mixed" his labor with it—that is, "joined to it something that is his own." (27)

(1d) He "thereby makes it his property," for "it hath, by this labour, something annexed to it that excludes the common right of other men. For this labour

---

[2] Marx, for example, never explicitly denies that laborers are entitled in justice to the fruits of their labor. (Indeed, it is natural to think that his condemnation of capitalist exploitation depends on a conviction that laborers are entitled to the *whole* fruits of their labor.) He is scornful of the theory of primitive acquisition. See *Capital*, vol. I, part VIII, chapter xxvi as translated from the third and revised from the fourth German editions (Chicago, Charles H. Ken, 1924). And the root idea of the labor theory seems inconsistent with the communism which is to result from the classless society in which labor has become unalienated. But I can find no place in which he specifically attacks the idea.

[3] In the Second of *Two Treatises on Government*. All references will be to the standard numbered paragraphs of this work.

* Editor's note: Number refers to paragraph 27, *Second Treatise*. See pp. 29–30 in this volume.

being the unquestionable property of the labourer, no man but he can have a right to what that is once joined to. . . ." (27)

(1e) This is so "at least where there is enough and as good left in common for others" (27), and where what one takes is no more than one can use. (31)

The root idea is here understood in terms of a derivation from prior property rights. Since one's body is one's property, and its produce (labor) is also one's property, it follows (?) that the labor's product is also one's property. Critics have generally focused on the final inference rather than the premises behind it, and they have had good sport with the metaphors of "mixing," "annexing," or "joining" one's labor to a thing.

But these metaphors really pose no more difficult a problem than is posed by the need to define the extent of one's "occupation" of a piece of land; both problems can be solved in much the same way. Labor is first distinguished from mere intent, declaration, or occupation. It is next distinguished from play and accidental improvement (e.g. playfully pushing a boulder into a boulder field and accidentally starting an avalanche which clears the field and then makes it suitable pasture for sheep).[4] One then simply calls attention to the fact that labor is purposive. Some efforts are for the purpose of enclosing a piece of land; some are for growing a crop; others are for creating an artifact to be possessed and used. The extent of the land (or whatever) with which one's labor "mixes" is thus quite naturally defined by the purposes for which one labors. Erecting a fence counts as a mixing of labor with the enclosed area, and cultivation counts as laboring on the soil. There are puzzling cases, embarrassing cases (what about the airspace over the land?). But on the whole, the metaphors are manageable ones.

The crucial problem with premises (c) and (d) is, as Nozick puts it, why anyone should think that mixing one's labor with a thing is a way of making the thing one's own rather than a way of losing one's labor.[5] It is evident that Locke was not content with these premises either. He keeps adding remarks which produce variants of the original argument. For example, consider this variant:

(2a) People have property in their bodies (as in argument 1).

(2b) Likewise, their labor is their property (as in argument 1).

(2c) "That labour put[s] a distinction between [the thing worked on] and [what is held in] common." (28)

(2d) The distinction is that labor "added something to [the thing] more than nature . . . had done. . . ." (28)

(2e) The thing labor adds—the difference it makes—is value. Things that are unappropriated are "of no use" (28) and labor is responsible for nine-tenths or perhaps ninety-nine hundredths of the value of the products of the earth. (40)

(2f) Therefore one's labor entitles one to property in the thing labored on.

Strictly, of course, the argument could at most only yield the conclusion

---

[4] My attention was called to this problem by David Ozar's paper, "Locke's Labor Theory of Property," presented at the Western Division Meetings of the American Philosophical Association, 1975.

[5] Robert Nozick, *Anarchy, State and Utopia* (New York, Basic Books, 1974), pp. 174–5.

that one is entitled to the value one's labor adds to the thing, and not to the thing itself. Locke's reply would apparently have been that the difference is minuscule (some 1 percent) and that in some cases the labor value and the thing so improved are inseparable. Nineteenth-century critics—anarchists, socialists, and reform capitalists alike—insist quite correctly, however, that the argument does not support property in land.[6] In the products of labor, yes. But in the case of land those are the fruits of cultivation, or herding, or building, and not the land itself. The difference here is not a small one and the two are not inseparable.

But is the argument sound? It apparently proceeds by assuming that the property in one's body "extends" first to (the body's product) labor, and then again to the product of labor *by the alteration in one's relation to the thing which is the consequence of the labor.* But how is this so? Granted that when one labors on a thing, one's relation to it has been changed—i.e. before the laboring, the thing could not truly be described as something one had labored on; after the laboring, it can be so described. But how does that change justify the claim that one has property rights in the thing?

I shall comment on this argument in detail in a moment, but first let me lay out the final variant of the labor theory which can be found in Locke. This one, though it is less often quoted, is the heart of the issue as I see it. It begins by repeating premises (2a) through (2e):

(3a) People have property in their bodies (as in arguments 1, 2).

(3b) Likewise, their labor is their property (as in arguments 1, 2).

(3c) "That labour put[s] a distinction between [the thing worked on] and [what is held in] common." (28)

(3d) The distinction is that labor "added something to [the thing] more than nature . . . had done. . . ." (28)

(3e) The thing labor adds—the difference it makes—is value. Things that are unappropriated are "of no use" (28) and labor is responsible for nine-tenths or perhaps ninety-nine hundredths of the value of the products of the earth. (40)

Then the new argument adds the following:

(3f) Since things are of no use until appropriated (28), and appropriation in most cases involves labor which would not be undertaken except for the expected benefits, to let others have the "benefits of another's pains" (34) would clearly be unjust.

(3g) This is so "at least where there is enough and as good left in common for others" (27) and where one takes no more than one can use (31). "For he that leaves as much as another can make use of, does as good as take nothing at all."

(3h) Therefore, from (a) through (e) one is entitled to the whole of the value one's labor adds to things, and from (f) and (g)—together with elements from (a) through (e)—one is entitled to the other expected benefits as well.

Here, in (3f) and (3g), is a variant of the root idea quite distinct from that expressed in (a) through (e). The proposal is that labor is something unpleasant

---

[6] See Henry George, *Progress and Poverty* (New York, Henry Schalkenbach Foundation, 1955), reprint of the 1905 edition, p. 337.

enough so that people only do it in the expectation of benefits (and since unlabored-on things are of little or no value anyway), it would be unjust not to let people have the benefits they take pains to get. This is so at least where one's appropriation has no significant effect on others.

Here (3g)—premise (1e) in the original argument—functions as much to disarm objections as to state a positive requirement of justice. Premises (f) and (g), then, taken together, constitute an argument for the benefits people expect, but cannot get title to from premises (a) through (e). If these benefits are ones people deserve by virtue of the (labor) pains they have taken, then that constitutes a good reason for granting the benefits. And if there are no countervailingly strong reasons to the contrary, granting them is justified. This explication of the root idea has seldom been attacked.

Locke gives, then, two distinct reasons for thinking that one's labor entitles one to property in the thing labored on: (1) that such rights derive from prior property rights in one's body and its labors; and (2) that such rights are required, in justice, as a return for the laborer's pains. Both reasons, taken together, are intended to establish security in the right to capital and the other rights normally associated with capital—namely, possessory, use, management, and income rights. Absence of term is also supposed to follow, and the prohibition of harmful use (probably) follows from the restrictions in (3g). Liability to execution for debt may perhaps be ground out of an analysis of the powers of alienation (promises governing exchanges). At least it is consistent with a rational system of exchanges. Transmissibility, however, does not follow directly from Locke's arguments, as has been noted by some.[7]

Criticism of Locke's Theory

Critics of these arguments have not carefully distinguished them, and have often contented themselves with attacks on the "mixing" metaphors in the first argument and the self-defeating character of the labor theory as applied to ownership of land (the fact that, once all the land is owned by a proper subset of the population, the landless, while they must work on the land, are denied the whole fruits of their labors by the results of the very arguments which were supposed to guarantee them).

Proudhon goes farther than this in two directions: by calling attention to what he takes to be an ambiguity in premises (3a) and (3b), and by scoffing at the "taking pains" part of (3f). Clearly, these are crucial lines of attack, for they go to the heart of each of the two interpretations of the labor theory's root idea. Neither line of attack has gotten the development it needs. I intend to remedy that in what follows, beginning in each case from Proudhon's sketchy remarks.

[7] See J. S. Mill, *Principles of Political Economy* in *The Collected Works of John Stuart Mill*, volume II (London, Routledge & Kegan Paul, 1965), book II, 1, § 3 (p. 208).

Property Rights in One's Body[8]

Some people have thought that premise (a) involves Locke's argument in an equivocal use of the term 'property.' Proudhon says: "The word property has two meanings: 1. It designates the quality which makes a thing what it is . . . 2. It expresses the right of absolute control over a thing. . . . To tell a poor man that he HAS property because he *HAS* arms and legs . . . is to play upon words, and to add insult to injury."[9] As Black's law dictionary points out, older writers sometimes used the word in the sense of "that which is proper to someone," and Salmond[10] cites Locke as among those who use it to refer to "all that is |one's| in law."

It is conceivable that Locke equivocated in his use of "property." But it is unlikely that Locke equivocated *in this passage;* and it is certain that the argument in no way *depends* on equivocation. (Nor does it depend on the concept of a mysterious soul-substance which "owns" its body.) Property rights in one's body can be perfectly well understood merely as the correlatives of other people's duties to forbear from acting so as to possess, use, and manage one's body. Property rights here, as in the standard cases of ownership, are fundamentally rights to *exclude* others. As such, assertions that my body is my property are not logically troublesome.

Locke says nothing about where these property rights come from, but I suspect it is wisest to regard them as simply summations of the relevant aspects of one's rights to life and liberty. Even so, a close look at the relations between these rights and the rights to the produce of one's labor produces some surprising results.

The fact is that without some modification of one or both propositions, "Everyone has property in his own body" and "Everyone is entitled to the fruit of his labors" are strictly incompatible. They are incompatible because, supposing both are true of everyone, then either (1) parents are entitled to property rights in their children (as the fruit of their labor), in which case not all people have property rights in their own bodies (namely, those with living parents who have not relinquished their rights in their children, or those whose parents have assigned the rights to others who are living and have not relinquished them); or (2) parents are not entitled to property rights in their children, in which case they are not (always) entitled to property rights in the fruits of their labor.

Whichever one of these alternatives is considered sound, Locke's argument must be revised to avoid the contradiction. If children do not have property

---

[8]The legal status and extent of such rights is currently under some strain—and therefore a topic of discussion—due to the rise of organ transplantation. The law has long forbidden the pledging or selling of body parts by their "owners" (while in some places permitting the sale of blood and sperm). But for a recent argument for a change in the law, see "The Sale of Human Body Parts," *Michigan Law Review,* 72: 1182–264 (1974).

[9]P. J. Proudhon, *What is Property?* |originally published in 1867| (New York, Howard Fertig, 1966), p. 61.

[10]*Salmond on Jurisprudence,* 12th edition (London, Sweet & Maxwell, 1966), chapter 13.

rights in their bodies, the necessary revisions produce a picture of human relationships repugnant to modern readers. (Though it is notable that this is, in part, purely a modern phenomenon. Writers as late as Grotius, for example, record without objection the recognition of parental property rights in children by some societies.[11]) Specifically, people would start life quite literally as their parents' chattels, and so continue until freed by manumission, default, or emancipation. It is clear that Locke would have accepted no such revision of the premises, if for no other reason than that it would eliminate property as a natural right except for the small class of people whose parents die intestate. Further, of course, there is no way to make the consequences of such revisions compatible with natural rights accounts of liberty and equality.

Repugnance to modern sensibilities is not, by itself, an argument against this revision of Locke's premises, of course. And there is certainly enough dispute about the validity of natural rights theory to mean that the revision cannot simply be dismissed by pointing out its incompatibility with the requirements of that theory. But the wholesale nature of the changes which would result from the adoption of the revised premises—changes which would conflict with fundamental principles held even on utilitarian grounds—suggest that there would have to be better reasons than merely the preservation of one of Locke's arguments for property rights to justify adoption of the revised premises.

But suppose instead of insisting that not everyone has rights to their bodies, one takes the other alternative and insists that people do not always have a right to the products of their labors? Specifically, that they do not have such rights when their labor produces other people. Very well. But how is such a restriction to be justified as anything other than an *ad hoc* device to square Locke's argument with conventional moral principles? There seem again to be two possibilities: (1) that there is something in the nature of labor which justifies a property claim for some products but not for others; or (2) that the labor claim is valid in all cases, just overriden in some by conflicting claims.

I know of no way to take the first possibility. It is true that writers have often spoken of some things as not acquirable by occupation or labor (the sea, the air). But these arguments are usually unsound (as when Grotius speaks of the sea as unbounded and therefore unoccupiable[12]). The air and the sea *can* be appropri-

---

[11]Hugo Grotius, *De Jure Belli ac Pacis,* translation of 1646 edition by F. W. Kelsey and others (Oxford, Clarendon Press, 1926), book II, chapter III, §IV, no. 1. The reader may also find Socrates' arguments about his status as a child of the Laws interesting in this connection. (I refer to the arguments against civil disobedience in Plato's *Crito.*) Contrast this with Aristotle's remark in *Nichomachean Ethics* (book V, chapter 6, at 1134b). And, of course, while Greek law was apparently less than literal in its treatment of children as chattels, early Roman law was very literal indeed about it. See Nicholas, *An Introduction to Roman Law,* pp. 65 ff. The *paterfamilias* could lawfully kill, as well as sell, a *filius familias* at his discretion—apparently as late as the second century A.D. Nor could a *filius familias* own property in law, though the custom was to let him use the produce of his labor as if it were his property. Only upon the death of one's father (supposing one had not been sold into slavery or emancipated) did a son become himself a *paterfamilias* and property owner.

[12]*Ibid.,* book II, chapter II, §VI-X.

ated by labor—bottled and compressed in the one case, drained off in the other. In any event, if anything is clearly a product of (one's body's) labor, a child is. It seems unlikely that anything will be found in the nature of the *labor* involved in conception, gestation, birth, and nurturing which will distinguish it sufficiently from the labor involved in cultivating a garden to justify using the latter in a Lockean argument but forbidding the use of the former.

The second possibility—the conflicting claims alternative—is surely the obvious line. One asserts first that persons have rights other than those to the fruits of their labor. This means others have duties corresponding to those rights. Such duties—e.g. my parents' duty to respect my liberty—may conflict with their property rights in me. Where a duty conflicts with a right it may (a) be overriden by the right; (b) be equal to and therefore effectively "cancel" the right; or (c) override the right. The question now to be answered is why the duty of parents to respect the liberty of their children either cancels or overrides their property rights in those children.

The long answer would have to go through the whole account of rights to life and liberty, showing their dominance over property rights. But fortunately there is a shorter argument available in this case. Locke makes the right to property in the fruits of one's labor *derivative* from one's rights to one's body (at least he does so in the standardly quoted line of argument). If the property rights in one's body are merely summations of—or another way of stating—the rights to liberty all humans are entitled to, then it is clear that we have grounds for restricting the consequences of a principle derived from those rights (namely, the principle that people are entitled to property in the fruits of their labor) to results which are compatible with the "originating" rights (namely, the liberty rights). That is, we can rule out as self-contradictory any consequence of a principle which contradicts the premises which generate that principle. If we begin from the premise that all people have property rights in their bodies, and from that generate the principle that they are entitled to the produce of their labors, we cannot accept an interpretation of that principle which permits a property right in the produce of labor to outweigh or cancel a person's property right in his or her body. For the latter sort of right is primary; it is *from* that that property rights to labor's produce derive.

This also solves nicely the problem of accounting for the *existence* of property rights in one's body. After all, in Locke's account, labor is supposed to be the only mode of original or primitive acquisition, and if anyone acquires property in people's bodies that way it is parents, not the people themselves. So where do these "prior" property rights come from? Thinking of them as restatements of rights to life and liberty gives a good answer. Of course it also means that property rights—in this one argument at least—*derive* from rights to life and liberty, and therefore one's success in establishing property rights by that argument depends on success in establishing those other rights. But this is a consequence natural rights theorists would accept gladly, I think.

The Failure of the "Property Rights in One's Body" Line of Argument. What they might not accept as gladly is the way the account just given makes painfully clear the need to further restrict the property rights so derived. If their source in people's liberty means that persons cannot be owned, does it not also mean that ownership of land must be restricted? "Place one hundred men on an island from which there is no escape, and whether you make one of these men the absolute owner of the other ninety-nine or the absolute owner of the soil of the island, will make no difference either to him or to them."[13] Where ownership of anything (land, water, etc.) has the effect of abridging the liberty (property in one's body) from which the Lockean argument derives the rights of ownership over things other than one's body, the argument cannot permit such ownership.

Worse still, the basic question remains unsettled: How is it that the property rights to one's body "transfer" or extend to property in the products of one's labor? In so far as one's labor is inseparable (by way of ownership rights) from one's body, it is understandable how the first "extension"—from ownership of the body to ownership of the labor—is warranted. But the same can hardly be said for the second extension—from ownership of the labor to ownership of labor's products. The products of one's labors are clearly separable from one's body. And Nozick's question remains: Why is it that investing one's labor in something causes one to come to own that thing? Why does it not instead just mean that one has lost the investment?

Here defenders of the labor theory tend to make a burden-of-proof argument. Why not? they say. Surely my working on something *changes* things. I now stand in a relation to the thing labored on which differentiates me from all other persons. I produced its human value (or nine-tenths or ninety-nine hundredths of it). Surely that makes it *mine.*

Unfortunately, this will not work. The phrase "It is mine" is ambiguous here. As a reference to the fact that it (the produce of one's labor) *is* just that—and not the produce of anyone else's, or a product of chance—the claim "It is mine" is of course true, but merely a repetition of the assertion of the unique relation which now holds between you and the thing. The crucial question remains unanswered: What reason is there to conclude that this altered relationship constitutes, or warrants, or gives any support at all to the claim that you have ownership rights in the thing? Why does it not just mean that you are entitled to public admiration? Or the gratitude of your fellows? Or perhaps nothing more than the appropriate change in the great book which describes the world? It is labor theorists who are making the assertion here—that the changes produced by their labors entitle them to property rights. The burden of proof is on them to show how it is so, and they have not done so. I see no reason to think that they can. I suspect that what they *can* show is the reasonability (in some cases) of saying that labor grounds a *recipient claim right* to the thing. That is, that the fact of one's labor can sometimes establish that one is owed possession or use or management in the sense that, should one not get it, one could appropriately react as though an *unspecifiable* duty-bearer had violated one's claim rights. But that is not a property right, and so whether or not the labor theory establishes it is irrelevant here.

[13]George, *Progress and Poverty,* p. 347.

*Entitlement to the Products of
One's Labor*

But isn't one *entitled* to those products none the less? Most people since Locke have said, assumed, or implied an affirmative answer, and shifted to the other major argument from labor to do it. Locke puts it in the form of an entitlement for one's "pains" in creating something valuable out of raw and largely useless material. I took the *trouble* to make it; I deserve some reward for my efforts; I *earned* it by my efforts. The sentiment is a familiar and powerful one. But to see just how little it proves—at least in the way Locke uses it—consider this exchange between Proudhon and Mill.

Proudhon scoffs at the whole idea, quoting someone else: "The rich have the arrogance to say. 'I built this wall, I earned this land with my labor.' Who set you the tasks? we may reply, and by what right do you demand payment from us for labor which we did not impose on you?" Proudhon says, "All sophistry falls to the ground in the presence of this argument."[14] Mill salvages the "sophistry," in a passage specifically *not* referring to property in *land,* in the following way: "It is no hardship to anyone, to be excluded from what others have produced: |the producers| were not bound to produce it for his use, and he loses nothing by not sharing in what otherwise would not have existed at all."[15]

Mill has gotten, I think, as close as one can get to an account of how Locke's "taking pains" argument justifies a property claim: when the labor is (1) beyond what is required, morally, that one do for others; (2) produces something which would not have existed except for it; and (3) its product is something which others lose nothing by being excluded from; then (4) it is not wrong for producers to exclude others from the possession, use, etc. of the fruits of their labors. It is not so much that the producers *deserve* the produce of their labors. It is rather that no one else does, and it is not wrong for the laborer to have them. Then, in so far as instituting a system of property rights which guarantees to laborers the fruits of their labor is a justifiable way of excluding others (as under the three conditions above), such property rights are justifiable.

The Prior Demands of Morality. Notice, however, the severe restrictions on what this argument can justify. First, the labor has to be above and beyond what morality requires a person to do for others. And that can be a very large condition indeed under some circumstances. For morality not only requires the fulfillment of obligations, but the exemplification of at least some moral character traits and occasional concessions to the principle of maximizing goods. Morality encourages and permits much else, but it *requires* that much—at least in the sense that not to do

---

[14] Proudhon, *What is Property?*, p. 84.

[15] Mill, *Principles of Political Economy,* book II, chapter 2, §6 (page 230). The passage continues, with respect to land, "But it is some hardship to be born into the world and to find all nature's gifts previously engrossed, and no place left for the newcomer." For a recent discussion which closely parallels Mill—especially with regard to the "no loss" requirement—see George I. Mavrodes, "Property," *Personalist,* 53: 245–62 (1972).

it makes one liable for reprobation.[16] And though others may not "deserve" the benefits morality requires one to confer on them, it is none the less wrong to withhold them. When excluding others from the fruits of one's labor amounts to withholding such benefits from others, then such withholding cannot be justified—at least not by the labor argument alone.

The Supplemental Value Requirement. Second, the labor must produce something which would not have existed except for it. This restriction is simply designed to call attention to the difference between the land one labors on and what is produced. Under some circumstances (such as the draining of a swamp, the filling of an estuary, etc.), one may fairly claim that one's labor has produced usable land itself. But under most circumstances, it is not the land itself that labor produces, but something *from* the land. Similarly for the water in a well, stream, or lake. The entitlement to labor's products cannot extend (except by convention) to the means of production—at least to the extent that the means of production are not themselves the products of labor.

The No-Loss Requirement. Third, the property rights to which one accedes by virtue of labor must not constitute a loss to others. Many disputes about the legitimacy of property rights can be understood as veiled disagreements about the interpretation of this requirement. If it is taken to mean that no one must be put at a relative disadvantage by another's accession to property rights, then it is doubtful whether one could legitimately claim ownership of any significant product of one's labors. Even a toothbrush, in so far as it is an advantage, puts its possessor in a position of relative superiority over those who do not possess one.

But surely this stretches the concept of a "loss" too far. The point of this restriction is to exclude a laborer's taking away others' existing goods. Equality of bad teeth is not an existing good, except in competitive situations where good teeth are a competitive advantage. So I have not "taken away" a good from others by my possession of a toothbrush. Land and the means of production, however, are a different matter. No doubt unused land represents a benefit to people only in so far as it is an opportunity of one sort or another. None the less, the elimination of those opportunities by the acquisition of land which does not leave "enough and as good" for others *is* a loss to those others. The point of Locke's restriction, as applied to land and finite non-renewable resources generally, is clear on this issue. (Its

---

[16]What is required by morality is, broadly, what one is justifiably liable for reprobation for not doing (though one may not usually demand approbation for *doing* it). What is not required, but merely permitted or encouraged, is what can*not* be liable for reprobation for not doing, and for doing which one ought to get approbation. The requirements of morality are generally expressed as duties or obligations. This is harmless enough as long as one does not overlook the character traits whose absence makes a person subject to reproof (as opposed merely to the absence of positive endorsements), and the times when a failure to choose the *best* available alternative (as opposed to one which is merely adequate) also makes the agent subject to sanction.

application to cases, of course, will depend largely on the explication of what it means to leave "enough" for others. And this will be a difficult problem indeed for any society which is [in any sense] overpopulated, or in which an equal sharing of some available resource would mean that the most industrious would get significantly less than they could use.)

There is still a large conflict, however, between the way various anti-property theorists might regard the notion of "loss" and the explication just given. In a competitive situation, it will be urged, to be put at a competitive disadvantage is a loss in precisely the way the inability to acquire land is a lost opportunity. And acquisition of property rights which puts others at a competitive disadvantage is therefore a "taking away of an existing good"—namely, competitive parity.

It seems to me that this is correct, and that it does not, like the concept of relative disadvantage, stretch the notion of a "loss" beyond recognition. There may be nothing "good" about having teeth as rotten as your neighbor's. Thus when he improves his relative to yours, the equality lost is not necessarily the loss of a good. But in a competitive situation the loss of competitive equality, or any deterioration of one's competitive position, *is* necessarily the loss of a good.

The extent to which the principle of entitlement to the fruits of one's labor can justify property rights is thus greatly limited in *competitive situations*—so much so, I suspect, as to defeat most of the point of Locke's arguments. In competitive situations, the restrictions on ownership must be extended to at least the major means of production. Locke's argument then becomes a foundation for socialism rather than "possessive individualism." Land, other natural resources, and the major means of production (sources of energy, transportation, communication, heavy industry, and important tools or knowledge too difficult for the individual to manufacture from available resources), cannot be privately owned. If they are acquired privately, they either deprive others of opportunity, or put them at a competitive disadvantage. In either case the requirement that no one suffer loss by the producer's acquisition of property is violated.

Entitlement Reconsidered

It will surely be urged in reply, however, that there is something very wrong with this explication of the root idea of the labor theory. Proudhon's attack boils down to "I didn't ask you to work, so I should not have to pay you in the form of property rights for the work you did." Mill's reply is, "As long as it is no loss to you—no "payment"—why should you care?" All this is very well as rhetoric, it will be said, but when the consequences of Mill's reply themselves undermine the theory, something is wrong. For after all, why *shouldn't* the industrious gain competitive advantages over the non-industrious? Locke himself remarks that "[God] gave [the earth] to the use of the industrious and rational. . . ."[17] He clearly had it

---

[17] Locke, *Second Treatise*, paragraph 34.

in mind that there could be no justice in a system which did not distinguish, in the distribution of goods, between the producers of those goods and the non-producers. But why is this so? It cannot be for the reason that Mill gives (that the inequality constitutes no loss to the unindustrious), for whenever they are thereby put at a competitive disadvantage, they do suffer a loss. And to say that the producers *deserve* the property because they earned it with their labor is just to repeat, with emphasis, the original premise—the root idea of the labor theory one is trying to explicate.

Further, when the reply here is taken out of the language of the work ethic and one substitutes for 'industrious' the terms (equally accurate as things actually happen) 'aggressive,' 'intelligent,' and 'strong,' and substitutes for 'unindustrious' the terms 'passive,' 'unintelligent,' and 'weak,' the reply loses some appeal. Why should the aggressive inherit the earth, after all? They have, but has it been a good thing? Why should the people with the natural advantage of intelligence (whether acquired by inheritance or by environment) inherit the earth? Have they *earned* the means which permit their acquisition? And so on.

(It should be noted that the social Darwinist rationale for the right of the strong to the advantages conferred by property reduces to an absurdity. As Rashdall points out, property rights—especially when they protect possession and inheritance—quite clearly protect the weak against the strong. [18])

The final blow to the argument is this: it may be that in some situations a laborer's accession to liberty rights is no loss to others, but the accession to a *claim right*, or a power, or an immunity, is usually a different matter. The creation of the corresponding duties, liabilities, and disabilities in others usually constitutes a loss of *liberty* for them. Rights justified by this argument cannot, then, include claim rights, powers, or immunities *if and in so far as* the existence of those sorts of rights actually constitutes a loss to others. And all of the varieties of ownership distinguished at the outset involve not only liberties but claim rights or powers or immunities as well.

Yet even when all this is said, it must be admitted that a person's commitment to the root idea of the labor theory may not have been disturbed very much by the argument so far. Head shaking, protestations that the analysis has "gone too fast" or must have overlooked some alternatives, and general carping about the poverty of philosophy are more typical reactions. This is not an unusual result when an analysis has been unable to find rational support for a widely held moral conviction. But the persistence of the conviction after all this is enough to give one cause to consider another possibility: that the whole effort to find arguments to justify the labor theory may have been wrongheaded.

Laborer's Entitlement as a Fundamental Principle. Suppose it is urged that one should not try to go behind the root idea of the labor theory at all—that this

---

[18]Hastings Rashdall, "The Philosophical Theory of Property," in J. V. Bartlett (ed.), *Property: Its Duties and Rights*, 2nd edition (London, Macmillan, 1915), pp. 54–6.

root idea is just a fundamental or primitive moral principle which neither needs nor is capable of justification. Once this suggestion is made, the argument shifts to the issue of what it means to say that a moral idea is primitive or fundamental, and the justification for thinking that the labor theory contains such an idea.

Now there are several senses in which an idea may be said to be so fundamental as to defy moral justification. First, an idea may so permeate the whole "moral conceptualization" of the world that to discard it would be to discard altogether the enterprise of making moral judgments. The notion that agents are responsible for their acts has been thought to be this sort of fundamental idea, as has the generalizability of moral judgments. "Going behind" either of these ideas to talk about their moral justifiability might thus be held to be circular; they are simply constitutive of the concept of morality *per se*.

Second, an idea may be necessary to the conceptualization of an important range of cases *within* moral life—necessary in the sense that without it one loses one's grip on the particular moral problem the cases present. The concept of desert might be thought fundamental in this way to the problem of penalties and punishment (as opposed to reformation or deterrence). Without it, one hardly knows how to proceed. Thus it might be urged that in a discussion of restorative or retributive justice the justifiability of the notion that people can deserve certain things is assumed. One treats that notion as fundamental and does not go behind it; it is just constitutive of the concept under discussion.

Third, an idea may be regarded as fundamental in the sense that it is the best choice of the alternatives available for a justificatory "starting point." Justifications cannot prove everything; they have to start somewhere—with something which is itself unproved. The best starting point, of course, is one which is indisputable. But for anything beyond purely formal systems, it is hard to find indisputable axioms. Instead, one must usually settle for something which is not actually *in* serious dispute and which can otherwise perform the role of an axiom (for example, axioms must be self-consistent, be stated clearly and unambiguously, and be suitably powerful or "at the bottom" of many justificatory issues).

I think it is clear that the root idea of the labor theory cannot qualify as fundamental in either of the first two senses: there is no logical circularity involved in asking for a moral justification of it, and it is certainly not presupposed by the conceptualization of the problems raised by the justification of property rights (witness ancient discussions of property acquisition). So we are left with the possibility that it may be fundamental in the third sense—that is, that it is the best (or a member of the best set of) justificatory "starting point(s)."

This contention has some initial plausibility. The general, unquestioning approval of the idea is a modern (Western?) phenomenon, but one which is very firmly established. So the condition that the starting point not actually be in dispute seems satisfied. Further, the idea that laborers are entitled to the products of their labor seems (initially) to satisfy some of the other requirements of an axiom: generality; self-consistency; the ability to generate determinate conclusions when applied to cases. But in each case this initial plausibility crumbles upon inspection.

For example, if there is general agreement that laborers should get property rights in the fruits of their labor, there is also general agreement that this should not be at the expense of others. Proudhon's challenge, "I did not ask you to work so why should I have to pay you for what you did?" is as generally agreed to as the root idea of the labor theory. That is surely part of the reason Locke and Mill were so careful to include the "no loss" requirement in their arguments. So any attempt to treat the root idea as a plausible first principle *on the basis of people's actual commitment to it* would, if it were to be consistent, have to include a qualification equivalent to the "no loss" requirement. Thus nothing would have been gained by treating the root idea as a first principle (since with the no loss requirement, its justification goes through anyway).

Further, there is an insuperable problem with the generality of the idea. Laborers are supposed to be entitled to property in the *very things* they produce (and where these are inseparable from the raw materials worked on, property in the things worked on). But it has already been shown that this supposition must be revised in the case of the children parents produce. And it is equally clear that it will not do for the whole class of employees and the equally large class of people who perform services for others. It is perhaps true that most employees work on things already owned by others, and since labor is only claimed to be a mode of original acquisition, for that reason they cannot come to own the very things they produce or work on. But why is it not generally agreed that scholars have property rights in the ideas they produce (as opposed to the books the ideas are published in)? Surely it is not because the ideas are owned by someone else. Nor is it because scholars do not claim those ideas as "their own," for they do so claim them. Nor is it because scholars have all waived possible property rights prior to beginning to work (as might be the case for certain government or corporate employees engaged in research), for some of them have not done so. Why, in short, is it sometimes generally agreed that people should have property rights in their ideas (in the form of copyrights and patents), but not always? And why is it generally accepted that patents and copyrights lapse automatically after a period of time, while ownership of land acquired by labor would not be expected to?[19] *Once it is acknowledged that some labor is expected to yield property rights in the very things labored on, while other labor is not*, the root idea of the labor theory must be seen as a poor choice for a fundamental principle. In the form in which it can claim general acceptance, it simply does not "cover" all the cases. The obvious covering principle is that laborers *deserve* something for their labor. Perhaps in some cases what they deserve is property in the thing labored on; in other cases property in some sort of fee for the labor; and in still other cases, not property at all but simply the recognition, admiration,

[19]Nozick makes interesting remarks on these issues on *Anarchy, State and Utopia* (New York, Basic Books, 1974), at pp. 141 and 182. See also Ayn Rand, "Patents and Copyrights," in her *Capitalism: The Unknown Ideal* (New York, New American Library, 1966), pp. 125–9. For a review of current legal theory on intellectual property, see the Note by Joseph E. Kovacs, "Beyond the Realm of Copyright: Is There Legal Sanctuary for the Merchant of Ideas?" *Brooklyn Law Review*, 41: 284 (1974).

or gratitude of other people. If the principle of desert can settle when people deserve property rights in the products of their labor, then we will have a plausible reformulation of the labor theory. . . . But we should be clear that it will be a reformulation, not the traditional version.

The upshot of this is, then, that the Locke-Mill labor theory cannot serve as a fundamental, unjustified moral principle. If any principle related to labor has that status it is the notion that labor should be rewarded. This principle may in some cases justify recognizing a property right in the thing labored on. In other cases, it may not. In any case, to repeat, it is not the root idea of the labor theory of property acquisition—at least as traditionally formulated—which is at the bottom of such justifications.

Fair Taking: A Final Note. It is one thing to tell people they ought to give away things they have produced; it is quite another to tell them the things are not theirs to give. It is one thing to tell people that they ought not to take unfair advantage of others; it is another thing to tell them that they are not entitled to advantages taken fairly. And there is still something so far unsaid about the "fair taking" idea.

Proudhon's objections, and Mill's reply, concern situations in which people go about producing things wholly on their own—without being asked, and without initial reference to the desires, needs, or abilities of others. *Then* it is asked: how does their labor justify rights to what they produce? The answer, naturally enough, is in terms of objections people might raise against the producers. "You have destroyed *my* opportunities for acquisition." Or, "You have put me at a disadvantage."

But suppose we imagine a situation in which there are enough resources (initially) for each person to make full use of his or her abilities, people are equal in ability, and aware of the consequences for their own eventual opportunities and competitive positions if they allow others to "get ahead." This, I think, is the sort of picture last-ditch defenders of the labor theory conjure up. What, they ask, is wrong with securing for the industrious the fruits of their labor in that sort of situation? It is true that they will soon have a competitive advantage over the idlers, but so what? Surely they deserve it. And if their initial acquisitions make it possible for them to use more of the land, minerals, and other resources than they could initially, and the nonproducers see this, but still do not care to appropriate (by their labor) their original "shares," then what is unfair about letting the industrious take that too?

It must be granted that in the situation just described, the slothful do not deserve the produce of others. Nor do they deserve to be protected from the consequences of their own sloth (conditions justifying paternalism having been ruled out). And so it would not be wrong to give property rights—including claim rights—to the industrious. But this is hardly a comfort to the defenders of the labor theory. In the first place it is still too weak: at best, one can only derive a recipient right from it, and that is not a property right. Second, as described, the situation in which one can take advantage "fairly" is so rare as to be of very little practical importance beyond certain special colonizing enterprises.[20] Third, the "fairness" of the situation is wrecked with the arrival of the second generation. Even if inheritance is not permitted, the members of the first generation and those of the second who come to maturity first clearly leave the remainder, no matter how industrious, with reduced opportunities. So the "industrious colonist" metaphor does not advance the range of allowable property rights very far.

Deserving to Own: Reformulating the Labor Theory

One is left, again, with little more than the persistence of the root idea—and the vehemence of its advocates. One explanation for this may be found in a psychological fact: that labor is (in some circumstances) *psychological* appropriation—appropriation in the sense of a "felt incorporation" of the thing labored on "into" one's person. If it is true that I "am" (psychologically) what I want to become as well as what I have become, then one can say with similar validity that I am what I have made. I am what I was, what I do, what I want to do, and what I produce. These are all greatly abbreviated locutions for complex facts about personality, but the ones which refer to the consequences of labor are no less sound than the others. The trouble is that while such facts may be able to support a claim for a recipient right, I see no way for them to go beyond that. It is not a happy situation.

I want, therefore, to explore one final possibility—the idea that there might be some principle of desert, related specifically to labor, which will satisfy the insistent demand that despite all the difficulties, something like the labor theory must be sound.[21] The idea is obviously very closely tied to Locke's notion of justice for those who "take pains" or who add value to things by their own efforts, on their own initiative. But as far as I can tell, the argument to follow is not one that either Locke or Mill actually intended to make.

[20] A word needs to be said here about thought-experiments in ethics. State-of-nature imagery is sometimes compared to notions in the physical sciences such as uniform motion. Uniform motion is an imaginary phenomenon, but useful for the foundation of an explanatory and predictive account of motion as it actually occurs in experience. Similarly, it is said, though no state of nature exists (or probably ever did exist), the concept can help construct a justification for states of affairs which actually do or could exist. The parallel is plausible, but dangerous. Motion exists. Uniform motion is a linear extrapolation to the vanishing point, as it were, of certain properties of real motion. To the extent that the notion of a state of nature is similarly an extrapolation, the parallel looks sound. But when it turns out that *only* in the "unreal" conditions can a given type of social arrangement be justified (e.g. private ownership of all available land), then the use of the imaginary situation in moral theory becomes something of a menace to clear thinking.

[21] I am indebted to Robert Nozick and Ruth Barcan Marcus for providing the stimulus to my reflections on this line of argument.

Desert as a Fundamental Principle

To begin, suppose we acknowledge that the notion of desert is a constituent of the notion of morality *per se*. This may not be immediately obvious, but consider: Morality is concerned with (among other things) questions of what people ought to do and be. And among the things which people ought to do and be it is certainly held that there are some moral requirements—that is, things for which sanctions of various sorts will be invoked if people fail to do what they ought, or fail to be what they ought. (There may be other things which are morally good or bad but which are not either required or forbidden.) Now it is understood that, by definition, moral sanctions—reprobation, blame, punishment, and their opposites—are not just instrumental acts, to be invoked whenever they will yield a desirable result. They are to be applied only to those who "deserve" or are "worthy" of the sanction. One must be morally blame*worthy*, or praise*worthy* for it to be appropriate for a moral sanction to be imposed. Thus just as surely as the notion of moral requirements and prohibitions (and the concomitant sanctions) necessarily involves the notion of agents who can be said to be responsible for their acts, so too it necessarily involves the notion of desert. To ask whether desert is an intelligible concept is to call into question the whole enterprise of passing moral judgment on people for their conduct. If agents can be morally responsible for their acts, they can by definition deserve reward or punishment for them. That is part of what it means to say someone is a responsible agent. And if they cannot deserve moral sanctions, they cannot be morally responsible for their conduct. The whole enterprise of making moral judgments is indefensible. Unless we are wholesale moral sceptics, then, we have to acknowledge the intelligibility—indeed the necessity—of the concept of moral desert.

But what does deserving something mean? That is, what "principles of moral desert" can be articulated simply by analyzing the concept itself? Here Joel Feinberg's careful analysis is useful.[22] First, it is clear that claims that people deserve this or that must have a "basis." That is, "[i]f a person is deserving of some sort of treatment, he must, necessarily, be so *in virtue* of some possessed characteristic or prior activity. . . . Of course, [one] may not know the basis of [another's] desert, but if [one] denies that there is any basis, then he has forfeited the right to use the terminology of desert."[23]

The basis for a desert-claim, however, is to be distinguished from the basis for a claim that a person is eligible, or qualified, or entitled to something (where entitled means having a claim right to a thing).[24] And the basis for a desert-claim must, in general, be some fact about the person who is said to be deserving. One can imagine a case in which one *ought* (morally) to reward X simply because it

---

[22]Joel Feinberg, "Justice and Personal Desert," in his book *Doing and Deserving* (Princeton University Press, 1970), pp. 55–87.

[23]*Ibid.*, p. 58.

[24]*Ibid.*, pp. 58–9.

would make X's parents very happy; but that is not a basis for saying that X *deserves a reward*.[25]

What is a basis for a desert-claim? Happily, we need not be able to give a comprehensive answer to that question to see that, by definition again, personal deeds and character *may* be bases. We sometimes give reasons for *not* using them. ("I suppose it was 'good' of him to return the money, but after all he owed it to me. People don't deserve anything special for doing their duty.") But we do not normally give reasons *for* using personal deeds and character as desert bases because what else, after all, could be a basis for *personal* desert? So it must be the case that a person's "adding value" to the world—in the sense of discovering, inventing, or improving something which helps others—*can* be a basis for a desert-claim. And once we add the stipulations that the deed be both morally permissible and beyond what is morally required of the person, I cannot imagine any objection to the assertion that such "adding of value" *must* be a basis for a desert-claim. Then, finally, since the very notion of personal desert is that "good things" (prizes, rewards, benefits) are what befit good deeds or good character (when they are desert bases), the following principle must be sound simply by definition:

> *A person who, in some morally permissible way, and without being morally required to do so, "adds value" to others' lives deserves some benefit for it.*[26]

I have gone over these definitional matters with no doubt tedious care because philosophers have been justifiably leery of the notion of desert. I do not want to leave the impression that anything has been hidden. For I now want to claim to have shown that the desert principle just enunciated meets the requirements for a fundamental principle of the first sort . . . It certainly also meets the requirements for the other two sorts . . . It does this, in short, because the concept of desert is constitutive of the concept of morality *per se,* and because the principle of desert given above is entailed by that very concept of desert.

Some Features of This Principle of Desert

Once this much is granted, there are several things which can be said immediately about this principle of desert. In the first place, it must be a double-edged principle: if a benefit is due for adding value, presumably a penalty is due for

---

[25] *Ibid.*, pp. 58–9.

[26] One must be very careful here not to slip into saying that one who deserves X is *entitled* to it—where 'entitled' means 'has a claim right.' People may deserve things which they have no claim right to (i.e. which others have no duty to provide); and they may have claim rights to things which they do not deserve. Desert must also be distinguished from eligibility. See Feinberg, "Justice and Personal Desert," pp. 58–9.

subtracting value. Such symmetry is a conceptual requirement for *this* principle of desert (though not for all), because the context in which the concept of desert here operates calls for a "polar" notion of desert.[27] "Adding value" is taken to be a good deed; good deeds have their opposites. (Here that would mean "subtracting value.") If benefits are what befit good deeds, penalties are what befit bad ones. The principle of desert stated here cannot consistently affirm the former without also affirming the latter. On the assumption that there are some morally permissible acts which both add and subtract values—by improving the lot of some at the expense of others—then it follows that sometimes both a benefit and a penalty are due. This results in an argument for a tax on entrepreneurs whose activities deplete the community's stock of unowned resources or limit the opportunity of others without their consent; and it results in an argument for compensation to any persons who suffer a demonstrable net personal loss. The size of such penalties may in effect cancel the benefit entirely, of course.

Second, we must hold the principle of desert to be totally inapplicable to cases in which gains are gotten by violating moral prohibitions—e.g. by unjustifiably overriding the rights of others. And this is so no matter how much more good than bad is eventually produced. It is, after all, a principle of personal desert being considered, and if the balance of good over bad does not justify overriding the right, then it is hardly consistent to think that the wrongdoer deserves a benefit for whatever good is done. Consider immoral medical experiments on unwilling human subjects. (The case is different for rights which are justifiably overriden. Compensation is still due, but the notion of desert is applicable.)

Third, the desert principle must include a proportionality requirement: Benefit or penalty to be proportional to the value added or subtracted by the labor. I say for the value produced rather than for the (value of the) labor expended, for conceptual reasons. By the term of the desert principle as stated, value accrued or lost without labor does not count. Labor is a necessary condition for desert. But it is not sufficient. Labor alone—labor which neither adds to nor diminishes value— does not deserve anything. So the benefit must be proportional to the value produced by the labor (and if that is not separable from the total value of the product, then proportional to the total value of the product). Similarly, penalties are to be proportional to the loss produced by the labor.[28]

---

[27] *Ibid.*, pp. 62 ff. Feinberg distinguishes contexts in which desert is a "polar" concept (e.g. reward and punishment contexts) from those in which it is not (e.g. deserving the trophy for winning the race). He would, I think, agree that in the context under discussion here, desert was necessarily polar. In an appendix to his article (*ibid.*, pp. 88–94), Feinberg discusses economic benefits as deserved, and concludes that they are best regarded (if deserts at all) as compensations. But he does not consider arguments of the form I shall advance here.

[28] Suppose we used a different principle of desert—one which said people deserved something (benefit for effort? penalty for ineptitude?) for *un*productive labor as well as for productive labor. Then would the proportionality requirement look like this?

benefit = value of labor + value of labor's product;
penalty = value (disvalue?) of labor + disvalue of labor's product.

Compare Nozick's suggestions for a retributive principle for punishment in *Anarchy, State and Utopia*, pp. 59–63.

Fourth, and finally, the principle of desert must have a way of fitting the type of benefit to the type of labor or to the laborer. After all, a candy bar is not (usually) a fitting reward for someone who does not like sweets.

I suggest that each of these four elements must be regarded as a constitutive feature of the principle of desert under discussion. That is, the meaning of the principle of desert used here cannot be fully and self-consistently explicated without including them.

Property Rights as Fitting Benefits

It is the fourth element which raises the possibility for a new argument. Are there some types of labor for which property rights are the *only* fitting benefit? Or less strongly, are there some sorts of labor for which property rights are the *most* fitting benefits? (Care must be taken here not to let the standard for fittingness turn the argument into a version of the appeal to utility. For example, to argue that certain benefits are fitting because without them people would not do the things we want them to do is to give a utility argument, not a labor-desert argument. The standard of fittingness must come instead from the nature of the labor, the laborer, or the products of labor. And it is not immediately obvious how this will work.)

Suppose we begin by recalling once again that labor (as opposed to random expenditure of effort and play) is goal-directed activity. It is undertaken for some purpose—for the satisfaction of some desire. Now, it is clear that the satisfaction of some such desires might in principle require property rights, while the satisfaction of others does not. If the whole purpose (or an indispensable part of the purpose) of the laborer's efforts is to get and keep as property what the labor produces, then if the laborer deserves a benefit for his or her efforts, and if property rights in the thing produced do not exceed the proportionality requirement, then they are obviously the only (or part of the only) fitting benefit.

Note that this does not mean that people can come to deserve property rights by simply having them as part of their goals when they undertake to do something. What they do must deserve a benefit, and a benefit of a size comparable to the value of the property rights they want (whether full, liberal ownership or some more restricted variety). Once this is understood, the labor-desert argument looks quite sound. Further, the use of the goal of labor as the mark against which to measure the fittingness of benefits allows for an account of why and when money rewards can be substituted for rights to the very thing produced. For example, if my object in gardening is to have the satisfaction of eating things I have grown, then substitutes (like money to buy other produce) won't do. On the other hand, if all I want is vegetables of a certain quality, at certain times, at a certain convenience, then it may well be a matter of indifference whether my entitlement is to property in the very things I have produced or to money to buy equivalent products.

Similarly for the issue of when, and why, the recognition, admiration, and gratitude of one's peers are more fitting than either money or property in the thing produced. Some things, after all, are not done for fortune. They may be done for fame, for example. One may want to be admired—known for something. In that case, reward of money and anonymity is a poor substitute for what is sought. (Think of James Watson's desire to be the first to understand DNA.[29])

The Labor-Desert Argument for Property

What does this mean for private property rights? Well, it means that when people deserve a benefit for their labor, and when (in terms of the purposes of their efforts) nothing but property in the things produced will do, and when the value of such rights meets the test of proportionality, then they deserve property in those things. When, on the other hand, substitutes will do every bit as well, they then deserve either the things produced or an equally satisfactory substitute. And finally, where property in the things produced is not what is sought at all, and cannot be an adequate substitute for what is sought, the laborers deserve something else (perhaps recognition, gratitude).

Put more formally, this version of the labor argument is as follows:

(1) When it is beyond what morality requires them to do for others, people deserve some benefit for the value their (morally permissible) labor produces, and conversely, they deserve some penalty for the disvalue their labor produces.

(2) The benefits and penalties deserved are those proportional to the values and disvalues produced, and those fitting for the type of labor done.

(3) When, in terms of the purposes of the labor, nothing but property rights in the things produced can be considered a fitting benefit for the labor, and when the benefit provided by such rights is proportional to the value produced by the labor, the property rights are deserved;

when, in terms of the purposes of the labor, either property rights in the things produced or something else can be considered a fitting and proportional benefit, then either the property rights or one of the acceptable alternatives is deserved;

when, in terms of the purposes of the labor, property rights in the things produced cannot be considered a fitting reward, or when the benefits of such rights are in excess of the values produced by the labor, the rights are not deserved.

(4) Any diminution of value produced by labor must be assessed against the laborer as a penalty deserved for the loss thus produced. (Penalties must, of course, be proportional to the loss produced, and a fitting remedy for that loss—fitting not in terms of the purposes of the labor which produced it, but in terms of the purposes with regard to which it can be considered a loss.)

It should be noted that (1) meets the standards for a fundamental principle of the sorts explicated above, . . . and the remaining steps are deduced from the concepts of desert, fittingness, benefit, and loss. I think this line of argument is

---

[29]James D. Watson, *The Double Helix* (New York, Mentor Books, 1968).

sound, and is in fact what the labor theory reduces to. I think, further, that it satisfies the stubborn desire we have to make the labor theory work. But several things should be noted about what it does and does not prove.

In the first place, this labor argument—by itself—gives no unequivocal grounds for the private ownership of the things produced unless there is no substitute for it acceptable in terms of the goals of the labor. This means that where the production of things is a means to an end—security, power, status, the ability to guarantee the same for one's children, etc.—and where the state can provide those things *as laborers' deserts* without granting ownership rights over the very things produced, this version of the labor theory does not provide a justification for private ownership of the things produced. It is thus in principle compatible with socialist economic arrangements.

Second, the no-loss requirement—here understood as the double-edged aspect of the desert principle—places a heavy tax and/or compensation requirement on entrepreneurs whose activities reduce total welfare, or opportunities, or which otherwise disadvantage their fellows. But here it can be seen that the type of thing produced has a great deal to do with such restrictions. For one thing, the problems with "intellectual property" become clearer. In the case of technological problems for which there is a unique solution (or a very small, well-defined class of solutions), an invention by one person—if it is then fully owned by that person— significantly diminishes the opportunities of others. We therefore have grounds for sharply limiting or taxing patent and copyright arrangements, just as we have grounds for limiting or taxing the acquisition of land and exhaustible natural resources generally. On the other hand, we have no grounds for penalizing someone *just because* he or she has invented or created something unique. Inventions *per se* do not diminish the net number of opportunities to invent *other* things, any more than the writing of *Moby Dick* diminished the opportunities of subsequent novelists. The classes of possibilities are not finite. And in the case of art, each work, by its very existence, creates new possibilities—for further work which "refers to" or "uses" it, for example.

Third, it should be noticed that the labor–desert argument does nothing to establish entitlement in cases where the laborer's efforts have not benefitted anyone else. Deserving a benefit for producing something which only you profit from is a strange notion. So the applicability of the argument is confined to cases in which the product of one's labor itself (independently of whether one owns it) adds value to others' lives. Cases in which others are neither benefitted nor harmed by the labor (e.g. by one's use of some nonscarce sand to make an hourglass purely for personal amusement) must be dealt with in terms of the Locke-Mill version of the labor theory. . . .

Fourth, and finally, there is a strange result of this line of argument which demands notice. If the fittingness of a reward is tied only to the satisfaction of the laborer's purposes, then what is to be done by way of rewarding people whose purpose is *just* to work, *just* to produce useful or beautiful things, or to discover the truth about things? Whether or not anyone ever works solely for such motives, surely many people often work partly for them. Is such labor to be its own reward entirely, just because the laborers do not happen to want more? Or is there some additional way of justifying the fittingness of (an additional) reward?

It is here, of course, that honors, recognition, gratitude, and status rewards are often used. And the fittingness of these rewards (as well as other benefits) is no more difficult to understand than the appropriateness of returning love with love and kindness with kindness. Other responses are simply not compatible with our ideals of moral character. However one argues for the justifiability of an ideal (whether solely on utilitarian grounds or not), it would not be easy, I think, to defend a notion of the good person which entailed a disposition to treat hatred or indifference as an appropriate response to another's love, or vindictiveness, disgust or apathy as an appropriate response to another's kindness.[30] In short, we need not fear that this principle of desert—this version of the labor theory—will shortchange the selfless.

To summarize, then, this tortuous analysis of the labor theory: the version proposed by Mill—with the no-loss requirement as explicated here—is sound, but of very limited applicability in its traditional form. It works most satisfactorily in the case of the sorts of personal possessions (e.g., a small rock collection) whose ownership harms no one. When reformulated with the desert principle, however, the labor theory possesses most of the power of the original intuition. This does not mean that the no-loss requirement has been relaxed. Indeed, the penalty clause of the desert principle provides a strong ground for tax and compensation requirements on entrepreneurs. But the reinterpretation provided by the desert principle at last allows a clear account of why and when laborers—solely by virtue of their labor, and not just because there are no objections to it—deserve to own what they produce.

---

[30] Of course, the other's kindness may itself be inappropriate, but that raises a separate issue.

Property, Title and
Redistribution
●

A. M. Honoré

This discussion paper is concerned with the relationship between the institution of private property and the notion of economic equality. Is it inconsistent, or morally obtuse to recognize the value of the institution and at the same time to argue that each member of a society is entitled to an equal or approximately equal standard of living? I shall be particularly concerned with the argument of R. Nozick, in Anarchy, State and Utopia[1] to the effect that under a system of "just entitlements" such as he specifies there is no room to admit that the state has the right or duty to redistribute benefits so as to secure an equal or more equal spread, because "the particular rights over things fill the space of rights, leaving no room for general rights to be in a certain material condition."[2] Though Nozick's "just entitlements"[3] are not confined to titles to property I shall so confine myself. Rights of a more personal character could in theory be the subjects of redistribution and indeed Nozick discusses the case for transplanting organs from A to B in order to correct physical maldistribution of parts of the body.[4] Fascinating as such speculations may be, the physical and technical difficulties involved in such a programme would be stupendous and the moral objections to the invasion of people's bodies for whatever purpose are much stronger than they are when what is proposed is to tax or, in some cases, to expropriate. Nor can one concede the argument that the redistribu-

A. M. Honoré, "Property, Title and Redistribution," first published in Equality and Freedom: Past, Present and Future, ed. by Carl Wellman. ARSP. Archives for Philosophy of Law and Social Philosophy: Beiheft (Supplement) Neue Folge (New Series) No. 10, pp. 107–115. Wiesbaden, W. Germany: Franz Steiner Verlag, 1977. Reprinted by permission of the author and the publisher.

A. M. Honoré teaches law at Oxford University and is an author, with H. L. A. Hart, of Causation in the Law.

[1] Oxford 1974.
[2] Nozick p. 238.
[3] Nozick pp. 150–182.
[4] Nozick p. 206.

tion of part of what A has earned to B goes beyond the invasion of property rights and amounts to a system of forced labour[5] by which A is compelled to work part of his day for B, so that redistribution of property is really an invasion of the status and freedom of the person taxed or expropriated. This is no more compelling than the Marxist argument that a wage-earner whose surplus product is appropriated by the employer is a sort of wage slave. The objection to this is not that the income-earner freely works under a system in which he knows that part of what he produces will be appropriated by his employer or transferred to other people by means of taxes. He may have no choice, if he is to earn a living, but to accept a system which he dislikes. The argument is open to attack rather because it rests on the morally questionable view that a person is entitled to keep exclusively and indefinitely for himself whatever he makes or produces. This would be true of a man working in complete isolation; no serious argument has been advanced to show that it is true of a social being.

Nozick's argument depends on accepting this questionable view. Against those who favour a principle of social justice by which things are to be distributed according to need, desert, the principle of equal claims or the like, he argues that the just allocation is the historically justifiable one. This can be ascertained, in relation to any given item of property, by asking whether the holder acquired it by a just title or derived his title justly from another who so held it, either originally or by derivation from such a just acquirer. Consequently just distribution depends on just acquisition and transfer, and redistribution is confined to those instances in which the original acquisition or the subsequent transmission of the property was unjust.

All therefore turns on what count as just principles of acquisition and transfer of title. According to *Nozick* —

1. a person who acquires a holding in accordance with the principle of justice in acquisition is entitled to that holding

2. a person who acquires a holding in accordance with the principle of justice in transfer from some one else entitled to the holding is entitled to the holding

3. no one is entitled to a holding except by (repeated) applications of 1 and 2

The complete principle of distributive justice would say simply that a distribution is just if everyone is entitled to the holdings they possess under the distribution.

What is presupposed by this set of rules for tracing title is apparently only that the principles of acquisition and transfer should be morally respectable. For

---

[5] Nozick pp. 169 f, arguing that redistributive arrangements give B a sort of Property right in A. This mistake stems from the Lockean argument that we own ourselves and *hence* what we make etc. If human beings are free they cannot own themselves; their relationship to themselves and their bodies is more like one of "sovereignty" which cannot be alienated or foregone, though it can be restricted by (lawful) contract or treaty.

acquisition something like *Locke's* theory of property is understood.[6] Transfers in a free society will be consensual. But that is only the appearance. What *Nozick* additionally presupposes, without seeking to justify, is that the interest acquired and transmitted is the ownership of property as conceived in western society on the model of Roman law.[7] He is assuming, first, that the acquirer obtains an exclusive right to the thing acquired, that he is entitled, having cleared the land, made the tool etc. to deny access and use to everyone else. Secondly he is supposing that the right acquired is of indefinite duration. The man who has made the clearing can remain there for his lifetime. He is not obliged to move on after so many years, and leave the fruits of his labour to another, nor does he lose his right by leaving. Thirdly the right is supposed to be transmissible inter vivos and on death, so that it can be sold, given, inherited, mortgaged and the like again without limit of time. Under such a system of property law, of course, the initial acquisition is decisive. Once A has cleared the land his neighbours, friends, associates and, if it comes to that, his family are obliged to look on while he enjoys and transmits his "entitlement" to whomsoever he chooses, irrespective of the fact that in a wider context they, along with him, form part of a single group[8] which is dedicated, among other objects, to the preservation of all. This system of property law, whatever its economic merits, is not self-evidently just. If the interest acquired (western type ownership) is greater than can be morally justified, then however just the methods by which A acquires the thing in question and transfers it to X, the distribution of property under which the thing is allocated to X is not thereby saved from criticism. Indeed, quite the contrary. If the interest awarded to owners under the system is greater than can reasonably be justified on moral, as opposed to economic grounds, any distribution of property will be inherently unjust. Hence the intervention of the state will be needed if justice is to be done.

There is no doubt that the *Nozick* rules about just acquisition, transfer and distribution reproduce in outline western systems of property law based on the liberal conception of ownership. According to these notions, ownership is a permanent, exclusive and transmissible interest in property. But this type of property system is neither the only conceivable system, nor the easiest to justify from a moral point of view, nor does it predominate in those societies which are closest to a "state of nature."

In so far as the *Nozick* principles are meant to reproduce western property law they are incomplete in that they omit provision for lapse of title and for compulsory acquisition. Lapse of title is not perhaps of great moral importance, but it is worth noting that legal rules about limitation of actions and prescription embody the idea that an owner who neglects his property may be deprived of it. The acquirer (squatter or the like) obtains it by a sort of private expropriation. More important is expropriation by the state or public authority. It is not at all clear why

[6] Nozick pp. 174 ff.

[7] For an analysis see Honoré, "Ownership," in: Guest, *Oxford Essays in Jurisprudence* (London 1961).

[8] For an analysis see Honoré ARSP 61 (1975) 161.

the parts of western property law favourable to the private owner should be reproduced in the system of entitlements to the exclusion of those which favour the claims of the community. The latter, after all, balance the former. The individualistic bias of property law is corrected by the admission of state claims to tax and expropriate.

Aside from the omission of rules about lapse and compulsory acquisition one may note that *Nozick's* principles rest on the assumption that whether a justification exists for acquiring or transferring property can be decided in abstraction from the historical and social context. A just acquisition in 1066 or 1620 remains a just root of title in 1975. If this were really so one would have to say either that the acquisition of slaves is seen in retrospect always to have been unjust and that the state would have been justified in intervening in a slave-owning society to correct the injustice, or that the descendants of slave-owners are entitled to own the descendants of freed slaves. So with colonies, *mutatis mutandis.* Are we to say that as a result of the post-war movement to free colonies we now see that the acquisition of colonies, apparently valid at the time in international law and morality, was always wrong and that the international society would have been justified, had it been so minded, in intervening even in the nineteenth century to free the existing colonies and prevent further acquisitions? If so, how can we be sure that there are not equally unjustified forms of property ownership in present-day society which in fact justify state intervention in a redistributive sense? And how can we be sure in any future society that these objectionable forms of acquisition are not present? In which case, outside Utopia, the thesis advanced by *Nozick* has no application. But if the acquisition of slaves and colonies was initially just, surely some provision should be made in his system for the redistribution of entitlements when the moral basis on which they originally rested has become eviscerated. These instances would count morally as cases of lapse of title owing to changing views of right and wrong. Legally they would furnish examples of just expropriation. There would have to be a further exception in *Nozick's* system to cater for changing conditions of fact. Suppose, apart from any question of the justification for colonies, that in the nineteenth century Metropolitania occupied a deserted tract which it proceeded to colonize, building roads and irrigating the land. As a result a numerous indigenous population crowded in from the neighbouring areas. These people now claim to be free and to decide their own destinies. Whether or not colonization is in general thought a permissible form of "entitlement" the changed situation must surely change one's moral evaluation of Metropolitania's title to the formerly deserted tract. So with the Mayflowerite who bagged a large stretch of unoccupied land in 1620. If the situation is now that irrespective of title the tracts in question are occupied by people who have nowhere else to live surely the moral basis of the title of the Mayflowerite's successors must at least be open to debate. Once there was more than enough to go round, now there is not. And is the case very different if the thousands without property instead of occupying the colonies or tracts in question crowd the periphery and make claims on the unused resources inside: All this is intended to make the simple point that it is obtuse to suppose that the justification for acquiring or transmitting property could be settled once and for all at the date of acquisition or transfer. Legally it may be so, subject to the rules of lapse and expropriation. This is because of the need to frame rules of law in such a way as to ensure certainly of title. They are meant however to be applied in a context in which social and moral criticism may be directed against their operation and in which their defects may be corrected by legislation or similar means. Apart from positive law, can it seriously be maintained that the rules about what constitutes a just acquisition or transfer both express unchanging verities and, in their application to the facts of a given acquisition or transfer, are exempt from reassessment in the light of changed circumstances?

Systems of property law which diverge from the orthodox western type based on liberal conceptions of ownership are conceivable, morally defensible and have actually obtained in certain societies. To begin with the conceivable, let us take an imaginary case. Suppose that, in a "state of nature" a group of people live near a river and subsist on fish, which they catch by hand, and berries. There is great difficulty in catching fish by hand. Berries are however fairly plentiful. There are bits of metal lying around and I discover how to make one of them into a fishhook. With this invention I quadruple my catch of fish. My neighbours cannot discover the knack and I decline to tell them. They press me to lend them the fishhook or to give them lessons in acquiring the technique. I have however acquired western notions of property law and Lockean ideas about entitlement, I point out that I have a just title to the fishhook, since according to *Nozick's* version of *Locke* they are no worse off as a result of my invention. I am therefore entitled to the exclusive, permanent and transmissible use of the fishhook. My neighbors may try their hands at finding out how to make one, of course, but if they fail they may look forward to eating berries and from time to time a bit of fish while I and those persons whom I choose to invite to a meal propose to enjoy ourselves with daily delicacies. If they object that this is unfair I shall point out (though the relevance is not obvious) that they are not actually starving. Nor am I monopolizing materials. There are other pieces of metal lying around. They are no worse off than they were before or than they would have been without my find (in fact they *are* worse off, relatively to me). As to the parrot cry that they protect me and my family from marauders, wild animals and the like, so that I ought to share my good fortune with them, I reply that they have not grasped what is implied by a system of just entitlements. Are they saying that I am not entitled to the fishhook?

One of my brighter neighbours might well answer me as follows. "I do not deny that you have a right to the fishhook. As you say you made it and you invented the system of using it to catch fish. But it does not follow that, as you assert, your right to it is exclusive, permanent and transmissible. Your views seem to be coloured by reading books about sophisticated societies. In those societies men are dedicated to increasing production, come what may, and in order to achieve that they accept institutions which to us seem very unfair. We are simple people used to sharing our fortunes and misfortunes. We recognize that you have a right to the fishhook but not that the right has the unlimited content which you assign to it. You ought to allow each of us to use it in turn. Naturally as the maker and inventor you are entitled to a greater share in the use than the rest of us individually, and if you like to call that share 'ownership' we shall not object. But please stop looking up the definition of 'ownership' in foreign books. These notions will only disrupt our way of life."

The point my neighbour is making is that a system of private property can be inherently distributive. In the system envisaged there is an "owner" in the sense of a person whose right to the use of the thing is greater than that of others, who has a residual claim if others do not want to use the thing, and in whom powers of management will be vested. He will be responsible for lending the fishhook out, it will be returned to him each evening, he will keep it in repair. But these powers of use, management and reversion fall short of western conception of ownership. In such a system the redistributive power of the state will be unnecessary unless the members of the group fail to keep the rules. For the rules themselves ensure an even distribution of property, subject to the recognition of desert and choice—a recognition which is not allowed to subvert the principle of sharing.

Is the projected system of property law obviously unjust? How does it compare with western notions of ownership? From the point of view of justice, though perhaps not of economic efficiency, it seems to compare rather favourably. It is designed to give effect to the interdependence of the members of the group and to recognize overtly that they cannot survive in isolation. It rejects the notion that I do no harm to a member of my group if as a result of my effort I am better off, and he is no worse off than he would otherwise be. That notion, which is common to the outlook of *Nozick* and *Rawls,* however much they otherwise differ, rests on the assumption that a person who is *comparatively* worse off is not worse off. But he is, and the precise wrong he suffers is that of being treated as an unequal by the more fortunate member or members of the group.

The fruits of an invention which raises production have therefore, in the projected system, to be shared, either by a system of compulsory loan or, in a weaker version, by a system of surplus sharing, under which what an owner "has in excess of his needs or is not using must be made available to other members of his group."[9]

The sort of system envisaged is unlikely to survive the division of labour, viz. specialisation. The members of the group other than the inventor are likely to feel that he can fish better than they and that they would do well to get him to fish for them. But then they must pay him. At first perhaps the payment is a fraction of the catch. Later the inventor is bemused by the idea that he is entitled to the whole product of his invention. So he argues that his neighbours owe him the whole of his catch and, if they want any of it, must pay in some other way, as by repairing his hut. As he has possession on his side his views may prevail. We slide insensibly, therefore, from a participatory to an exclusive system of property law, and it is difficult to keep alive, in a society of economic specialisation, the notion that each participates in a common enterprise. The remedy for this is not, or is only to a minor extent, a return to rotatory labour. It is rather that the community as a whole,

[9]Herskowitz, below n. 12, p. 372.

the state, must act as the surrogate of the participatory principles. The inventor of the fishhook will have to be taxed. In that way the economic advantages of specialisation can be combined with a just, or juster distribution of the benefits derived from it. The tax will be used to give the other members of the group benefits corresponding to their former rights to use the fishhook.

There is no point in attempting to work out in detail what a participatory system of property law would be like. The idea is easy to grasp. If such a system is morally sound, then it follows that in a western-type system the intervention of the state, so far from being, as *Nozick* thinks, ruled out except in peripheral instances, (initially unjust acquisitions, subsequently unjust transfers) is essential in order to achieve justice in distribution.[10] Whether one says that this is because in a western-type system all the holdings are unjust (because they are holdings of an unjust sort of property interest) or that they were initially just but that their permanent retention cannot be justified, is debatable: the former seems more appealing. In any event either *Nozick's* conclusion is empty because the premises are never fulfilled, or if the premises are fulfilled, they do not lead to the conclusion to which they seem to lead.

If it is accepted that the sort of property system described is conceivable and morally defensible, that is sufficient to rebut the argument which denies a redistributive function to the state. It is not irrelevant, however, to draw attention to the fact that among the variety of property arrangements found in simple societies there are some which approximate to the distributive arrangement outlined. Among other things this will serve to rebut any argument that I am relying on a gimmicky obligatory principle of transfer.[11] A convenient outline of the variety of such property systems is to be found in *M. J. Herskowitz'* work.[12] They are of course multifold: apart from arrangements which resemble the western institution of ownership there are to be found types of group (e.g. family or clan) ownership, public ownership, rotating individual use (e.g. of fishing grounds) and also the sort of arrangement here envisaged, namely what may be called private ownership subject to compulsory loan or sharing. Thus among the Bushmen[13] "all kinds of food are private property" and "one who takes without the permission of the owner is liable to punishment for theft" but "one who shoots a buck or discovers a terrain where vegetable food is to be gathered is nevertheless expected to share with those who have nothing," so that "all available food, though from the point of view of customary law privately owned, is actually distributed among the members of a given group." The dividing is done by the owner and the skin, sinews

[10]Nozick, pp. 174 ff. However one interprets Locke's requirement that the acquirer must leave enough and as good in common for others (Second Treatise sec. 27) the intention behind it is not satisfied unless entitlements are adjusted from time to time according to what *then* remains for others.

[11]Nozick p. 157.

[12]M. J. Herskowitz, *Economic Anthropology* (New York 1952), part IV. Property.

[13]Herskowitz pp. 321–2, citing L. Schapera, *The Khosian Peoples of South Africa, Bushmen and Hottentots* (London 1930) p. 148.

etc. belong to him to deal with as he pleases. Among the Indians of the Pacific North-West[14] a man is said to have "owned" an economically important tract and this "ownership" was expressed by his "giving permission," to his fellows to exploit the locality each season but "no instance was ever heard of an 'owner' refusing to give the necessary permission. Such a thing is inconceivable." The individual "ownership" is a sort of stewardship or ownership in trust carrying with it management and the right to use but not excluding the right of others to a similar use. Among certain tribes of Hottentots[15] a person who dug a waterhole or opened a spring made this his property and all who wished to use it had to have his permission, but he was under an obligation to see that no stranger or stranger's stock was denied access to it. Among the Tswana[16] where the chief allocates (and in that sense "owns") the land he will allot cattle-posts to individuals, but not exclusively. The allocee, whose position is closest to that of the private owner, "must share with a number of other people the pastures of the place where his cattle-post is situated, although no one else may bring his cattle there without permission." Yet occupation does give a certain prior right. "If a man builds a hut and so indicates that it is not merely for temporary use, he established a form of lien over the place, and can return to it at any time."

There are also examples of what I have termed surplus sharing, which give effect to the principle that what a person has in excess of his needs, or is not using must be made available to other members of the group. Among the Eskimos the principle that "personal possession is conditioned by actual use of the property" comes into play. A fox-trap lying idle may be taken by anyone who will use it. In Greenland a man already owning a tent or large boat does not inherit another, since it is assumed that one person can never use more than one possession of this type. "Though what a person uses is generally acknowledged to be his alone any excess must be at the disposal of those who need it and can make good use of it."[17]

These examples show that there is nothing unnatural about distributive property arrangements in a simple society. The mechanism, or one of the possible mechanisms by which such arrangements are secured, is that of what it seems preferable to call private ownership subject to a trust or a duty to permit sharing. The "ownership" is not of course ownership of the classical western type, but neither is it "primitive communism." Its essential feature is that the titles to acquisition are much the same as in modern societies—finding, invention, occupation, making and the like—and the types of transfer—sale, gift, inheritance—are not necessarily dissimilar, but the type of interest acquired and transmitted is different. The principle of sharing is written into the delineation of interests of property.

[14]Herskowitz pp. 332–3, citing P. Drucker "Rank, Wealth and Kinship in Northwest Coast Society," *Amer. Anth.* 41 (1939) p. 59.

[15]Herskowitz pp. 343–4, citing Schapera, above n. 13, at pp. 286–291.

[16]Herskowitz p. 344, citing L. Schapera and A. J. H. Goodwin "Work and Wealth" in *The Bantu-Speaking Tribes of South Africa* (ed. L. Schapera) pp. 156–7.

[17]Herskowitz pp. 373–4 citing K. Birket-Smith, *The Eskimos* (London 1936) pp. 148–151.

There is no special reason to think that our moral consciousness is superior to that of simple societies. So if compulsory sharing commends itself to some of them it should not be dismissed out of hand for societies in which the division of labour has made those simple arrangements out of date: but in these, given the weakened social cohesion which the division of labour introduces, the central authority (the state) is needed to see that sharing takes place.

2

Profits

Should everyone try to maximize profits?

Can everyone gain under capitalism?

Who are the losers?

What are the social costs of the "free market"?

What should be done about the modern corporation and about work?

The Progress of Opulence
•
Adam Smith

Of the Division of Labor

It is the great multiplication of the productions of all the different arts, in consequence of the division of labor, which occasions, in a well-governed society, that universal opulence which extends itself to the lowest ranks of the people. Every workman has a great quantity of his own work to dispose of beyond what he himself has occasion for; and every other workman being exactly in the same situation, he is enabled to exchange a great quantity of his own goods for a great quantity, or, what comes to the same thing, for the price of a great quantity of theirs. He supplies them abundantly with what they have occasion for, and they accommodate him as amply with what he has occasion for, and a general plenty diffuses itself through all the different ranks of the society.

Observe the accommodation of the most common artificer or day laborer in a civilized and thriving country, and you will perceive that the number of people of whose industry a part, though but a small part, has been employed in procuring him this accommodation exceeds all computation. The woolen coat, for example, which covers the day laborer, as coarse and rough as it may appear, is the produce of the joint labor of a great multitude of workmen. The shepherd, the sorter of the wool, the wool comber or carder, the dyer, the scribbler, the spinner, the weaver, the fuller, the dresser, with many others, must all join their different arts in order to complete even this homely production. How many merchants and carriers, besides, must have been employed in transporting the materials from some of those workmen to others who often live in a very distant part of the country! How much commerce and navigation in particular, how many shipbuilders, sailors, sailmakers, ropemakers, must have been employed in order to bring together the different drugs made use of by the dyer, which often come from the remotest corners of the world! What a variety of labor too is necessary in order to produce the tools of the

From Adam Smith, *The Wealth of Nations,* first published in 1776.
     Adam Smith (1723–1790) was born and lived most of his life in Scotland. He was professor of moral philosophy at the University of Glasgow and author also of a *Theory of Moral Sentiments,* a work of moral psychology. He provided in *The Wealth of Nations* a formulation of the laws of the market and a vast treatise on commercial development.

meanest of those workmen! To say nothing of such complicated machines as the ship of the sailor, the mill of the fuller, or even the loom of the weaver, let us consider only what a variety of labor is requisite in order to form that very simple machine, the shears with which the shepherd clips the wool. The miner, the builder of the furnace for smelting the ore, the feller of the timber, the burner of the charcoal to be made use of in the smelting house, the brickmaker, the bricklayer, the workmen who attend the furnace, the millwright, the forger, the smith, must all of them join their different arts in order to produce them. Were we to examine, in the same manner, all the different parts of his dress and household furniture, the coarse linen shirt which he wears next his skin, the shoes which cover his feet, the bed which he lies on, and all the different parts which compose it, the kitchen grate at which he prepares his victuals, the coals which he makes use of for that purpose, dug from the bowels of the earth, and brought to him perhaps by a long sea and a long land carriage, all the other utensils of this kitchen, all the furniture of his table, the knives and forks, the earthen or pewter plates upon which he serves up and divides his victuals, the different hands employed in preparing his bread and his beer, the glass window which lets in the heat and the light, and keeps out the wind and the rain, with all the knowledge and art requisite for preparing that beautiful and happy invention without which these northern parts of the world could scarcely have afforded a very comfortable habitation, together with the tools of all the different workmen employed in producing those different conveniences; if we examine, I say, all these things, and consider what a variety of labor is employed about each of them, we shall be sensible that without the assistance and co-operation of many thousands, the very meanest person in a civilized country could not be provided, even according to what we very falsely imagine as the easy and simple manner in which he is commonly accommodated. Compared, indeed, with the more extravagant luxury of the great, his accommodation must no doubt appear extremely simple and easy; and yet it may be true, perhaps, that the accommodation of a European prince does not always so much exceed that of an industrious and frugal peasant, as the accommodation of the latter exceeds that of many an African king, the absolute master of the lives and liberties of ten thousand naked savages.

Of the Principle Which Gives Occasion to the Division of Labor

This division of labor, from which so many advantages are derived, is not originally the effect of any human wisdom which foresees and intends that general opulence to which it gives occasion. It is the necessary, though very slow and gradual, consequence of a certain propensity in human nature which has in view no such extensive utility: the propensity to truck, barter, and exchange one thing for another.

Whether this propensity be one of those original principles in human nature, of which no further account can be given; or whether, as seems more probable, it be the necessary consequence of the faculties of reason and speech, it belongs not to our present subject to inquire. It is common to all men, and to be found in no other race of animals, which seem to know neither this nor any other species of contracts. Two greyhounds, in running down the same hare, have sometimes the appearance of acting in some sort of concert. Each turns her toward his companion, or endeavors to intercept her when his companion turns her toward himself. This, however, is not the effect of any contract, but of the accidental concurrence of their passions in the same object at that particular time. Nobody ever saw a dog make a fair and deliberate exchange of one bone for another with another dog. Nobody ever saw one animal by its gestures and natural cries signify to another, this is mine, that yours; I am willing to give this for that. When an animal wants to obtain something either of a man or of another animal, it has no other means of persuasion but to gain the favor of those whose service it requires. A puppy fawns upon its dam, and a spaniel endeavors by a thousand attractions to engage the attention of its master who is at dinner, when it wants to be fed by him. Man sometimes uses the same arts with his brethren, and when he has no other means of engaging them to act according to his inclinations, endeavors by every servile and fawning attention to obtain their good will. He has not time, however, to do this upon every occasion. In civilized society he stands at all times in need of the co-operation and assistance of great multitudes, while his whole life is scarcely sufficient to gain the friendship of a few persons. In almost every other race of animals each individual, when it is grown up to maturity, is entirely independent, and in its natural state has occasion for the assistance of no other living creature. But man has almost constant occasion for the help of his brethren, and it is in vain for him to expect it from their benevolence only. He will be more likely to prevail if he can interest their self-love in his favor, and show them that it is for their own advantage to do for him what he requires of them. Whoever offers to another a bargain of any kind proposes to do this. Give me that which I want, and you shall have this which you want, is the meaning of every such offer; and it is in this manner that we obtain from one another the far greater part of those good offices which we stand in need of. It is not from the benevolence of the butcher, the brewer, or the baker that we expect our dinner, but from their regard to their own interest. We address ourselves not to their humanity, but to their self-love, and never talk to them of our own necessities, but of their advantages. Nobody but a beggar chooses to depend chiefly upon the benevolence of his fellow citizens. Even a beggar does not depend upon it entirely. The charity of well-disposed people, indeed, supplies him with the whole fund of his subsistence. But though this principle ultimately provides him with all the necessities of life for which he has occasion, it neither does nor can provide him with them as he has occasion for them. The greater part of his occasional wants are supplied in the same manner as those of other people, by treaty, by barter, and by purchase. With the money which one man gives him he purchases food. The old clothes which another bestows upon him he exchanges for other old clothes which suit him better, or for lodging, or for food, or for money, with which he can buy either food, clothes, or lodging as he has occasion.

As it is by treaty, by barter, and by purchase that we obtain from one another the greater part of those mutual good offices which we stand in need of, so it is this same trucking disposition which originally gives occasion to the division of labor. In a tribe of hunters or shepherds a particular person makes bows and arrows, for example, with more readiness and dexterity than any other. He frequently exchanges them for cattle or for venison with his companions; and he finds at last that he can in this manner get more cattle and venison than if he himself went to the field to catch them. From a regard to his own interest, therefore, the making of bows and arrows grows to be his chief business, and he becomes a sort of armorer. Another excels in making the frames and covers of their little huts or movable houses. He is accustomed to be of use in this way to his neighbors, who reward him in the same manner with cattle and with venison, till at last he finds it his interest to dedicate himself entirely to his employment and to become a sort of house carpenter. In the same manner a third becomes a smith or a brazier; a fourth, a tanner or dresser of hides or skins, the principal part of the clothing of savages. And thus the certainty of being able to exchange all that surplus part of the produce of his own labor, which is over and above his own consumption, for such parts of the produce of other men's labor as he may have occasion for, encourages every man to apply himself to a particular occupation, and to cultivate and bring to perfection whatever talent or genius he may possess for that particular species of business.

The difference of natural talents in different men is, in reality, much less than we are aware of; and the very different genius which appears to distinguish men of different professions, when grown up to maturity, is not upon many occasions so much the cause as the effect of the division of labor. The difference between the most dissimilar characters, between a philosopher and a common street porter, for example, seems to arise not so much from nature, as from habit, custom, and education. When they came into the world, and for the first six or eight years of their existence, they were, perhaps, very much alike, and neither their parents nor playfellows could perceive any remarkable difference. About that age, or soon after, they come to be employed in very different occupations. The difference of talents comes then to be taken notice of, and widens by degrees, till at last the vanity of the philosopher is willing to acknowledge scarcely any resemblance. But without the disposition to truck, barter, and exchange, every man must have procured to himself every necessity and convenience of life which he wanted. All must have had the same duties to perform and the same work to do and there could have been no such difference of employment as could alone give occasion to any great difference of talents.

As it is this disposition which forms that difference of talents, so remarkable among men of different professions, so it is this same disposition which renders that difference useful. Many tribes of animals acknowledged to be all of the same species derive from nature a much more remarkable distinction of genius than what, antecedent to custom and education, appears to take place among men. By nature a philosopher is not in genius and disposition half so different from a street porter, as a mastiff is from a greyhound, or a greyhound from a spaniel, or this last from a shepherd's dog. Those different tribes of animals, however, though all of the same species, are of scarcely any use to one another. The strength of the mastiff is not in the least supported either by the swiftness of the greyhound, or by the sagacity of the spaniel, or by the docility of the shepherd's dog. The effects of those different geniuses and talents, for want of the power or disposition to barter and exchange, cannot be brought into a common stock, and do not in the least contribute to the better accommodation and convenience of the species. Each animal is still obliged to support and defend itself, separately and independently, and derives no sort of advantage from that variety of talents with which nature has distinguished its fellows. Among men, on the contrary, the most dissimilar geniuses are of use to one another; the different produces of their respective talents, by the general disposition to truck, barter and exchange, being brought as it were into a common stock, where every man may purchase whatever part of the produce of other men's talents he has occasion for.

Of the Origin and Use of Money

When the division of labor has been once thoroughly established, it is but a very small part of a man's wants which the produce of his own labor can supply. He supplies the far greater part of them by exchanging that surplus part of the produce of his own labor, which is over and above his own consumption, for such parts of the produce of other men's labor as he has occasion for. Every man thus lives by exchanging, or becomes in some measure a merchant, and the society itself grows to be what is properly a commercial society.

But when the division of labor first began to take place, this power of exchanging must frequently have been very much clogged and embarrassed in its operations. One man, we shall suppose, has more of a certain commodity than he himself has occasion for, while another has less. The former consequently would be glad to dispose of, and the latter to purchase, a part of this superfluity. But if this latter should chance to have nothing that the former stands in need of, no exchange can be made between them. The butcher has more meat in his shop than he himself can consume, and the brewer and the baker would each of them be willing to purchase a part of it. But they have nothing to offer in exchange, except the different productions of their respective trades, and the butcher is already provided with all the bread and beer which he has immediate occasion for. No exchange can, in this case, be made between them. He cannot be their merchant, nor they his customers; and they are all of them thus mutually less serviceable to one another. In order to avoid the inconvenience of such situations, every prudent man in every period of society, after the first establishment of the division of labor, must naturally have endeavored to manage his affairs in such a manner, as to have at all times by him, besides the peculiar produce of his own industry, a certain quantity of some one commodity or other, such as he imagined few people would be likely to refuse in exchange for the produce of their industry.

Many different commodities, it is probable, were successively both thought of and employed for this purpose. In the rude ages of society, cattle are said to have been the common instrument of commerce; and, though they must have been a most inconvenient one, yet in old times we find things were frequently valued according to the number of cattle which had been given in exchange for them. The armor of Diomedes, says Homer, cost only nine oxen; but that of Glaucus cost a hundred oxen. Salt is said to be the common instrument of commerce and exchanges in Abyssinia; a species of shells in some parts of the coast of India; dried cod at Newfoundland; tobacco in Virginia; sugar in some of our West Indian colonies; hides or dressed leather in some other countries; and there is at this day a village in Scotland where it is not uncommon, I am told, for a workman to carry nails instead of money to the baker's shop or the alehouse.

In all countries, however, men seem at last to have been determined by irresistible reasons to give the preference, for this employment, to metals above every other commodity. Metals can not only be kept with as little loss as any other commodity, scarcely anything being less perishable than they are, but they can likewise, without any loss, be divided into any number of parts, as by fusion those parts can easily be reunited again—a quality which no other equally durable commodities possess, and which more than any other quality renders them fit to be the instruments of commerce and circulation. The man who wanted to buy salt, for example, and had nothing but cattle to give in exchange for it, must have been obliged to buy salt to the value of a whole ox, or a whole sheep, at a time. He could seldom buy less than this, because what he was to give for it could seldom be divided without loss; and if he had a mind to buy more, he must, for the same reasons, have been obliged to buy double or triple the quantity, the value, to wit, of two or three oxen, or of two or three sheep. If, on the contrary, instead of sheep or oxen, he had metals to give in exchange for it, he could easily proportion the quantity of the metal to the precise quantity of the commodity which he had immediate occasion for.

Different metals have been made use of by different nations for this purpose. Iron was the common instrument of commerce among the ancient Spartans; copper among the ancient Romans; and gold and silver among all rich and commercial nations. . . .

. . . Money has become in all civilized nations the universal instrument of commerce, by the intervention of which goods of all kinds are bought and sold, or exchanged for one another.

What are the rules which men naturally observe in exchanging them either for money or for one another, I shall now proceed to examine. These rules determine what may be called the relative or exchangeable value of goods.

The word VALUE, it is to be observed, has two different meanings, and sometimes expresses the utility of some particular object, and sometimes the power of purchasing other goods which the possession of that object conveys. The one may be called "value in use"; the other, "value in exchange." The things which have the greatest value in use have frequently little or no value in exchange; and on the contrary, those which have the greatest value in exchange have frequently little or no value in use. Nothing is more useful than water, but it will purchase scarcely anything; scarcely anything can be had in exchange for it. A diamond, on the contrary, has scarcely any value in use; but a very great quantity of other goods may frequently be had in exchange for it. . . .

Of the Real and Nominal Price of Commodities, or of Their Price in Labor, and Their Price in Money

Every man is rich or poor according to the degree in which he can afford to enjoy the necessities, conveniences, and amusements of human life. But after the division of labor has once thoroughly taken place, it is but a very small part of these with which a man's own labor can supply him. The far greater part of them he must derive from the labor of other people, and he must be rich or poor according to the quantity of that labor which he can command, or which he can afford to purchase. The value of any commodity, therefore, to the person who possesses it, and who means not to use or consume it himself, but to exchange it for other commodities, is equal to the quantity of labor which it enables him to purchase or command. Labor, therefore, is the real measure of the exchangeable value of all commodities.

The real price of everything, what everything really costs to the man who wants to acquire it, is the toil and trouble of acquiring it. What everything is really worth to the man who has acquired it, and who wants to dispose of it or exchange it for something else, is the toil and trouble which it can save to himself, and which it can impose upon other people. What is bought with money or with goods is purchased by labor, as much as what we acquire by the toil of our own body. That money or those goods indeed save us this toil. They contain the value of a certain quantity of labor which we exchange for what is supposed at the time to contain the value of an equal quantity. Labor was the first price, the original purchase-money that was paid for all things. It was not by gold or silver, but by labor, that all the wealth of the world was originally purchased; and its value, to those who possess it, and who want to exchange it for some new productions, is precisely equal to the quantity of labor which it can enable them to purchase or command.

Wealth, as Mr. Hobbes says, is power. But the person who either acquires, or succeeds to a great fortune, does not necessarily acquire or succeed to any political power, either civil or military. His fortune may, perhaps, afford him the means of acquiring both, but the mere possession of that fortune does not necessarily convey to him either. The power which that possession immediately and directly conveys to him is the power of purchasing—a certain command over all the labor or over all the produce of labor which is then in the market. His fortune is greater or less, precisely in proportion to the extent of this power, or the quantity either of other men's labor, or, what is the same thing, of the produce of other men's labor, which it enables him to purchase or command. The exchangeable value of everything must always be precisely equal to the extent of this power which it conveys to its owner.

But though labor be the real measure of the exchangeable value of all commodities, it is not that by which their value is commonly estimated. It is often difficult to ascertain the proportion between two different quantities of labor. The time spent in two different sorts of work will not always alone determine this proportion. The different degrees of hardship endured, and of ingenuity exercised, must likewise be taken into account. There may be more labor in an hour's hard work than in two hours' easy business; or in an hour's application to a trade which it cost ten years' labor to learn, than in a month's industry at an ordinary and obvious employment. But it is not easy to find any accurate measure either of hardship or ingenuity. In exchanging indeed the different productions of different sorts of labor for one another, some allowance is commonly made for both. It is adjusted, however, not by any accurate measure, but by the higgling and bargaining of the market, according to that sort of rough equality which, though not exact, is sufficient for carrying on the business of common life.

Every commodity, besides, is more frequently exchanged for, and thereby compared with, other commodities than with labor. It is more natural, therefore, to estimate its exchangeable value by the quantity of some other commodity than by that of the labor which it can purchase. The greater part of people too understand better what is meant by a quantity of a particular commodity, than by a quantity of labor. The one is a plain, palpable object; the other an abstract notion, which, though it can be made sufficiently intelligible, is not altogether so natural and obvious.

But when barter ceases, and money has become the common instrument of commerce, every particular commodity is more frequently exchanged for money than for any other commodity. The butcher seldom carries his beef or his mutton to the baker, or the brewer, in order to exchange them for bread or for beer; but he carries them to the market, where he exchanges them for money, and afterwards exchanges that money for bread and for beer. The quantity of money which he gets for them regulates too the quantity of bread and beer which he can afterwards purchase. It is more natural and obvious to him, therefore, to estimate their value by the quantity of money, the commodity for which he immediately exchanges them, than by that of bread and beer, the commodities for which he can exchange them only by the intervention of another commodity; and rather to say that his butcher's meat is worth threepence or fourpence a pound, than that it is worth three or four pounds of bread, or three or four quarts of small beer. Hence it comes to pass that the exchangeable value of every commodity is more frequently estimated by the quantity of money, than by the quantity either of labor or of any other commodity which can be had in exchange for it.

Gold and silver, however, like every other commodity, vary in their value, are sometimes cheaper and sometimes dearer, sometimes of easier and sometimes of more difficult purchase. The quantity of labor which any particular quantity of them can purchase or command, or the quantity of other goods which it will exchange for, depends always upon the fertility or barrenness of the mines which happen to be known about the time when such exchanges are made. The discovery of the abundant mines of America reduced, in the sixteenth century, the value of gold and silver in Europe to about a third of what it had been before. As it cost less labor to bring those metals from the mine to the market, so when they were brought thither they could purchase or command less labor; and this revolution in their value, though perhaps the greatest, is by no means the only one of which history gives some account. But as a measure of quantity, such as the natural foot, fathom, or handful, which is continually varying in its own quantity, can never be an accurate measure of the quantity of other things; so a commodity, which is itself continually varying in its own value, can never be an accurate measure of the value of other commodities. Equal quantities of labor, at all times and places, may be said to be of equal value to the laborer. In his ordinary state of health, strength, and spirits, in the ordinary degree of his skill and dexterity, he must always lay down the same portion of his ease, his liberty, and his happiness. The price which he pays must always be the same, whatever may be the quantity of goods which he receives in return for it. Of these, indeed, it may sometimes purchase a greater and sometimes a smaller quantity; but it is their value which varies, not that of the labor which purchases them. At all times and places that is dear which it is difficult to come at, or which it costs much labor to acquire; and that cheap which is to be had easily, or with very little labor. Labor alone, therefore, never varying in its own value, is alone the ultimate and real standard by which the value of all commodities can at all times and places be estimated and compared. It is their real price; money is their nominal price only.

But though equal quantities of labor are always of equal value to the laborer, yet to the person who employs him they appear sometimes to be of greater and sometimes of smaller value. He purchases them sometimes with a greater and sometimes with a smaller quantity of goods, and to him the price of labor seems to vary like that of all other things. It appears to him dear in the one case, and cheap in the other. In reality, however, it is the goods which are cheap in the one case, and dear in the other.

In this popular sense, therefore, labor, like commodities, may be said to have a real and a nominal price. Its real price may be said to consist in the quantity of the necessaries and conveniences of life which are given for it; its nominal price, in the quantity of money. The laborer is rich or poor, is well or ill rewarded, in proportion to the real, not to the nominal price of his labor.

The distinction between the real and the nominal price of commodities and labor is not a matter of mere speculation, but may sometimes be of considerable use in practice. The same real price is always of the same value; but on account of the variations in the value of gold and silver, the same nominal price is sometimes of very different values. When a landed estate, therefore, is sold with a reservation of a perpetual rent, if it is intended that this rent should always be of the same value, it is of importance to the family in whose favor it is reserved that it should not consist in a particular sum of money. Its value would in this case be liable to variations of two different kinds: first, to those which arise from the different quantities of gold and silver which are contained at different times in coin of the same denomination; and, secondly, to those which arise from the different values of equal quantities of gold and silver at different times. . . .

Of the Accumulation of Capital, or of Productive and Unproductive Labor

There is one sort of labor which adds to the value of the subject upon which it is bestowed; there is another which has no such effect. The former, as it produces a value, may be called productive; the latter, unproductive labor. Thus the labor of a manufacturer adds, generally, to the value of the materials which he works upon, that of his own maintenance, and of his master's profit. The labor of a menial servant, on the contrary, adds to the value of nothing. Though the manufacturer has his wages advanced to him by his master, he, in reality, costs him no expense, the value of those wages being generally restored, together with a profit, in the improved value of the subject upon which his labor is bestowed. But the maintenance of a menial servant never is restored. A man grows rich by employing a multitude of manufacturers; he grows poor by maintaining a multitude of menial servants. The labor of the latter, however, has its value, and deserves its reward as well as that of the former. But the labor of the manufacturer fixes and realizes itself in some particular subject or vendible commodity, which lasts for some time at least after that labor is past. It is, as it were, a certain quantity of labor stocked and stored up to be employed, if necessary, upon some other occasion. That subject, or what is the same thing, the price of that subject, can afterwards, if necessary, put into motion a quantity of labor equal to that which had originally produced it. The labor of the menial servant, on the contrary, does not fix or realize itself in any particular subject or vendible commodity. His services generally perish in the very instant of their performance, and seldom leave any trace or value behind them, for which an equal quantity of service could afterwards be procured.

The labor of some of the most respectable orders in the society is, like that of menial servants, unproductive of any value and does not fix or realize itself in any permanent subject, or vendible commodity, which endures after that labor is past, and for which an equal quantity of labor could afterwards be procured. The sovereign, for example, with all the officers both of justice and war who serve under him, the whole army and navy, are unproductive laborers. They are the servants of the public, and are maintained by a part of the annual produce of the industry of other people. Their service, how honorable, how useful, or how necessary soever, produces nothing for which an equal quantity of service can afterwards be procured. The protection, security, and defense of the commonwealth, the effect of their labor this year, will not purchase its protection, security, and defense for the year to come. In the same class must be ranked some both of the gravest and most important, and some of the most frivolous professions: churchmen, lawyers, physicians, men of letters of all kinds; players, buffoons, musicians, opera singers, opera dancers, etc. The labor of the meanest of these has a certain value, regulated by the very same principles which regulate that of every other sort of labor; and that of the noblest and most useful produces nothing which could afterwards purchase or procure an equal quantity of labor. Like the declamation of the actor, the harangue of the orator, or the tune of the musician, the work of all of them perishes in the very instant of its production.

Both productive and unproductive laborers, and those who do not labor at all, are all equally maintained by the annual produce of the land and labor of the country. This produce, how great soever, can never be infinite, but must have certain limits. Accordingly, therefore, as a smaller or greater proportion of it is in any one year employed in maintaining unproductive hands, the more in the one case and the less in the other will remain for the productive, and the next year's produce will be greater or smaller accordingly, the whole annual produce, if we except the spontaneous productions of the earth, being the effect of productive labor.

Though the whole annual produce of the land and labor of every country is, no doubt, ultimately destined for supplying the consumption of its inhabitants, and for procuring a revenue to them; yet when it first comes either from the ground, or from the hands of the productive laborers, it naturally divides itself into two parts. One of them, and frequently the largest, is, in the first place, destined for replacing a capital, or for renewing the provisions, materials, and finished work which had been withdrawn from a capital; the other for constituting a revenue either to the owner of this capital, as the profit of his stock; or to some other person, as the rent of his land. Thus, of the produce of land, one part replaces the capital of the farmer; the other pays his profit and the rent of the landlord, and thus constitutes a revenue both to the owner of this capital, as the profits of his stock, and to some other person, as the rent of his land. Of the produce of a great manufactory, in the same manner, one part, and that always the largest, replaces the capital of the undertaker of the work; the other pays his profit, and thus constitutes a revenue to the owner of this capital.

That part of the annual produce of the land and labor of any country which replaces a capital never is immediately employed to maintain any but productive hands. It pays the wages of productive labor only. That which is immediately destined for constituting a revenue, either as profit or as rent, may maintain indifferently either productive or unproductive hands.

Whatever part of his stock a man employs as a capital, he always expects it to be replaced to him with a profit. He employs it, therefore, in maintaining productive hands only, and after having served in the function of a capital to him, it constitutes a revenue to them. Whenever he employs any part of it in maintaining unproductive hands of any kind, that part is, from that moment, withdrawn from his capital and placed in his stock reserved for immediate consumption.

Unproductive laborers, and those who do not labor at all, are all maintained by revenue; either, first, by that part of the annual produce which is originally destined for constituting a revenue to some particular persons, either as the rent of land or as the profits of stock; or, secondly, by that part which, though originally destined for replacing a capital and for maintaining productive laborers only, yet when it comes into their hands, whatever part of it is over and above their necessary subsistence, may be employed in maintaining indifferently either productive or unproductive hands. Thus, not only the great landlord or the rich merchant, but even the common workman, if his wages are considerable, may maintain a menial servant; or he may sometimes go to a play or a puppet show, and so contribute his share toward maintaining one set of unproductive laborers; or he may pay some taxes, and thus help to maintain another set, more honorable and useful, indeed, but equally unproductive. No part of the annual produce, however, which had been originally destined to replace a capital, is ever directed toward maintaining unproductive hands, till after it has put into motion its full complement of productive labor, or all that it could put into motion in the way in which it was employed. The workman must have earned his wages by work done, before he can employ any part of them in this manner. That part too is generally but a small one. It is his spare revenue only, of which productive laborers have seldom a great deal. They generally have some, however, and in the payment of taxes the greatness of their number may compensate, in some measure, the smallness of their contribution. The rent of land and the profits of stock are everywhere, therefore, the principal sources from which unproductive hands derive their subsistence. These are the two sorts of revenue of which the owners have generally most to spare. They might both maintain indifferently either productive or unproductive hands. They seem, however, to have some predilection for the latter. The expense of a great lord feeds generally more idle than industrious people. The rich merchant, though with his capital he maintains industrious people only, yet by his expense, that is, by the employment of his revenue, he feeds commonly the very same sort as the great lord.

The proportion, therefore, between the productive and unproductive hands depends very much in every country upon the proportion between that part of the annual produce which, as soon as it comes either from the ground or from the hands of the productive laborers, is destined for replacing a capital, and that which is destined for constituting a revenue, either as rent, or as profit. This proportion is very different in rich from what it is in poor countries. . . .

It can seldom happen, indeed, that the circumstances of a great nation can be much affected either by the prodigality or misconduct of individuals, the profusion or imprudence of some being always more than compensated by the frugality and good conduct of others.

With regard to profusion, the principle which prompts to expense is the passion for present enjoyment, which, though sometimes violent and very difficult to be restrained, is in general only momentary and occasional. But the principle which prompts to save is the desire of bettering our condition, a desire which, though generally calm and dispassionate, comes with us from the womb, and never leaves us till we go into the grave. In the whole interval which separates those two moments, there is scarcely perhaps a single instant in which any man is so perfectly and completely satisfied with his situation as to be without any wish of alteration or improvement of any kind. An augmentation of fortune is the means by which the greater part of men propose and wish to better their condition. It is the means the most vulgar and the most obvious; and the most likely way of augmenting their fortune is to save and accumulate some part of what they acquire, either regularly and annually, or upon some extraordinary occasions. Though the principle of expense, therefore, prevails in almost all men upon some occasions, and in some men upon almost all occasions, yet in the greater part of men, taking the whole course of their life at an average, the principle of frugality seems not only to predominate, but to predominate very greatly.

With regard to misconduct, the number of prudent and successful under-takings is everywhere much greater than that of injudicious and unsuccessful ones. After all our complaints of the frequency of bankruptcies, the unhappy men who fall into this misfortune make but a very small part of the whole number engaged in trade and all other sorts of business, not much more perhaps than one in a thousand. Bankruptcy is perhaps the greatest and most humiliating calamity which can befall an innocent man. The greater part of men, therefore, are sufficiently careful to avoid it. Some, indeed, do not avoid it, as some do not avoid the gallows.

Great nations are never impoverished by private, though they sometimes are by public, prodigality and misconduct. The whole, or almost the whole, public revenue is in most countries employed in maintaining unproductive hands. Such are the people who compose a numerous and splendid court, a great ecclesiastical establishment, great fleets and armies, who in time of peace produce nothing, and in time of war acquire nothing which can compensate the expense of maintaining them, even while the war lasts. Such people, as they themselves produce nothing, are all maintained by the produce of other men's labor. When multiplied, therefore, to an unnecessary number, they may in a particular year consume so great a share of this produce as not to leave a sufficiency for maintaining the productive laborers who should reproduce it next year. The next year's produce, therefore, will be less than that of the foregoing, and if the same disorder should continue, that of the third year will be still less than that of the second. Those unproductive hands, who should be maintained by a part only of the spare revenue of the people, may consume so great a share of their whole revenue, and therefore oblige so great a number to encroach upon their capitals, upon the funds destined for the mainte-nance of productive labor, that all the frugality and good conduct of individuals may not be able to compensate the waste and degradation of produce occasioned by this violent and forced encroachment.

This frugality and good conduct, however, is upon most occasions, it appears from experience, sufficient to compensate not only the private prodigality and misconduct of individuals, but the public extravagance of government. The uniform, constant, and uninterrupted effort of every man to better his condition, the principle from which public and national, as well as private opulence is originally derived, is frequently powerful enough to maintain the natural progress of things toward improvement, in spite both of the extravagance of government, and of the greatest errors of administration. Like the unknown principle of animal life, it frequently restores health and vigor to the constitution, in spite, not only of the disease, but of the absurd prescriptions of the doctor.

The annual produce of the land and labor of any nation can be increased in its value by no other means, but by increasing either the number of its productive laborers, or the productive powers of those laborers who had before been employed. The number of its productive laborers, it is evident, can never be much increased but in consequence of an increase of capital, or of the funds destined for maintaining them. The productive powers of the same number of laborers cannot be increased, but in consequence either of some addition and improvement to those machines and instruments which facilitate and abridge labor; or of a more proper division and distribution of employment. In either case an additional capital is almost always required. It is by means of an additional capital only, that the undertaker of any work can either provide his workmen with better machinery, or make a more proper distribution of employment among them. When the work to be done consists of a number of parts, to keep every man constantly employed in one way requires a much greater capital than where every man is occasionally employed in every different part of the work. When we compare, therefore, the state of a nation at two different periods, and find that the annual produce of its land and labor is evidently greater at the latter than at the former, that its lands are better cultivated, its manufacturers more numerous and more flourishing, and its trade more extensive, we may be assured that its capital must have increased during the interval between those two periods, and that more must have been added to it by the good conduct of some, than had been taken from it either by the private misconduct of others, or by the public extravagance of government. But we shall find this to have been the case of almost all nations, in all tolerably quiet and peaceful times, even of those who have not enjoyed the most prudent and parsimonious governments. To form a right judgment of it, indeed, we must compare the state of the country at periods somewhat distant from one another. The progress is frequently so gradual that, at near periods, the improvement is not only not sensible, but from the declension either of certain branches of industry, or of certain districts of the country, things which sometimes happen though the country in general be in great prosperity, there frequently arises a suspicion that the riches and industry of the whole are decaying.

The annual produce of the land and labor of England, for example, is certainly much greater than it was a little more than a century ago, at the restoration of Charles II. Though, at present, few people, I believe, doubt of this, yet during this period, five years have seldom passed away in which some book or pamphlet has not been published, written, too, with such abilities as to gain some authority with the public, and pretending to demonstrate that the wealth of the nation was fast declining, that the country was depopulated, agriculture neglected, manufactures decaying, and trade undone. Nor have these publications been all party pamphlets, the wretched offspring of falsehood and venality. Many of them have been written by very candid and very intelligent people, who wrote nothing but what they believed, and for no other reason but because they believed it. . . .

Of the Natural Progress of Opulence

The great commerce of every civilized society is that carried on between the inhabitants of the town and those of the country. It consists in the exchange of rude for manufactured produce, either immediately, or by the intervention of money, or of some sort of paper which represents money. The country supplies the town with the means of subsistence and the materials of manufacture. The town repays this supply by sending back a part of the manufactured produce to the inhabitants of the country. The town, in which there neither is nor can be any reproduction of substances, may very properly be said to gain its whole wealth and subsistence from the country. We must not, however, upon this account, imagine that the gain of the town is the loss of the country. The gains of both are mutual and reciprocal, and the division of labor is in this, as in all other cases, advantageous to all the different persons employed in the various occupations into which it is subdivided. The inhabitants of the country purchase of the town a greater quantity of manufactured goods, with the produce of a much smaller quantity of their own labor, than they must have employed had they attempted to prepare them themselves. The town affords a market for the surplus produce of the country, or what is over and above the maintenance of the cultivators, and it is there that the inhabitants of the country exchange it for something else which is in demand among them. The greater the number and revenue of the inhabitants of the town, the more extensive is the market which it affords to those of the country; and the more extensive that market, it is always the more advantageous to a great number. The corn which grows within a mile of the town sells there for the same price with that which comes from twenty miles distance. But the price of the latter must generally not only pay the expense of raising and bringing it to market, but afford, too, the ordinary profits of agriculture to the farmer. The proprietors and cultivators of the country, therefore, which lies in the neighborhood of the town, over and above the ordinary profits of agriculture gain, in the price of what they sell, the whole value of the carriage of the like produce that is brought from more distant parts, and they save, besides, the whole value of this carriage in the price of what they buy. Compare the cultivation of the lands in the neighborhood of any considerable town with that of those which lie at some distance from it, and you will satisfy yourself how much the country is benefited by the commerce of the town. Among all the absurd speculations that have been propagated concerning the balance of trade, it has never been pretended that either the country loses by its commerce with the town, or the town by that with the country which maintains it.

As subsistence is, in the nature of things, prior to convenience and luxury, so the industry which procures the former must necessarily be prior to that which ministers to the latter. The cultivation and improvement of the country, therefore, which affords subsistence, must, necessarily, be prior to the increase of the town, which furnishes only the means of convenience and luxury. It is the surplus produce of the country only, or what is over and above the maintenance of the cultivators, that constitutes the subsistence of the town, which can therefore increase only with the increase of this surplus produce. The town, indeed, may not always derive its whole subsistence from the country in its neighborhood, or even from the territory to which it belongs, but from very distant countries; and this, though it forms no exception from the general rule, has occasioned considerable variations in the progress of opulence in different ages and nations.

That order of things which necessity imposes in general, though not in every particular country, is, in every particular country, promoted by the natural inclinations of man. If human institutions had never thwarted those natural inclinations, the towns could nowhere have increased beyond what the improvement and cultivation of the territory in which they were situated could support, till such time, at least, as the whole of that territory was completely cultivated and improved. Upon equal, or nearly equal, profits, most men will choose to employ their capitals rather in the improvement and cultivation of land, than either in manufactures or in foreign trade. The man who employs his capital in land has it more under his view and command, and his fortune is much less liable to accidents than that of the trader, who is obliged frequently to commit it, not only to the winds and the waves, but to the more uncertain elements of human folly and injustice, by giving great credits in distant countries to men with whose character and situation he can seldom be thoroughly acquainted. The capital of the landlord, on the contrary, which is fixed in the improvement of his land, seems to be as well secured as the nature of human affairs can admit of. The beauty of the country, besides the pleasures of a country life, the tranquillity of mind which it promises, and wherever the injustice of human laws does not disturb it, the independence which it really affords, have charms that more or less attract everybody; and as to cultivate the ground was the original destination of man, so in every stage of his existence he seems to retain a predilection for this primitive employment.

Without the assistance of some artificers, indeed, the cultivation of land cannot be carried on, but with great inconvenience and continual interruption. Smiths, carpenters, wheelwrights, and plowrights, masons, and bricklayers, tanners, shoemakers, and tailors are people whose service the farmer has frequent occasion for. Such artificers, too, stand, occasionally, in need of the assistance of one another; and as their residence is not, like that of the farmer, necessarily tied down to a precise spot, they naturally settle in the neighborhood of one another, and thus form a small town or village. The butcher, the brewer, and the baker soon join them, together with many other artificers and retailers, necessary or useful for supplying their occasional wants, and who contribute still further to augment the town. The inhabitants of the town and those of the country are mutually the servants of one another. The town is a continual fair or market, to which the inhabitants of the country resort, in order to exchange their rude for manufactured produce. It is this commerce which supplies the inhabitants of the town both with the materials of their work, and the means of their subsistence. The quantity of the finished work which they sell to the inhabitants of the country necessarily regulates the quantity of the materials and provisions which they buy. Neither their employment nor subsistence, therefore, can augment but in proportion to the augmentation of the demand from the country for finished work; and this demand can augment only in proportion to the extension of improvement and cultivation. Had human institutions, therefore, never disturbed the natural course of things, the progressive wealth and increase of the towns would, in every political society, be consequential, and in proportion to the improvement and cultivation of the territory or country.

In our North American colonies, where uncultivated land is still to be had upon easy terms, no manufactures for distant sale have ever yet been established in any of their towns. When an artificer has acquired a little more stock than is necessary for carrying on his own business in supplying the neighboring country, he does not, in North America, attempt to establish with it a manufacture for more distant sale, but employs it in the purchase and improvement of uncultivated land. From artificer he becomes planter, and neither the large wages nor the easy subsistence which that country affords to artificers can bribe him rather to work for other people than for himself. He feels that an artificer is the servant of his customers, from whom he derives his subsistence; but that a planter who cultivates his own land, and derives his necessary subsistence from the labor of his own family, is really a master, and independent of all the world.

In countries, on the contrary, where there is either no uncultivated land, or none that can be had upon easy terms, every artificer who has acquired more stock than he can employ in the occasional jobs of the neighborhood, endeavors to prepare work for more distant sale. The smith erects some sort of iron, the weaver some sort of linen or woolen manufactory. Those different manufactures come, in process of time, to be gradually subdivided, and thereby improved and refined in a great variety of ways, which may easily be conceived, and which it is therefore unnecessary to explain any further.

In seeking for employment of a capital, manufactures are, upon equal or nearly equal profits, naturally preferred to foreign commerce, for the same reason that agriculture is naturally preferred to manufactures. As the capital of the landlord or farmer is more secure than that of the manufacturer, so the capital of the manufacturer, being at all times more within his view and command, is more secure than that of the foreign merchant. In every period, indeed, of every society, the surplus part both of the rude and manufactured produce, or that for which there is no demand at home, must be sent abroad in order to be exchanged for something for which there is some demand at home. But whether the capital which carries this surplus produce abroad be a foreign or a domestic one is of very little importance. If the society has not acquired sufficient capital both to cultivate all its lands, and to manufacture in the most complete manner the whole of its rude produce, there is even a considerable advantage that the rude produce should be exported by a foreign capital, in order that the whole stock of the society may be employed in more useful purposes. The wealth of ancient Egypt, that of China and Indostan sufficiently demonstrate that a nation may attain a very high degree of opulence, though the greater part of its exportation trade be carried on by foreigners. The progress of our North American and West Indian colonies would have been much less rapid, had not capital but what belonged to themselves been employed in exporting their surplus produce.

According to the natural course of things, therefore, the greater part of the capital of every growing society is, first, directed to agriculture, afterwards to manufactures, and last of all to foreign commerce. This order of things is so very natural that, in every society that had any territory, it has always, I believe, been in some degree observed. Some of their lands must have been cultivated before any considerable towns could be established, and some sort of coarse industry of the manufacturing kind must have been carried on in those towns, before they could well think of employing themselves in foreign commerce.

But though this natural order of things must have taken place in some degree in every such society, it has, in all the modern states of Europe, been, in many respects, entirely inverted. The foreign commerce of some of their cities has introduced all their finer manufactures, or such as were fit for distant sale; and manufactures and foreign commerce together have given birth to the principal improvements of agriculture. The manners and customs which the nature of their original government introduced, and which remained after that government was greatly altered, necessarily forced them into this unnatural and retrograde order. . . .

Of Restraints upon the Importation from Foreign Countries of Such Goods as Can Be Produced at Home

By restraining, either by high duties, or by absolute prohibitions, the importation of such goods from foreign countries as can be produced at home, the monopoly of the home market is more or less secured to the domestic industry employed in producing them. Thus the prohibition of importing either live cattle or salt provisions from foreign countries secures to the graziers of Great Britain the monopoly of the home market for butcher's meat. The high duties upon the importation of corn, which in times of moderate plenty amount to a prohibition, give a like advantage to the growers of that commodity. The prohibition of the importation of foreign woolens is equally favorable to the woolen manufacturers. The silk manufacture, though altogether employed upon foreign materials, has lately obtained the same advantage. The linen manufacture has not yet obtained it, but is making great strides toward it. Many other sorts of manufacturers have, in the same manner, obtained in Great Britain, either altogether, or very nearly, a monopoly against their countrymen. The variety of goods of which the importation into Great Britain is prohibited, either absolutely, or under certain circumstances, greatly exceeds what can easily be suspected by those who are not well acquainted with the laws of the customs.

That this monopoly of the home market frequently gives great encouragement to that particular species of industry which enjoys it, and frequently turns toward that employment a greater share of both the labor and stock of the society than would otherwise have gone to it, cannot be doubted. But whether it tends either to increase the general industry of the society, or to give it the most advantageous direction, is not, perhaps, altogether so evident.

The general industry of the society never can exceed what the capital of the society can employ. As the number of workmen that can be kept in employment by any particular person must bear a certain proportion to his capital, so the number of those that can be continually employed by all the members of a great society must bear a certain proportion to the whole capital of that society and never can exceed that proportion. No regulation of commerce can increase the quantity of industry in any society beyond what its capital can maintain. It can only divert a part of it into a direction into which it might not otherwise have gone; and it is by no means certain that this artificial direction is likely to be more advantageous to the society than that into which it would have gone of its own accord.

Every individual is continually exerting himself to find out the most advantageous employment for whatever capital he can command. It is his own advantage, indeed, and not that of the society, which he has in view. But the study of his own advantage naturally, or rather necessarily, leads him to prefer that employment which is most advantageous to the society.

First, every individual endeavors to employ his capital as near home as he can, and consequently as much as he can in the support of domestic industry, provided always that he can thereby obtain the ordinary, or not a great deal less than the ordinary, profits of stock.

. . . A capital employed in the home trade . . . necessarily puts into motion a greater quantity of domestic industry and gives revenue and employment to a greater number of the inhabitants of the country than an equal capital employed in the foreign trade of consumption; and one employed in the foreign trade of consumption has the same advantage over an equal capital employed in the carrying trade. Upon equal, or only nearly equal, profits, therefore, every individual naturally inclines to employ his capital in the manner in which it is likely to afford the greatest support to domestic industry, and to give revenue and employment to the greatest number of people of his own country.

Secondly, every individual who employs his capital in the support of domestic industry necessarily endeavors so to direct that industry that its produce may be of the greatest possible value.

The produce of industry is what it adds to the subject or materials upon which it is employed. In proportion as the value of this produce is great or small, so will likewise be the profits of the employer. But it is only for the sake of profit that any man employs a capital in the support of industry; and he will always, therefore, endeavor to employ it in the support of that industry of which the produce is likely to be of the greatest value, or to exchange for the greatest quantity either of money or of other goods.

But the annual revenue of every society is always precisely equal to the exchangeable value of the whole annual produce of its industry, or rather is precisely the same thing with that exchangeable value. As every individual, therefore, endeavors as much as he can both to employ his capital in the support of domestic industry and so to direct that industry that its produce may be of the greatest value; every individual necessarily labors to render the annual revenue of the society as great as he can. He generally, indeed, neither intends to promote the public interest, nor knows how much he is promoting it. By preferring the support of domestic to that of foreign industry, he intends only his own security; and by directing that industry in such a manner as its produce may be of the greatest value, he intends only his own gain, and he is in this, as in many other cases, led by an invisible hand to promote an end which was no part of his intention. Nor is it always the worse for the society that it was no part of it. By pursuing his own interest he frequently promotes that of the society more effectually than when he really intends to promote it. I have never known much good done by those who affected to trade for the public good. It is an affectation, indeed, not very common among merchants, and very few words need be employed in dissuading them from it.

What is the species of domestic industry which his capital can employ, and of which the produce is likely to be of the greatest value, every individual, it is evident, can, in his local situation, judge much better than any statesman or lawgiver can do for him. The statesman, who should attempt to direct private people in what manner they ought to employ their capitals, would not only load himself with a most unnecessary attention, but assume an authority which could safely be trusted, not only to no single person, but to no council or senate whatever, and which would nowhere be so dangerous as in the hands of a man who had folly and presumption enough to fancy himself fit to exercise it.

To give the monopoly of the home market to the produce of domestic industry, in any particular art or manufacture, is in some measure to direct private people in what manner they ought to employ their capitals, and must, in almost all cases, be either a useless or a hurtful regulation. If the produce of domestic can be brought there as cheaply as that of foreign industry, the regulation is evidently useless. If it cannot, it must generally be hurtful. It is the maxim of every prudent master of a family, never to attempt to make at home what it will cost him more to make than to buy. . . .

What is prudence in the conduct of every private family can scarcely be folly in that of a great kingdom. . . .

Labour and Capital

•

Karl Marx

The Fetishism of Commodities and
the Secret Thereof

A commodity appears, at first sight, a very trivial thing, and easily understood. Its analysis shows that it is, in reality, a very queer thing, abounding in metaphysical subtleties and theological niceties. So far as it is a value in use, there is nothing mysterious about it, whether we consider it from the point of view that by its properties it is capable of satisfying human wants, or from the point that those properties are the product of human labour. It is as clear as noonday, that man, by his industry, changes the forms of the materials furnished by Nature, in such a way as to make them useful to him. The form of wood, for instance, is altered, by making a table out of it. Yet, for all that, the table continues to be that common, everyday thing, wood. But, so soon as it steps forth as a commodity, it is changed into something transcendent. It not only stands with its feet on the ground, but, in relation to all other commodities, it stands on its head, and evolves out of its wooden brain grotesque ideas, far more wonderful than "table-turning" ever was.

The mystical character of commodities does not originate, therefore, in their use-value. Just as little does it proceed from the nature of the determining factors of value. For, in the first place, however varied the useful kinds of labour, or

From Karl Marx, *Capital*, vol. I, first published in 1867. The text is from the translation of the Third German Edition by Samuel Moore and Edward Aveling, edited by Frederick Engels (London: 1889).

Born in Germany, Karl Marx (1818–1883) was a newspaper editor before fleeing to London, where he continued for many years to produce, often with the help of Frederick Engels, his vast body of writings on philosophy, society, and economics. Among the most important of his other works are the *Economic and Philosophical Manuscripts of 1844*, *Wage Labour and Capital*, *The Communist Manifesto*, the *Grundrisse*, and *A Contribution to the Critique of Political Economy*.

productive activities, may be, it is a physiological fact, that they are functions of the human organism, and that each such function, whatever may be its nature or form, is essentially the expenditure of human brain, nerves, muscles, etc. Secondly, with regard to that which forms the groundwork for the quantitative determination of value, namely, the duration of that expenditure, or the quantity of labour, it is quite clear that there is a palpable difference between its quantity and the quality. In all states of society, the labour time that it costs to produce the means of subsistence must necessarily be an object of interest to mankind, though not of equal interest in different stages of development. And lastly, from the moment that men in any way work for one another, their labour assumes a social form.

Whence, then, arises the enigmatical character of the product of labour, so soon as it assumes the form of commodities? Clearly from this form itself. The equality of all sorts of human labour is expressed objectively by their products all being equally valued; the measure of the expenditure of labour power by the duration of that expenditure takes the form of the quantity of value of the products of labour; and finally, the mutual relations of the producers, within which the social character of their labour affirms itself, take the form of a social relation between the products.

A commodity is therefore a mysterious thing, simply because in it the social character of men's labour appears to them as an objective character stamped upon the product of that labour; because the relation of the producers to the sum total of their own labour is presented to them as a social relation, existing not between themselves, but between the products of their labour. This is the reason why the products of labour become commodities, social things whose qualities are at the same time perceptible and imperceptible by the senses. In the same way the light from an object is perceived by us not as the subjective excitation of our optic nerve, but as the objective form of something outside the eye itself. But, in the act of seeing, there is at all events, an actual passage of light from one thing to another, from the external object to the eye. There is a physical relation between physical things. But it is different with commodities. There, the existence of the things *qua* commodities, and the value relation between the products of labour which stamps them as commodities, have absolutely no connection with their physical properties and with the material relations arising therefrom. There it is a definite social relation between men, that assumes, in their eyes, the fantastic form of a relation between things. In order, therefore, to find an analogy, we must have recourse to the mist-enveloped regions of the religious world. In that world the productions of the human brain appear as independent beings endowed with life, and entering into relation both with one another and the human race. So it is in the world of commodities with the products of men's hands. This I call the Fetishism which attaches itself to the products of labour, so soon as they are produced as commodities, and which is therefore inseparable from the production of commodities.

This Fetishism of commodities has its origin, as the foregoing analysis has already shown, in the peculiar social character of the labour that produces them.

As a general rule, articles of utility become commodities, only because they are products of the labour of private individuals or groups of individuals who carry on their work independently of each other. The sum total of the labour of all these private individuals forms the aggregate labour of society. Since the producers do not come into social contact with each other until they exchange their products, the specific social character of each producer's labour does not show itself except in the act of exchange. In other words, the labour of the individual asserts itself as a part of the labour of society only by means of the relations which the act of exchange establishes directly between the products, and indirectly, through them, between the producers. To the latter, therefore, the relations connecting the labour of one individual with that of the rest appear, not as direct social relations between individuals at work, but as what they really are, material relations between persons and social relations between things. It is only by being exchanged that the products of labour acquire, as values, one uniform social status, distinct from their varied forms of existence as objects of utility. This division of a product into a useful thing and a value becomes practically important, only when exchange has acquired such an extension that useful articles are produced for the purpose of being exchanged, and their character as values has therefore to be taken into account, beforehand, during production. From this moment the labour of the individual producer acquires socially a twofold character. On the one hand, it must, as a definite useful kind of labour, satisfy a definite social want, and thus hold its place as part and parcel of the collective labour of all, as a branch of a social division of labour that has sprung up spontaneously. On the other hand, it can satisfy the manifold wants of the individual producer himself, only in so far as the mutual exchangeability of all kinds of useful private labour is an established social fact, and therefore the private useful labour of each producer ranks on an equality with that of all others. The equalization of the most different kinds of labour can be the result only of an abstraction from their inequalities, or of reducing them to their common denominator, viz., expenditure of human labour power or human labour in the abstract. The twofold social character of the labour of the individual appears to him, when reflected in his brain, only under those forms which are impressed upon that labour in everyday practice by the exchange of products. In this way, the character that his own labour possesses of being socially useful takes the form of the condition that the product must be not only useful, but useful for others, and the social character that his particular labour has of being the equal of all other particular kinds of labour, takes the form that all the physically different articles that are the products of labour have one common quality, viz., that of having value.

Hence, when we bring the products of our labour into relation with each other as values, it is not because we see in these articles the material receptacles of homogeneous human labour. Quite the contrary: whenever, by an exchange, we equate as values our different products, by that very act, we also equate, as human labour, the different kinds of labour expended upon them. We are not aware of this, nevertheless we do it. Value, therefore, does not stalk about with a label describing what it is. It is value, rather, that converts every product into a social hieroglyphic. Later on, we try to decipher the hieroglyphic, to get behind the secret of our own social products; for to stamp an object of utility as a value, is just as much a social product as language. The recent scientific discovery that the products of labour, so far as they are values, are but material expressions of the human labour spent in their production marks, indeed, an epoch in the history of the development of the human race, but by no means dissipates the mist through which the social character of labour appears to us to be an objective character of the products themselves. The fact that in the particular form of production with which we are dealing, viz., the production of commodities, the specific social character of private labour carried on independently, consists in the equality of every kind of that labour, by virtue of its being human labour, which character, therefore, assumes in the product the form of value—this fact appears to the producers, notwithstanding the discovery above referred to, to be just as real and final, as the fact that, after the discovery by science of the component gases of air, the atmosphere itself remained unaltered.

What, first of all, practically concerns producers when they make an exchange, is the question, how much of some other product they get for their own? in what proportions are the products exchangeable? When these proportions have, by custom, attained a certain stability, they appear to result from the nature of the products, so that, for instance, one ton of iron and two ounces of gold appear as naturally to be of equal value as a pound of gold and a pound of iron, in spite of their physical and chemical qualities, appear to be of equal weight. The character of having value, when once impressed upon products, obtains fixity only by reason of their acting and reacting upon each other as quantities of value. These quantities vary continually, independently of the will, foresight, and action of the producers. To them, their own social action takes the form of the action of objects, which rule the producers instead of being ruled by them. It requires a fully developed production of commodities before, from accumulated experience alone, the scientific conviction springs up that all the different kinds of private labour, which are carried on independently of each other, and yet as spontaneously developed branches of the social division of labour, are continually being reduced to the quantitative proportions in which society requires them. And why? Because, in the midst of all the accidental and ever fluctuating exchange-relations between the products, the labour time socially necessary for their production forcibly asserts itself like an overriding law of Nature. The law of gravity thus asserts itself when a house falls about our ears. The determination of the magnitude of value by labour time is therefore a secret, hidden under the apparent fluctuations in the relative values of commodities. Its discovery, while removing all appearance of mere accidentality from the determination of the magnitude of the values of products, yet in no way alters the mode in which that determination takes place.

Man's reflections on the forms of social life, and consequently, also, his scientific analysis of those forms, take a course directly opposite to that of their actual historical development. He begins, *post festum* [after the event], with the results of the process of development ready to hand before him. The characters that stamp products as commodities, and whose establishment is a necessary preliminary to the circulation of commodities, have already acquired the stability of natural, self-understood forms of social life, before man seeks to decipher, not their historical character, for in his eyes they are immutable, but their meaning. Consequently it was the analysis of the prices of commodities that alone led to the determination of the magnitude of value, and it was the common expression of all commodities in money that alone led to the establishment of their characters as values. It is, however, just this ultimate money-form of the world of commodities that actually conceals, instead of disclosing, the social character of private labour, and the social relations between the individual producers. When I state that coats or boots stand in a relation to linen, because it is the universal incarnation of abstract human labour, the absurdity of the statement is self-evident. Nevertheless, when the producers of coats and boots compare those articles with linen, or, what is the same thing, with gold or silver, as the universal equivalent, they express the relation between their own private labour and the collective labour of society in the same absurd form.

The categories of bourgeois economy consist of such like forms. They are forms of thought expressing with social validity the conditions and relations of a definite, historically determined mode of production, viz., the production of commodities. The whole mystery of commodities, all the magic and necromancy that surrounds the products of labour as long as they take the form of commodities, vanishes therefore, as soon as we come to other forms of production.

Since Robinson Crusoe's experiences are a favourite theme with political economists, let us take a look at him on his island. Moderate though he be, yet some few wants he has to satisfy, and must therefore do a little useful work of various sorts, such as making tools and furniture, taming goats, fishing and hunting. Of his prayers and the like we take no account, since they are a source of pleasure to him, and he looks upon them as so much recreation. In spite of the variety of his work, he knows that his labour, whatever its form, is but the activity of one and the same Robinson, and, consequently, that it consists of nothing but different modes of human labour. Necessity itself compels him to apportion his time accurately between his different kinds of work. Whether one kind occupies a greater space in his general activity than another depends on the difficulties, greater or less as the case may be, to be overcome in attaining the useful effect aimed at. This our friend Robinson soon learns by experience, and having rescued a watch, ledger, and pen and ink from the wreck, commences, like a true-born Briton, to keep a set of books. His stock-book contains a list of the objects of utility that belong to him, of the operations necessary for their production; and lastly, of the labour time that definite quantities of those objects have, on an average, cost him. All the relations between Robinson and the objects that form this wealth of his own creation, are here so simple and clear as to be intelligible without exertion, even to Mr. Sedley Taylor. And yet those relations contain all that is essential to the determination of value.

Let us now transport ourselves from Robinson's island bathed in light to the European middle ages shrouded in darkness. Here, instead of the independent man, we find everyone dependent, serfs and lords, vassals and suzerains, laymen and clergy. Personal dependence here characterizes the social relations of production just as much as it does the other spheres of life organized on the basis of that production. But for the very reason that personal dependence forms the groundwork of society, there is no necessity for labour and its products to assume a fantastic form different from their reality. They take the shape, in the transactions of society, of services in kind and payments in kind. Here the particular and natural form of labour, and not, as in a society based on production of commodities, its general abstract form is the immediate social form of labour. Compulsory labour is just as properly measured by time, as commodity-producing labour; but every serf knows that what he expends in the service of his lord is a definite quantity of his own personal labour power. The tithe to be rendered to the priest is more matter of fact than his blessing. No matter, then, what we may think of the parts played by the different classes of people themselves in this society, the social relations between individuals in the performance of their labour appear at all events as their own mutual personal relations, and are not disguised under the shape of social relations between the products of labour.

For an example of labour in common or directly associated labour, we have no occasion to go back to that spontaneously developed form which we find on the threshold of the history of all civilized races. We have one close at hand in the patriarchal industries of a peasant family, that produces corn, cattle, yarn, linen, and clothing for home use. These different articles are, as regards the family, so many products of its labour, but as between themselves, they are not commodities. The different kinds of labour, such as tillage, cattle tending, spinning, weaving, and making clothes, which result in the various products, are in themselves, and such as they are, direct social functions, because functions of the family, which, just as much as a society based on the production of commodities, possesses a spontaneously developed system of division of labour. The distribution of the work within the family, and the regulation of the labour time of the several members, depend as well upon differences of age and sex as upon natural conditions varying with the seasons. The labour power of each individual, by its very nature, operates in this case merely as a definite portion of the whole labour power of the family, and therefore the measure of the expenditure of individual labour power by its duration, appears here by its very nature as a social character of their labour.

Let us now picture ourselves, by way of change, a community of free individuals, carrying on their work with the means of production in common, in which the labour power of all the different individuals is consciously applied as the combined labour power of the community. All the characteristics of Robinson's labour are here repeated, but with this difference, that they are social, instead of individual. Everything produced by him was exclusively the result of his own personal labour, and therefore simply an object of use for himself. The total product of our community is a social product. One portion serves as fresh means of production and remains social. But another portion is consumed by the members as means of subsistence. A distribution of this portion among them is consequently necessary. The mode of this distribution will vary with the productive organization of the community, and the degree of historical development attained by the producers. We will assume, but merely for the sake of a parellel with the production of commodities, that the share of each individual producer in the means of subsistence is determined by his labour time. Labour time would, in that case, play a double part. Its apportionment in accordance with a definite social plan maintains the proper proportion between the different kinds of work to be done and the various wants of the community. On the other hand, it also serves as a measure of the portion of the common labour borne by each individual, and of his share in the part of the total product destined for individual consumption. The social relations of the individual producers, with regard both to their labour and to its products, are in this case perfectly simple and intelligible, and that with regard not only to production but also to distribution.

The religious world is but the reflex of the real world. And for a society based upon the production of commodities, in which the producers in general enter into social relations with one another by treating their products as commodities and values, whereby they reduce their individual private labour to the standard of homogeneous human labour—for such a society, Christianity with its *cultus* of abstract man, more especially in its bourgeois developments, Protestantism, Deism, etc., is the most fitting form of religion. In the ancient Asiatic and other ancient modes of production, we find that the conversion of products into commodities, and therefore the conversion of men into producers of commodities, holds a subordinate place, which, however, increases in importance as the primitive communities approach nearer and nearer to their dissolution. Trading nations, properly so called, exist in the ancient world only in its interstices, like the gods of Epicurus in the Intermundia, or like Jews in the pores of Polish society. Those ancient social organisms of production are, as compared with bourgeois society, extremely simple and transparent. But they are founded either on the immature development of man individually, who has not yet severed the umbilical cord that unites him with his fellowmen in a primitive tribal community, or upon direct relations of subjection. They can arise and exist only when the development of the productive power of labour has not risen beyond a low stage, and when, therefore, the social relations within the sphere of material life, between man and man, and between man and Nature, are correspondingly narrow. This narrowness is reflected in the ancient worship of Nature, and in the other elements of the popular religions. The religious reflex of the real world can, in any case, only then finally vanish, when the practical relations of everyday life offer to man none but perfectly intelligible and reasonable relations with regard to his fellowmen and to Nature. . . .

The life-process of society, which is based on the process of material production, does not strip off its mystical veil until it is treated as production by freely associated men, and is consciously regulated by them in accordance with a settled plan. This, however, demands for society a certain material groundwork or set of conditions of existence which in their turn are the spontaneous product of a long and painful process of development.

Political Economy has indeed analysed, however incompletely, value and its magnitude, and has discovered what lies beneath these forms. But it has never once asked the question why labour is represented by the value of its product and labour-time by the magnitude of that value. These formulas, which bear stamped upon them in unmistakable letters, that they belong to a state of society in which the process of production has the mastery over man, instead of being controlled by him, such formulas appear to the bourgeois intellect to be as much a self-evident necessity imposed by Nature as productive labour itself. Hence forms of social production that preceded the bourgeois form are treated by the bourgeoisie in much in the same way as the Fathers of the Church treated pre-Christian religions. . . .

To what extent some economists are misled by the Fetishism inherent in commodities, or by the objective appearance of the social characteristics of labour, is shown, among other ways, by the dull and tedious quarrel over the part played by Nature in the formation of exchange-value. Since exchange-value is a definite social manner of expressing the amount of labour bestowed upon an object, Nature has no more to do with it, than it has in fixing the course of exchange.

The mode of production in which the product takes the form of a commodity, or is produced directly for exchange, is the most general and most embryonic form of bourgeois production. It therefore makes its appearance at an early date in history, though not in the same predominating and characteristic manner as nowadays. Here its Fetish character is comparatively easy to be seen through. But when we come to more concrete forms, even this appearance of simplicity vanishes. Whence arose the illusions of the monetary system? To it gold and silver, when serving as money, did not represent a social relation between producers, but were natural objects with strange social properties. And modern economy, which looks down with such disdain on the monetary system, does not its superstition come out as clear as noonday, whenever it treats of capital? How long is it since economy discarded the physiocratic illusion that rents grow out of the soil and not out of society?

But not to anticipate, we will content ourselves with yet another example relating to the commodity-form. Could commodities themselves speak, they would say: Our use-value may be a thing that interests men. It is no part of us as objects. What, however, does belong to us as objects is our value. Our natural intercourse as commodities proves it. In the eyes of each other we are nothing but exchange-values. Now listen how those commodities speak through the mouth of the economist. "Value"—(i.e. exchange-value) "is a property of things, riches"—(i.e. use-value) "of man. Value, in this sense, necessarily implies exchanges, riches do not." "Riches" (use-value) "are the attribute of men, value is the attribute of commodities. A man or a community is rich, a pearl or a diamond is valuable. . . . A pearl or a diamond is valuable" as a pearl or diamond. So far no chemist has ever discovered exchange-value either in a pearl or a diamond. The economical discoverers of this chemical element, who by the by lay special claim to critical acumen, find however that the use-value of objects belongs to them independently of their material properties, while their value, on the other hand, forms a part of them as objects. What confirms them in this view is the peculiar circumstance that the use-value of objects is realized without exchange, by means of a direct relation between the objects and man, while, on the other hand, their value is realized only by exchange, that is, by means of a social process. Who fails here to call to mind our good friend, Dogberry, who informs neighbour Seacoal, that, "To be a well-favoured man is the gift of fortune; but to read and write comes by nature." . . .

The Production of Surplus-Value

The product appropriated by the capitalist is a use-value, as yarn, for example, or boots. But, although boots are, in one sense, the basis of all social progress, and our capitalist is a decided "progressist," yet he does not manufacture boots for their own sake. Use-value is, by no means, the thing "qu'on aime pour lui-même" in the production of commodities. Use-values are only produced by capitalists, because, and in so far as, they are the material substratum, the depositaries of exchange-value. Our capitalist has two objects in view: in the first place, he wants to produce a use-value that has a value in exchange, that is to say, an article destined to be sold, a commodity; and secondly, he desires to produce a commodity whose value shall be greater than the sum of the values of the commodities used in its production, that is, of the means of production and the labour-power, that he purchased with his good money in the open market. His aim is to produce not only a use-value, but a commodity also; not only use-value, but value; not only value, but at the same time surplus-value.

It must be borne in mind, that we are now dealing with the production of commodities, and that, up to this point, we have only considered one aspect of the process. Just as commodities are, at the same time, use-values and values, so the process of producing them must be a labour-process, and at the same time, a process of creating value.

Let us now examine production as a creation of value.

We know that the value of each commodity is determined by the quantity of labour expended on and materialised in it, by the working-time necessary, under given social conditions, for its production. This rule also holds good in the case of the product that accrued to our capitalist, as the result of the labour-process carried on for him. Assuming this product to be 10 lbs. of yarn, our first step is to calculate the quantity of labour realised in it.

For spinning the yarn, raw material is required; suppose in this case 10 lbs. of cotton. We have no need at present to investigate the value of this cotton, for our capitalist has, we will assume, bought it at its full value, say of ten shillings. In this price the labour required for the production of the cotton is already expressed in terms of the average labour of society. We will further assume that the wear and tear of the spindle, which, for our present purpose, may represent all other instruments of labour employed, amounts to the value of 2s. If, then, twenty-four hours' labour, or two working days, are required to produce the quantity of gold represented by twelve shillings, we have here, to begin with, two days' labour already incorporated in the yarn.

We must not let ourselves be misled by the circumstance that the cotton has taken a new shape while the substance of the spindle has to a certain extent been used up. By the general law of value, if the value of 40 lbs. of yarn = the value of 40 lbs. of cotton + the value of a whole spindle, i.e., if the same working time is required to produce the commodities on either side of this equation, then 10 lbs. of yarn are an equivalent for 10 lbs. of cotton, together with one-fourth of a spindle. In the case we are considering the same working time is materialised in the 10 lbs. of yarn on the one hand, and in the 10 lbs. of cotton and the fraction of a spindle on the other. Therefore, whether value appears in cotton, in a spindle, or in yarn, makes no difference in the amount of that value. The spindle and cotton, instead of resting quietly side by side, join together in the process, their forms are altered, and they are turned into yarn; but their value is no more affected by this fact than it would be if they had been simply exchanged for their equivalent in yarn.

The labour required for the production of the cotton, the raw material of the yarn, is part of the labour necessary to produce the yarn, and is therefore contained in the yarn. The same applies to the labour embodied in the spindle, without whose wear and tear the cotton could not be spun.

Hence, in determining the value of the yarn, or the labour-time required for its production, all the special processes carried on at various times and in different places, which were necessary, first to produce the cotton and the wasted portion of the spindle, and then with the cotton and spindle to spin the yarn, may together be looked on as different and successive phases of one and the same process. The whole of the labour in the yarn is past labour; and it is a matter of no importance that the operations necessary for the production of its constituent elements were carried on at times which, referred to the present, are more remote than the final operation of spinning. If a definite quantity of labour, say thirty days, is requisite to build a house, the total amount of labour incorporated in it is not altered by the fact that the work of the last day is done twenty-nine days later than that of the first. Therefore the labour contained in the raw material and the instruments of labour can be treated just as if it were labour expended in an earlier stage of the spinning process, before the labour of actual spinning commenced.

The values of the means of production, i.e., the cotton and the spindle, which values are expressed in the price of twelve shillings, are therefore constituent parts of the value of the yarn, or, in other words, of the value of the product.

Two conditions must nevertheless be fulfilled. First, the cotton and spindle must concur in the production of a use-value; they must in the present case become yarn. Value is independent of the particular use-value by which it is borne, but it must be embodied in a use-value of some kind. Secondly, the time occupied in the labour of production must not exceed the time really necessary under the given social conditions of the case. Therefore, if no more than 1 lb. of cotton be requisite to spin 1 lb. of yarn, care must be taken that no more than this weight of cotton is consumed in the production of 1 lb. of yarn; and similarly with regard to the spindle. Though the capitalist have a hobby, and use a gold instead of a steel spindle, yet the only labour that counts for anything in the value of the yarn is that which would be required to produce a steel spindle, because no more is necessary under the given social conditions.

We now know what portion of the value of the yarn is owing to the cotton and the spindle. It amounts to twelve shillings or the value of two days' work. The next point for our consideration is, what portion of the value of the yarn is added to the cotton by the labour of the spinner.

We have now to consider this labour under a very different aspect from that which it had during the labour-process; there, we viewed it solely as that particular kind of human activity which changes cotton into yarn; there, the more the labour was suited to the work, the better the yarn, other circumstances remaining the same. The labour of the spinner was then viewed as specifically different from other kinds of productive labour, different on the one hand in its special aim, viz., spinning, different, on the other hand, in the special character of its operations, in the special nature of its means of production and in the special use-value of its product. For the operation of spinning, cotton and spindles are a necessity, but for making rifled cannon they would be of no use whatever. Here, on the contrary, where we consider the labour of the spinner only so far as it is value-creating, i.e., a source of value, his labour differs in no respect from the labour of the man who bores cannon, or (what here more nearly concerns us), from the labour of the cotton-planter and spindle-maker incorporated in the means of production. It is solely by reason of this identity, that cotton planting, spindle making and spinning, are capable of forming the component parts, differing only quantitatively from each other, of one whole, namely, the value of the yarn. Here, we have nothing more to do with the quality, the nature and the specific character of the labour, but merely with its quantity. And this simply requires to be calculated. We proceed upon the assumption that spinning is simple, unskilled labour, the average labour of a given stage of society. Hereafter we shall see that the contrary assumption would make no difference.

While the labourer is at work, his labour constantly undergoes a transformation: from being motion, it becomes an object without motion; from being the labourer working, it becomes the thing produced. At the end of one hour's spinning, that act is represented by a definite quantity of yarn; in other words, a definite quantity of labour, namely that of one hour, has become embodied in the cotton. We say labour, i.e., the expenditure of his vital force by the spinner, and not spinning labour, because the special work of spinning counts here, only so far as it is the expenditure of labour-power in general, and not in so far as it is the specific work of the spinner.

In the process we are now considering it is of extreme importance, that no more time be consumed in the work of transforming the cotton into yarn than is necessary under the given social conditions. If under normal, i.e., average social conditions of production, a pounds of cotton ought to be made into b pounds of yarn by one hour's labour, then a day's labour does not count as 12 hours' labour unless 12 a pounds of cotton have been made into 12 b pounds of yarn; for in the creation of value, the time that is socially necessary alone counts.

Not only the labour, but also the raw material and the product now appear in quite a new light, very different from that in which we viewed them in the labour-process pure and simple. The raw material serves now merely as an absorbent of a definite quantity of labour. By this absorption it is in fact changed into yarn, because it is spun, because labour-power in the form of spinning is added to it; but the product, the yarn, is now nothing more than a measure of the labour absorbed by the cotton. If in one hour 1⅔ lbs. of cotton can be spun into 1⅔ lbs. of yarn, then 10 lbs. of yarn indicate the absorption of 6 hours' labour. Definite quantities of product, these quantities being determined by experience, now represent nothing but definite quantities of labour, definite masses of crystallized labour-time. They are nothing more than the materialisation of so many hours or so many days of social labour.

We are here no more concerned about the facts, that the labour is the specific work of spinning, that its subject is cotton and its product yarn, than we are about the fact that the subject itself is already a product and therefore raw material. If the spinner, instead of spinning, were working in a coal mine, the subject of his labour, the coal, would be supplied by Nature; nevertheless, a definite quantity of extracted coal, a hundred weight for example, would represent a definite quantity of absorbed labour.

We assumed, on the occasion of its sale, that the value of a day's labour-power is three shillings, and that six hours' labour are incorporated in that sum; and consequently that this amount of labour is requisite to produce the necessaries of life daily required on an average by the labourer. If now our spinner by working for one hour, can convert $1\frac{2}{3}$ lbs. of cotton into $1\frac{2}{3}$ lbs. of yarn,[1] it follows that in six hours he will convert 10 lbs. of cotton into 10 lbs. of yarn. Hence, during the spinning process, the cotton absorbs six hours' labour. The same quantity of labour is also embodied in a piece of gold of the value of three shillings. Consequently by the mere labour of spinning, a value of three shillings is added to the cotton.

Let us now consider the total value of the product, the 10 lbs. of yarn. Two and a half days' labour have been embodied in it, of which two days were contained in the cotton and in the substance of the spindle worn away, and half a day was absorbed during the process of spinning. This two and a half days' labour is also represented by a piece of gold of the value of fifteen shillings. Hence, fifteen shillings is an adequate price for the 10 lbs. of yarn, or the price of one pound is eighteen pence.

Our capitalist stares in astonishment. The value of the product is exactly equal to the value of the capital advanced. The value so advanced has not expanded, no surplus-value has been created, and consequently money has not been converted into capital. The price of the yarn is fifteen shillings, and fifteen shillings were spent in the open market upon the constituent elements of the product, or, what amounts to the same thing, upon the factors of the labour-process; ten shillings were paid for the cotton, two shillings for the substance of the spindle worn away, and three shillings for the labour-power. The swollen value of the yarn is of no avail, for it is merely the sum of the values formerly existing in the cotton, the spindle, and the labour-power: out of such a simple addition of existing values, no surplus-value can possibly arise.[2] These separate values are now all concentrated in one thing; but so they were also in the sum of fifteen shillings, before it was split up into three parts, by the purchase of the commodities.

There is in reality nothing very strange in this result. The value of one pound of yarn being eighteenpence, if our capitalist buys 10 lbs. of yarn in the market, he must pay fifteen shillings for them. It is clear that, whether a man buys

[1] These figures are quite arbitrary.

[2] This is the fundamental proposition on which is based the doctrine of the Physiocrats as to the unproductiveness of all labour that is not agriculture: it is irrefutable for the orthodox economist.

his house ready built, or gets it built for him, in neither case will the mode of acquisition increase the amount of money laid out on the house.

Our capitalist, who is at home in his vulgar economy, exclaims: "Oh! but I advanced my money for the express purpose of making more money." The way to Hell is paved with good intentions, and he might just as easily have intended to make money, without producing at all.[3] He threatens all sorts of things. He won't be caught napping again. In future he will buy the commodities in the market, instead of manufacturing them himself. But if all his brother capitalists were to do the same, where would he find his commodities in the market? And his money he cannot eat. He tries persuasion. "Consider my abstinence; I might have played ducks and drakes with the 15 shillings; but instead of that I consumed it productively, and made yarn with it." Very well, and by way of reward he is now in possession of good yarn instead of a bad conscience; and as for playing the part of a miser, it would never do for him to relapse into such bad ways as that; we have seen before to what results such asceticism leads. Besides, where nothing is, the king has lost his rights; whatever may be the merit of his abstinence, there is nothing wherewith specially to remunerate it, because the value of the product is merely the sum of the values of the commodities that were thrown into the process of production. Let him therefore console himself with the reflection that virtue is its own reward. But no, he becomes importunate. He says: "The yarn is of no use to me: I produced it for sale." In that case let him sell it, or, still better, let him for the future produce only things for satisfying his personal wants, a remedy that his physician McCulloch has already prescribed as infallible against an epidemic of over-production. He now gets obstinate. "Can the labourer," he asks, "merely with his arms and legs, produce commodities out of nothing? Did I not supply him with the materials, by means of which, and in which alone, his labour could be embodied? And as the greater part of society consists of such ne'er-do-wells, have I not rendered society incalculable service by my instruments of production, my cotton and my spindle, and not only society, but the labourer also, whom in addition I have provided with the necessaries of life? And am I to be allowed nothing in return for all this service?" Well, but has not the labourer rendered him the equivalent service of changing his cotton and spindle into yarn? Moreover, there is here no question of service.[4] A service is nothing more than the useful effect of a use-value, be it a commodity, or be it of labour. But here we are dealing with exchange-value. The capitalist paid to the labourer a value of 3 shillings, and the labourer gave him back an exact equivalent in the value of 3 shillings, added by him to the cotton: he gave him value for value. Our friend, up to this time so purse-proud,

[3] Thus from 1844-47 he withdrew part of his capital from productive employment, in order to throw it away in railway speculations; and so also, during the American Civil War, he closed his factory, and turned his work-people into the streets, in order to gamble on the Liverpool cotton exchange.

[4] "Extol thyself, put on finery and adorn thyself . . . but whoever takes more or better than he gives, that is usury, and is not service, but wrong done to his neighbour, as when one steals and robs. All is not service and benefit to a neighbour that is called service and benefit. For an

suddenly assumes the modest demeanour of his own workmen, and exclaims: "Have I myself not worked? Have I not performed the labour of superintendence and of overlooking the spinner? And does not this labour, too, create value?" His overlooker and his manager try to hide their smiles. Meanwhile, after a hearty laugh, he re-assumes his usual mien. Though he chanted to us the whole creed of the economists, in reality, he says, he would not give a brass farthing for it. He leaves this and all such like subterfuges and juggling tricks to the professors of political economy who are paid for it. He himself is a practical man; and though he does not always consider what he says outside his business, yet in his business he knows what he is about.

Let us examine the matter more closely. The value of a day's labour-power amounts to 3 shillings, because on our assumption half a day's labour is embodied in that quantity of labour-power, i.e., because the means of subsistence that are daily required for the production of labour-power, cost half a day's labour. But the past labour that is embodied in the labour-power, and the living labour that it can call into action; the daily cost of maintaining it, and its daily expenditure in work, are two totally different things. The former determines the exchange-value of the labour-power, the latter is its use-value. The fact that half a day's labour is necessary to keep the labourer alive during 24 hours, does not in any way prevent him from working a whole day. Therefore, the value of labour-power, and the value which that labour-power creates in the labour process, are two entirely different magnitudes; and this difference of the two values was what the capitalist had in view, when he was purchasing the labour-power. The useful qualities that labour-power possesses, and by virtue of which it makes yarn or boots, were to him nothing more than a conditio sine qua non; for in order to create value, labour must be expended in a useful manner. What really influenced him was the specific use-value which this commodity possesses of being *a source not only of value, but of more value than it has itself*. This is the special service that the capitalist expects from labour-power, and in this transaction he acts in accordance with the "eternal laws" of the exchange of commodities. The seller of labour-power, like the seller of any other commodity, realises its exchange-value, and parts with its use-value. He cannot take the one without giving the other. The use-value of labour-power, or in other words, labour, belongs just as little to its seller, as the use-value of oil after it has been sold belongs to the dealer who has sold it. The owner of the money has paid the value of a day's labour-power; his, therefore, is the use of it for a day; a day's labour belongs to him. The circumstance, that on the one hand the daily sustenance of labour-power costs only half a day's labour, while on the other hand the very same labour-power can work during a whole day, that consequently the

adulteress and adulterer do one another great service and pleasure. A horseman does an incendiary a great service, by helping him to rob on the highway, and pillage land and houses. The papists do ours a great service, in that they don't drown, burn, murder all of them, or let them all rot in prison; but let some live, and only drive them out, or take from them what they have. The devil himself does his servants inestimable service. . . . To sum up, the world is full of great, excellent, and daily service and benefit." (Martin Luther: "An die Pfarrherrn, wider den Wucher zu predigen," Wittenberg, 1540.)

value which its use during one day creates, is double what he pays for that use, this circumstance is, without doubt, a piece of good luck for the buyer, but by no means an injury to the seller.

Our capitalist foresaw this state of things, and that was the cause of his laughter. The labourer therefore finds, in the workshop, the means of production necessary for working, not only during six, but during twelve hours. Just as during the six hours' process our 10 lbs. of cotton absorbed six hours' labour, and became 10 lbs. of yarn, so now, 20 lbs. of cotton will absorb 12 hours' labour and be changed into 20 lbs. of yarn. Let us now examine the product of this prolonged process. There is now materialised in this 20 lbs. of yarn the labour of five days, of which four days are due to the cotton and the lost steel of the spindle, the remaining day having been absorbed by the cotton during the spinning process. Expressed in gold, the labour of five days is thirty shillings. This is therefore the price of the 20 lbs. of yarn, giving, as before, eighteenpence as the price of a pound. But the sum of the values of the commodities that entered into the process amounts to 27 shillings. The value of the yarn is 30 shillings. Therefore the value of the product is $\frac{1}{9}$ greater than the value advanced for its production; 27 shillings have been transformed into 30 shillings; a surplus-value of 3 shillings has been created. The trick has at last succeeded; money has been converted into capital.

Every condition of the problem is satisfied, while the laws that regulate the exchange of commodities, have been in no way violated. Equivalent has been exchanged for equivalent. For the capitalist as buyer paid for each commodity, for the cotton, the spindle and the labour-power, its full value. He then did what is done by every purchaser of commodities; he consumed their use-value. The consumption of the labour-power, which was also the process of producing commodities, resulted in 20 lbs. of yarn, having a value of 30 shillings. The capitalist, formerly a buyer, now returns to market as a seller, of commodities. He sells his yarn at eighteenpence a pound, which is its exact value. Yet for all that he withdraws 3 shillings more from circulation than he originally threw into it. This metamorphosis, this conversion of money into capital, takes place both within the sphere of circulation and also outside it; within the circulation, because conditioned by the purchase of the labour-power in the market; outside the circulation, because what is done within it is only a stepping-stone to the production of surplus-value, a process which is entirely confined to the sphere of production. Thus "tout est pour le mieux dans le meilleur des mondes possibles."

By turning his money into commodities that serve as the material elements of a new product, and as factors in the labour-process, by incorporating living labour with their dead substance, the capitalist at the same time converts value, i.e., past, materialised, and dead labour into capital, into value big with value, a live monster that is fruitful and multiplies.

If we now compare the two processes of producing value and of creating surplus-value, we see that the latter is nothing but the continuation of the former beyond a definite point. If on the one hand the process be not carried beyond the point, where the value paid by the capitalist for the labour-power is replaced by an exact equivalent, it is simply a process of producing value; if, on the other hand, it be continued beyond that point, it becomes a process of creating surplus-value.

If we proceed further, and compare the process of producing value with the labour-process, pure and simple, we find that the latter consists of the useful labour, the work, that produces use-values. Here we contemplate the labour as producing a particular article; we view it under its qualitative aspect alone, with regard to its end and aim. But viewed as a value-creating process, the same labour-process presents itself under its quantitative aspect alone. Here it is a question merely of the time occupied by the labourer in doing the work; of the period during which the labour-power is usefully expended. Here, the commodities that take part in the process, do not count any longer as necessary adjuncts of labour-power in the production of a definite, useful object. They count merely as depositaries of so much absorbed or materialised labour; that labour, whether previously embodied in the means of production, or incorporated in them for the first time during the process by the action of labour-power, counts in either case only according to its duration; it amounts to so many hours or days as the case may be.

Moreover, only so much of the time spent in the production of any article is counted, as, under the given social conditions, is necessary. The consequences of this are various. In the first place, it becomes necessary that the labour should be carried on under normal conditions. If a self-acting mule is the implement in general use for spinning, it would be absurd to supply the spinner with a distaff and spinning wheel. The cotton too must not be such rubbish as to cause extra waste in being worked, but must be of suitable quality. Otherwise the spinner would be found to spend more time in producing a pound of yarn than is socially necessary, in which case the excess of time would create neither value nor money. But whether the material factors of the process are of normal quality or not, depends not upon the labourer, but entirely upon the capitalist. Then again, the labour-power itself must be of average efficacy. In the trade in which it is being employed, it must possess the average skill, handiness and quickness prevalent in that trade, and our capitalist took good care to buy labour-power of such normal goodness. This power must be applied with the average amount of exertion and with the usual degree of intensity; and the capitalist is as careful to see that this is done, as that his workmen are not idle for a single moment. He has bought the use of the labour-power for a definite period, and he insists upon his rights. He has no intention of being robbed. Lastly, and for this purpose our friend has a penal code of his own, all wasteful consumption of raw material or instruments of labour is strictly forbidden, because what is so wasted, represents labour superfluously expended, labour that does not count in the product or enter into its value.

We now see, that the difference between labour, considered on the one hand as producing utilities, and on the other hand, as creating value, a difference which we discovered by our analysis of a commodity, resolves itself into a distinction between two aspects of the process of production.

The process of production, considered on the one hand as the unity of the labour-process and the process of creating value, is production of commodities;

considered on the other hand as the unity of the labour-process and the process of producing surplus-value, it is the capitalist process of production, or capitalist production of commodities.

We stated, on a previous page, that in the creation of surplus-value it does not in the least matter, whether the labour appropriated by the capitalist be simple unskilled labour of average quality or more complicated skilled labour. All labour of a higher or more complicated character than average labour is expenditure of labour-power of a more costly kind, labour-power whose production has cost more time and labour, and which therefore has a higher value, than unskilled or simple labour-power. This power being of higher value, its consumption is labour of a higher class, labour that creates in equal times proportionally higher values than unskilled labour does. Whatever difference in skill there may be between the labour of a spinner and that of a jeweller, the portion of his labour by which the jeweller merely replaces the value of his own labour-power, does not in any way differ in quality from the additional portion by which he creates surplus-value. In the making of jewellery, just as in spinning, the surplus-value results only from a quantitative excess of labour, from a lengthening-out of one and the same labour-process, in the one case, of the process of making jewels, in the other of the process of making yarn.[5]

But on the other hand, in every process of creating value, the reduction of skilled labour to average social labour, e.g., one day of skilled to six days of unskilled labour, is unavoidable. We therefore save ourselves a superfluous operation, and simplify our analysis, by the assumption, that the labour of the workman employed by the capitalist is unskilled average labour. . . .

Absolute and Relative Surplus-Value

In considering the labour-process, we began . . . by treating it in the abstract, apart from its historical forms, as a process between man and nature. We . . . stated . . . "If we examine the whole labour-process, from the point of view of its result, it is plain that both the instruments and the subject of labour are means of production, and that the labour itself is productive labour." . . . We further added: "This method of determining, from the standpoint of the labour-process alone, what is productive labour, is by no means directly applicable to the case of the

[5] The distinction between skilled and unskilled labour rests in part on pure illusion, or, to say the least, on distinctions that have long since ceased to be real, and that survive only by virtue of a traditional convention; in part on the helpless condition of some groups of the working-class, a condition that prevents them from exacting equally with the rest the value of their labour-power. Accidental circumstances here play so great a part, that these two forms of labour sometimes change places. Where, for instance, the physique of the working-class has deteriorated, and is, relatively speaking, exhausted, which is the case in all countries with a well developed capitalist production, the lower forms of labour, which demand great expenditure of muscle, are in general considered as skilled, compared with much more delicate forms of labour; the latter sink down to the level of unskilled labour.

capitalist process of production." We now proceed to the further development of this subject.

So far as the labour-process is purely individual, one and the same labourer unites in himself all the functions, that later on become separated. When an individual appropriates natural objects for his livelihood, no one controls him but himself. Afterwards he is controlled by others. A single man cannot operate upon nature without calling his own muscles into play under the control of his own brain. As in the natural body head and hand wait upon each other, so the labour-process unites the labour of the hand with that of the head. Later on they part company and even become deadly foes. The product ceases to be the direct product of the individual, and becomes a social product, produced in common by a collective labourer, i.e., by a combination of workmen, each of whom takes only a part, greater or less, in the manipulation of the subject of their labour. As the co-operative character of the labour-process becomes more and more marked, so, as a necessary consequence, does our notion of productive labour, and of its agent the productive labourer, become extended. In order to labour productively, it is no longer necessary for you to do manual work yourself; enough, if you are an organ of the collective labourer, and perform one of its subordinate functions. The first definition given above of productive labour, a definition deduced from the very nature of the production of material objects, still remains correct for the collective labourer, considered as a whole. But it no longer holds good for each member taken individually.

On the other hand, however, our notion of productive labour becomes narrowed. Capitalist production is not merely the production of commodities, it is essentially the production of surplus-value. The labourer produces, not for himself, but for capital. It no longer suffices, therefore, that he should simply produce. He must produce surplus-value. That labourer alone is productive, who produces surplus-value for the capitalist, and thus works for the self-expansion of capital. If we may take an example from outside the sphere of production of material objects, a schoolmaster is a productive labourer when, in addition to belabouring the heads of his scholars, he works like a horse to enrich the school proprietor. That the latter has laid out his capital in a teaching factory, instead of in a sausage factory, does not alter the relation. Hence the notion of a productive labourer implies not merely a relation between work and useful effect, between labourer and product of labour, but also a specific, social relation of production, a relation that has sprung up historically and stamps the labourer as the direct means of creating surplus-value. To be a productive labourer is, therefore, not a piece of luck, but a misfortune. . . .

The prolongation of the working day beyond the point at which the labourer would have produced just an equivalent for the value of his labour-power, and the appropriation of that surplus-labour by capital, this is production of absolute surplus-value. It forms the general groundwork of the capitalist system, and the starting point for the production of relative surplus-value. The latter presupposes that the working day is already divided into two parts, necessary labour, and surplus-labour. In order to prolong the surplus-labour, the necessary labour is shortened by methods whereby the equivalent for the wages is produced in less time. The production of absolute surplus-value turns exclusively upon the length of the working day; the production of relative surplus-value, revolutionises out and out the technical processes of labour, and the composition of society. It therefore presupposes a specific mode, the capitalist mode of production, a mode which, along with its methods, means, and conditions, arises and developes itself spontaneously on the foundation afforded by the formal subjection of labour to capital. In the course of this development, the formal subjection is replaced by the real subjection of labour to capital. . . .

From one standpoint, any distinction between absolute and relative surplus-value appears illusory. Relative surplus-value is absolute, since it compels the absolute prolongation of the working day beyond the labour-time necessary to the existence of the labourer himself. Absolute surplus-value is relative, since it makes necessary such a development of the productiveness of labour, as will allow of the necessary labour-time being confined to a portion of the working day. But if we keep in mind the behaviour of surplus-value, this appearance of identity vanishes. Once the capitalist mode of production is established and becomes general, the difference between absolute and relative surplus-value makes itself felt, whenever there is a question of raising the rate of surplus-value. Assuming that labour-power is paid for at its value, we are confronted by this alternative: given the productiveness of labour and its normal intensity, the rate of surplus-value can be raised only by the actual prolongation of the working day; on the other hand, given the length of the working day, that rise can be effected only by a change in the relative magnitudes of the components of the working day, viz., necessary labour and surplus-labour; a change which, if the wages are not to fall below the value of labour-power, presupposes a change either in the productiveness or in the intensity of the labour.

If the labourer wants all his time to produce the necessary means of subsistence for himself and his race, he has no time left in which to work gratis for others. Without a certain degree of productiveness in his labour, he has no such superfluous time at his disposal; without such superfluous time, no surplus-labour, and therefore no capitalists, no slave-owners, no feudal lords, in one word, no class of large proprietors. . . .

The General Law of Capitalist Accumulation

Section 1: In this chapter we consider the influence of the growth of capital on the lot of the labouring class. The most important factor in this inquiry is the composition of capital and the changes it undergoes in the course of the process of accumulation.

The composition of capital is to be understood in a twofold sense. On the side of value, it is determined by the proportion in which it is divided into constant capital or value of the means of production, and variable capital or value of labour power, the sum total of wages. On the side of material, as it functions in the process of production, all capital is divided into means of production and living labour power. This latter composition is determined by the relation between the mass of the means of production employed, on the one hand, and the mass of labour necessary for their employment on the other. I call the former the value-composition, the latter the technical composition of capital. Between the two there is a strict correlation. To express this, I call the value-composition of capital, in so far as it is determined by its technical composition and mirrors the changes of the latter, the organic composition of capital. Wherever I refer to the composition of capital, without further qualification, its organic composition is always understood.

The many individual capitals invested in a particular branch of production have, one with another, more or less different compositions. The average of their individual compositions gives us the composition of the total capital in this branch of production. Lastly, the average of these averages, in all branches of production, gives us the composition of the total social capital of a country, and with this alone are we, in the last resort, concerned in the following investigation.

Growth of capital involves growth of its variable constituent or of the part invested in labour power. A part of the surplus value turned into additional capital must always be re-transformed into variable capital, or additional labour-fund. If we suppose that, all other circumstances remaining the same, the composition of capital also remains constant (i.e., that a definite mass of means of production constantly needs the same mass of labour power to set it in motion), then the demand for labour and the subsistence-fund of the labourers clearly increase in the same proportion as the capital, and the more rapidly, the more rapidly the capital increases. Since the capital produces yearly a surplus value, of which one part is yearly added to the original capital; since this increment itself grows yearly along with the augmentation of the capital already functioning; since lastly, under special stimulus to enrichment, such as the opening of new markets, or of new spheres for the outlay of capital in consequence of newly developed social wants, etc., the scale of accumulation may be suddenly extended, merely by a change in the division of the surplus value or surplus product into capital and revenue, the requirements of accumulating capital may exceed the increase of labour power or of the number of labourers; the demand for labourers may exceed the supply, and, therefore, wages may rise. This must, indeed, ultimately be the case if the conditions supposed above continue. For since in each year more labourers are employed than in its predecessor, sooner or later a point must be reached, at which the requirements of accumulation begin to surpass the customary supply of labour, and, therefore, a rise of wages takes place. A lamentation on this score was heard in England during the whole of the fifteenth, and the first half of the eighteenth centuries. The more or less favourable circumstances in which the wage-working class supports and multiplies itself, in no way alter the fundamental character of capitalist production. As simple reproduction constantly reproduces the capital-relation itself, i.e., the relation of capitalists on the one hand, and wage-workers on the other, so reproduction on a progressive scale, i.e., accumulation, reproduces the capital-relation on a progressive scale, more capitalists or larger capitalists at this pole, more wage-workers at that. The reproduction of a mass of labour power, which must incessantly reincorporate itself with capital for that capital's self-expansion; which cannot get free from capital, and whose enslavement to capital is only concealed by the variety of individual capitalists to whom it sells itself, this reproduction of labour power forms, in fact, an essential of the reproduction of capital itself. Accumulation of capital is, therefore, increase of the proletariat. . . .

The law of capitalist production, that is at the bottom of the pretended "natural law of population," reduces itself simply to this: The correlation between accumulation of capital and rate of wages is nothing else than the correlation between the unpaid labour transformed into capital, and the additional paid labour necessary for the setting in motion of this additional capital. It is therefore in no way a relation between two magnitudes, independent one of the other: on the one hand, the magnitude of the capital; on the other, the number of the labouring population; it is rather, at bottom, only the relation between the unpaid and the paid labour of the same labouring population. If the quantity of unpaid labour supplied by the working-class, and accumulated by the capitalist class, increases so rapidly that its conversion into capital requires an extraordinary addition of paid labour, then wages rise, and, all other circumstances remaining equal, the unpaid labour diminishes in proportion. But as soon as this diminution touches the point at which the surplus labour that nourishes capital is no longer supplied in normal quantity, a reaction sets in: a smaller part of revenue is capitalized, accumulation lags, and the movement of rise in wages receives a check. The rise of wages therefore is confined within limits that not only leave intact the foundations of the capitalistic system, but also secure its reproduction on a progressive scale. The law of capitalistic accumulation, metamorphosed by economists into a pretended law of Nature, in reality merely states that the very nature of accumulation excludes every diminution in the degree of exploitation of labour, and every rise in the price of labour, which could seriously imperil the continual reproduction, on an ever-enlarging scale, of the capitalistic relation. It cannot be otherwise in a mode of production in which the labourer exists to satisfy the needs of self-expansion of existing values, instead of, on the contrary, material wealth existing to satisfy the needs of development on the part of the labourer. As in religion man is governed by the products of his own brain, so in capitalistic production, he is governed by the products of his own hand. . . .

But if a surplus labouring population is a necessary product of accumulation or of the development of wealth on a capitalist basis, this surplus population becomes, conversely, the lever of capitalistic accumulation, nay, a condition of existence of the capitalist mode of production. It forms a disposable industrial reserve army, that belongs to capital quite as absolutely as if the latter had bred it at its own cost. Independently of the limits of the actual increase of population, it creates, for the changing needs of the self-expansion of capital, a mass of human material always ready for exploitation. With accumulation, and the development of the productiveness of labour that accompanies it, the power of sudden expansion of capital grows also; it grows, not merely because the elasticity of the capital already functioning increases, not merely because the absolute wealth of society expands, of which capital only forms an elastic part, not merely because credit, under every special stimulus, at once places an unusual part of this wealth at the disposal of production in the form of additional capital; it grows, also, because the technical conditions of the process of production themselves—machinery, means of transport, etc.—now admit of the rapidest transformation of masses of surplus product into additional means of production. The mass of social wealth, overflowing with the advance of accumulation, and transformable into additional capital, thrusts itself frantically into old branches of production, whose market suddenly expands, or into newly formed branches, such as railways, etc., the need for which grows out of the development of the old ones. In all such cases, there must be the possibility of throwing great masses of men suddenly on the decisive points without injury to the scale of production in other spheres. Overpopulation supplies these masses. The course characteristic of modern industry, viz., a decennial cycle (interrupted by smaller oscillations) of periods of average activity, production at high pressure, crisis and stagnation, depends on the constant formation, the greater or less absorption, and the re-formation of the industrial reserve army or surplus population. In their turn, the varying phases of the industrial cycle recruit the surplus population, and become one of the most energetic agents of its reproduction. This peculiar course of modern industry, which occurs in no earlier period of human history, was also impossible in the childhood of capitalist production. The composition of capital changed but very slowly. With its accumulation, therefore, there kept pace, on the whole, a corresponding growth in the demand for labour. Slow as was the advance of accumulation compared with that of more modern times, it found a check in the natural limits of the exploitable labouring population, limits which could only be got rid of by forcible means to be mentioned later. The expansion by fits and starts of the scale of production is the preliminary to its equally sudden contraction; the latter again evokes the former, but the former is impossible without disposable human material, without an increase in the number of labourers independently of the absolute growth of the population. This increase is effected by the simple process that constantly "sets free" a part of the labourers; by methods which lessen the number of labourers employed in proportion to the increased production. The whole form of the movement of modern industry depends, therefore, upon the constant transformation of a part of the labouring population into unemployed or half-employed hands. The superficiality of Political Economy shows itself in the fact that it looks upon the expansion and contraction of credit, which is a mere symptom of the periodic changes of the industrial cycle, as their cause. As the heavenly bodies, once thrown into a certain definite motion, always repeat this, so is it with social production as soon as it is once thrown into this movement of alternate expansion and contraction. Effects, in their turn, become causes, and the varying accidents of the whole process, which always reproduces its own conditions, take on the form of periodicity. When this periodicity is once consolidated, even Political Economy then sees that the production of a relative surplus population—i.e., surplus with regard to the average needs of the self-expansion of capital—is a necessary condition of modern industry. . . .

The industrial reserve army, during the periods of stagnation and average prosperity, weighs down the active labour-army; during the periods of overproduction and paroxysm it holds its pretensions in check. Relative surplus population is therefore the pivot upon which the law of demand and supply of labour works. It confines the field of action of this law within the limits absolutely convenient to the activity of exploitation and to the domination of capital. . . .

Section 4: The relative surplus population exists in every possible form. Every labourer belongs to it during the time when he is only partially employed or wholly unemployed. Not taking into account the great periodically recurring forms that the changing phases of the industrial cycle impress on it, now an acute form during the crisis, then again a chronic form during dull times—it has always three forms, the floating, the latent, the stagnant. . . .

The lowest sediment of the relative surplus population finally dwells in the sphere of pauperism. Exclusive of vagabonds, criminals, prostitutes, in a word, the "dangerous" classes, this layer of society consists of three categories. First, those able to work. One need only glance superficially at the statistics of English pauperism to find that the quantity of paupers increases with every crisis, and diminishes with every revival of trade. Second, orphans and pauper children. These are candidates for the industrial reserve army, and are, in times of great prosperity, as 1860, e.g., speedily and in large numbers enrolled in the active army of labourers. Third, the demoralized and ragged, and those unable to work, chiefly people who succumb to their incapacity for adaptation, due to the division of labour; people who have passed the normal age of the labourer; the victims of industry, whose number increases with the increase of dangerous machinery, of mines, chemical works, etc., the mutilated, the sickly, the widows, etc. Pauperism is the hospital of the active labour-army and the dead weight of the industrial reserve army. Its production is included in that of the relative surplus population, its necessity in theirs; along with the surplus population, pauperism forms a condition of capitalist production, and of the capitalist development of wealth. It enters into the *faux frais* [unnecessary expenditure] of capitalist production; but capital knows how to throw these, for the most part, from its own shoulders on to those of the working-class and the lower middle class.

The greater the social wealth, the functioning capital, the extent and energy of its growth, and, therefore, also the absolute mass of the proletariat and the productiveness of its labour, the greater is the industrial reserve army. The same causes which develop the expansive power of capital develop also the labour power at its disposal. The relative mass of the industrial reserve army increases therefore with the potential energy of wealth. But the greater this reserve army in proportion to the active labour-army, the greater is the mass of a consolidated surplus population, whose misery is in inverse ratio to its torment of labour. The more extensive, finally, the lazarus-layers of the working-class, and the industrial reserve army, the greater is official pauperism. *This is the absolute general law of capitalist accumulation.* Like all other laws it is modified in its working by many circumstances, the analysis of which does not concern us here.

The folly of the economic wisdom that preaches to the labourers the accommodation of their number to the requirements of capital is now patent. The mechanism of capitalist production and accumulation constantly effects this adjustment. The first word of this adaptation is the creation of a relative surplus population, or industrial reserve army. Its last word is the misery of constantly extending strata of the active army of labour, and the dead weight of pauperism.

The law by which a constantly increasing quantity of means of production, thanks to the advance in the productiveness of social labour, may be set in movement by a progressively diminishing expenditure of human power, this law, in a capitalist society—where the labourer does not employ the means of production, but the means of production employ the labourer—undergoes a complete inversion and is expressed thus: the higher the productiveness of labour, the greater is the pressure of the labourers on the means of employment, the more precarious, therefore, becomes their condition of existence, viz., the sale of their own labour power for the increasing of another's wealth, or for the self-expansion of capital. The fact that the means of production, and the productiveness of labour, increase more rapidly than the productive population, expresses itself, therefore, capitalistically in the inverse form that the labouring population always increases more rapidly than the conditions under which capital can employ this increase for its own self-expansion. . . .

Within the capitalist system all methods for raising the social productiveness of labour are brought about at the cost of the individual labourer; all means for the development of production transform themselves into means of domination over, and exploitation of, the producers; they mutilate the labourer into a fragment of a man, degrade him to the level of an appendage of a machine, destroy every remnant of charm in his work and turn it into a hated toil; they estrange from him the intellectual potentialities of the labour process in the same proportion as science is incorporated in it as an independent power; they distort the conditions under which he works, subject him during the labour process to a despotism the more hateful for its meanness; they transform his lifetime into working-time, and drag his wife and child beneath the wheels of the Juggernaut of capital. But all methods for the production of surplus value are at the same time methods of accumulation; and every extension of accumulation becomes again a means for the development of those methods. It follows therefore that in proportion as capital accumulates, the lot of the labourer, be his payment high or low, must grow worse. The law, finally, that always equilibrates the relative surplus population, or industrial reserve army, to the extent and energy of accumulation, this law rivets the labourer to capital more firmly than the wedges of Vulcan did Prometheus to the rock. It establishes an accumulation of misery, corresponding with accumulation of capital. Accumulation of wealth at one pole is, therefore, at the same time accumulation of misery, agony of toil, slavery, ignorance, brutality, mental degradation, at the opposite pole, i.e., on the side of the class that produces its own product in the form of capital. . . .

What Are the Rules of the Game?
•

Joan Robinson

With all these economic doctrines, decaying and reviving, jostling each other, half understood, in the public mind, what basic ideas are acceptable, and what rules of policy are derived from them?

I

In the midst of all the confusion, there is one solid unchanging lump of ideology that we take so much for granted that it is rarely noticed—that is, nationalism.

The very nature of economics is rooted in nationalism. As a pure subject it is too difficult to be a rewarding object of study; the beauty of mathematics and the satisfaction of discoveries in the natural sciences are denied to the practitioners of this scrappy, uncertain, ill-disciplined subject. It would never have been developed except in the hope of throwing light upon questions of policy. But policy means nothing unless there is an authority to carry it out, and authorities are national. The subject by its very nature operates in national terms. Marxism also, though theoretically universalist, had to be poured into national moulds when revolutionary administrations were set up. The aspirations of the developing countries are more for national independence and national self-respect than just for bread to eat.

The hard-headed Classicals made no bones about it. They were arguing against the narrow nationalism of Mercantilists in favour of a more far-sighted

Joan Robinson, *Economic Philosophy*, Chapter VI. (C. A. Watts and Co. Ltd., 1962), pp. 126–48. Copyright Joan Robinson 1962. Reprinted by permission. Footnotes referring to other passages in the book have been omitted and the numbers adjusted.

Joan Robinson is emeritus professor of economics at Cambridge University and the author of *Economics of Imperfect Competition, An Essay on Marxian Economics,* and many other books.

policy, but they were in favour of Free Trade because it was good for Great Britain, not because it was good for the world.

The neo-classical doctrine purported to be universalist. *Utility* knows no frontiers. When Edgworth proposed to add up units of happiness he proposed that every individual should count for one. He did not say that every Englishman should count for one.

But, as it works out, the very fact that the *utility* doctrine cut across class makes it all the more nationalistic. As Gunnar Myrdal has argued[1] the appeal to national solidarity which supports the Welfare State itself makes solidarity of the human race all the more difficult to achieve.

The neo-classicals' ideology purported to be based on universal benevolence, yet they naturally fell into the habit of talking in terms of National Income and the welfare of the people. Our nation, our people were quite enough to bother about.

Nowadays, a conscientious writer like Professor Meade, before setting out the merits of the free market, is careful to say "In order that the monetary and pricing system should work with equity it is necessary to achieve a fair distribution of income and property" and to point out that inequality makes the system not only inequitable but also inefficient, so that a pre-condition for desiring to preserve it is "to take the radical measures to ensure a tolerably equitable distribution of income and property."[2] But he does not for a moment consider any other distribution than that between the citizens of Great Britain. It seems just as natural as breathing to limit equity and efficiency to our own shores.

The great central doctrine of the neo-classical school—the case for Free Trade—though it is sophistical when it pretends that no *nation* can ever benefit itself by protection, is impregnable when it maintains that no groups of producers can do themselves good by protection except by doing, at least temporarily, harm to others. But the economists did not argue that it is the duty of richer nations to increase the sum of *utility* in the world by subsidizing imports from the poorer ones.

A genuinely universalist point of view is very rare. The nearest we get to it, usually, is to argue that in a generally prosperous world *we* are likely to do better than in a miserable one. The prosperity of others is not desirable for *their* sake, but as a contribution to *our* comfort; when their prosperity seems likely to threaten ours, it is not desirable at all. This seems such a natural way of thinking, so right and proper, that we do not even notice that it *is* a particular way of thinking; we have breathed this air from birth and it never occurs to us to wonder what it smells of.

In recent times the growth of statistics has provided much food for nationalistic ideology. Several "League tables" are published periodically, of average National Income, rate of growth, percentage of saving, productivity,

[1] See *An International Economy*.
[2] *Planning and the Price Mechanism*, p. 35.

growth of productivity, etc., and we look anxiously at our placing. When the poor old U.K., as often happens, appears rather low, we are filled with chagrin; or else we set about picking holes in the statistics to show that the placing is wrong; or we point to all sorts of unfair advantages that the wretched foreigners have, which make the comparisons misleading.

In a world of international competition there is a solid reason for being anxious to keep up with the growth of productivity in other trading nations; if we lost markets through being undersold we should find it very hard to avoid reducing our consumption, and a cut in national real income is very disagreeable.

The League tables also can be used to show what is possible, so that an observer who wants in any case to advocate, say, more investment, can appeal to them to silence an opponent who is arguing that it just cannot be done.

These are rational uses of the comparisons. But the main appeal of the League tables is much more simply and directly to an instinct for keeping up with the Joneses projected on to the international plane.

International competition and national policy have been a great spur to economic development. Behind the façade of *laisser-faire* theory the governments of all capitalist nations have boosted trade and production, conquered territories and adopted institutions to help their own citizens to gain advantage. Free-Trade doctrine itself, as Marshall shrewdly observed, was really a projection of British national interests.

The enormous strides made by production under the régime of international competition have brought us to the paradoxical situation that we are in today. Never before has communication been so complete. Never before has educated public opinion in every country been so conscious of the rest of the world. Never before was it worthwhile to think about poverty as a world problem; it is only now that it seems possible, by the application of science to health, birth control and production, to relieve the whole human race from its worst miseries.

Yet never before has so great a proportion of economic energy and scientific study been devoted to means of destruction. We combine doctrines of universal benevolence with the same patriotism that inspired the horsemen of Ghengis Khan.

"When Nature formed mankind for society," as Adam Smith said, she endowed him with some feeling of sympathy with his fellows. Evolution produces a conscience. But biology ceases at the frontier of the tribe. Evolution will not answer the greatest of all moral questions, Who is my neighbour? At this point Humanity must take over from Nature, but it does not show at the moment any signs of doing so.

National patriotism certainly is a great force for good. Up to the frontier it is unifying. It overcomes the sectional patriotism of racial and religious groups and so makes for internal harmony. Marxists regret the extent to which it overcomes class antagonism. But internal neighbourliness is won by projecting aggression outside. Many things that would be considered disgraceful at home are justified in the name of national interest. As Dr. Johnson said, "Patriotism is the last refuge of a scoundrel." We are a very long way from developing a national conscience which would turn patriotism into a desire to behave well. Of course in this country, particularly, we make a great fuss about national conscience, but it consists mainly in insisting upon everyone ascribing our national policy to highly moral motives, rather than in examining what our motives really are. To take a modern example, when the Devlin Report described Nyasaland as a "police state" there was certainly great indignation. But the indignation, for the most part, was not that a British dependency should be in a condition that lent itself to that description, but rather that anyone should be so lost to proper feeling as to use those words about a British dependency.

As individuals, we value people for what they give to the world, not for what they get out of it. We see clearly enough in each other (though not always each in himself) that outward prestige is a poor substitute for inward content. We see that aggression is a sign of weakness and boasting of a lack of self-confidence. Yet greed, vainglory and oppression are quite acceptable in national terms.

It is true that there is a great deal of international economic benevolence being displayed at the present time, but it always has to be justified as a national interest. We help India (as much as we do) not because we want to multiply "units of happiness" by giving starving people a square meal, but because we hope it will keep up the prestige of the West against the Soviet Union. Judging by the Press, when the hunger that is relieved is in China, we are not particularly pleased about it.

The Keynesian revolution broke through the pretended internationalism of Free-Trade doctrines and helped to introduce a genuine internationalism into our thinking. The post-war international agreements, though strongly influenced by Free-Trade ideals, left escape-clauses for countries suffering from balance of payments difficulties, and for under-developed countries; and they permitted home employment policy to take precedence over international obligations. In principle, though very little has been done about it, regulation of trade in primary commodities is accepted as an objective of policy (though the Free-Trade fanatics still decry it) and when our own balance of payments improves by impoverishing primary producers, at least we recognize that it is nothing to be proud of.

This awareness of the variety of problems that face other nations, and the abandonment of the pseudo-universalist Free-Trade doctrine, is a great advance in enlightenment. It is also a great increase in mental discomfort. Without the anodyne of *laisser faire* the moral problem, on a world scale, stares us in the face.

2

On the home front also we are newly aware of choices that have to be made and newly deprived of simple principles for making them. The ideology of Full Employment as an end in itself is too thin, too easy to see through. The idea that there is a right, natural, indicated, equilibrium relation between investment and consumption; or between home and foreign investment; or between govern-ment and private investment; or a right, natural, equilibrium level of real wages, or of the rate of interest, is discredited by the very fact that national employment policy is admitted to be necessary.

In any case, once it is accepted that a "high and stable level of employment" is going to be provided (leaving aside the question of just how high it should be and whether a few wobbles will not be induced to alleviate the stability) then the question of employment as such ceases to be interesting. It was necessary to argue about it only when the official view was that nothing could be done. Now the argument must be about *what* should be done.

The neo-classical heritage still has a great influence, not only on the teaching of economics but in forming public opinion generally, or at least in providing public opinion with its slogans. But when it comes to an actual issue, it has nothing concrete to say. Its latter-day practitioners take refuge in building up more and more elaborate mathematical manipulations and get more and more annoyed at anyone asking them what it is that they are supposed to be manipulating.

In so far as economic doctrines have an influence on the choice of objectives for national policy, on the whole it is obscurantist rather than helpful.

The *utility* concept purports to look behind the "veil of money" but *utility* cannot be measured, while money values can, and economists have a bias in favour of the measurable like the tanner's bias in favour of leather.

The very fallacies that economics is supposed to guard against, economists are the first to fall into. Their central concept, National Income, is a mass of contradictions. Consumption, for instance, is customarily identified with sale of consumers' goods, and a high rate of "consumption" is identified with a high standard of life. But consumption, in the plain meaning of the term, in the sense that it is connected with the satisfaction of natural wants, does not take place at the moment when goods are handed over the counter, but during longer or shorter periods after that event. This time-dimension is completely left out of the figures. It is left out not because anyone denies its importance but because of the mere difficulty of catching it in a statistical net.

Fashion in clothes is a kind of sport where non-material values enter in, though on utilitarian principles the pain of many losers probably outweighs the pleasure of the few winners. However that may be, in goods whose purpose is to provide material satisfaction, durability is a great gain; if the time-dimension of consumption falls as the quantity-dimension of sales rises, it is a serious error to take the latter as a measure of changes in the standard of life.

Again, according to the doctrine of *utility*, goods are assumed to satisfy wants that exist independently of them. It was for this reason that goods were held to be a Good Thing. It is by no means obvious that goods which carry their own wants with them, through cunning advertisement, are a Good Thing. Surely we should be quite as well off without the goods and without the wants? This is the kind of question that, very naturally, is painfully irritating to National-Income statisticians. (National-Income studies are, of course, extremely valuable in their proper sphere, that is, in measuring changes in output, as an indication of business activity, and changes in productivity as a measure of efficiency.)

The great point of the *utility* theory was to answer Adam Smith's question about water and diamonds—to distinguish *total utility* which is supposed to measure satisfaction and *marginal utility* which is measured by price. Marshall's diagrammatic representation of consumer's surplus is bogus, of course—a pseudo-quantitative treatment of something which by its nature cannot be measured. But the idea behind it is based on common sense. The opportunity to buy a commodity, compared with a situation in which it does not exist, may offer an advantage to consumers which is in no way measured by the sums actually spent on it. Yet in National-Income accounting, goods have to be entered in terms of their exchange values, not their *utilities*. This would be a matter only for philosophical speculation were it not that policy is affected by propaganda for the standard of life as it appears in the figures, and there is a continuous and systematic pressure for goods with a sales value against those which are free. The fight that has to be put up, for instance, to keep wild country from being exploited for money profit is made more difficult because its defenders can be represented as standing up for "non-economic" values (which is considered soft-headed, foolish and unpatriotic) though the economists should have been the first to point out that *utility*, not money, is economic value and that the *utility* of goods is not measured by their prices.

The *laisser-faire* bias that still clings around orthodoxy also helps to falsify true values. When Keynes (in his "moderately conservative" mood) maintained that, provided overall full employment is guaranteed "there is no objection to be raised against the classical analysis of the manner in which private self-interest will determine what in particular is produced,"[3] he had forgotten that in an earlier chapter he had written "There is no clear evidence from experience that the investment policy which is socially advantageous coincides with that which is most profitable."[4] At that point he was considering the bias of private enterprise in favour of quick profits. There is a still more fundamental bias in our economy in favour of products and services for which it is easy to collect payment. Goods that can be sold in packets to individual customers, or services that can be charged for at so much per head, provide a field for profitable enterprise. Investments in, say, the layout of cities, cannot be enjoyed except collectively and are not easy to make any money out of; while negative goods, such as dirt and noise, can be dispensed without any compensation being required.

When you come to think of it, what can easily be charged for and what cannot, is just a technical accident. Some things, such as drainage and street lighting, are so obviously necessary that a modicum is provided in spite of the fact that payment has to be collected through the rates, but it is only the most glaring necessities that are met in this way, together with some traditional amenities, like flower-beds in the parks, that are felt to be necessary to municipal self-respect.

Funds for investment in profitable concerns are very largely provided out of the profits made on past investments. When we buy a packet of goods we pay

[3] *General Theory,* pp. 378–9.
[4] Ibid., p. 157.

the costs of producing it (including a return to the lenders of the finance that has gone into equipment for making it) and a bit extra as well, which goes to undistributed profits to finance more investments. In many cases the price also includes a contribution to taxes to be spent on general administration, social services, interest on the national debt, defence, and so forth. The difference between profit margins and indirect taxes, in terms of their economic functioning, is not at all clear cut; one is no more and no less a "burden" than the other. The difference between them is that the outlay of profit margins on dividends, amenities or profitable investment, under nominal control of the shareholders, is in the hands of boards of directors, while the outlay of rates and taxes is in the hands of city corporations and government departments, under nominal control of the electorate. The idea that one is necessarily more "economic" than the other has no foundation except in ideological prejudice.

Professor Galbraith depicts the situation in America, where both the output of saleable goods and the neglect of nonsaleable services are even more extreme than here—

> The family which takes its mauve and cerise, air-conditioned, power-steered, and power-braked car out for a tour passes through cities that are badly paved, made hideous by litter, blighted buildings, bill-boards, and posts for wires that should long since have been put underground. They pass on into a countryside that has been rendered largely invisible by commercial art. (The goods which the latter advertise have an absolute priority in our value system. Such aesthetic considerations as a view of the countryside accordingly come second. On such matters we are consistent.) They picnic on exquisitely packaged food from a portable icebox by a polluted stream and go on to spend the night at a park which is a menace to public health and morals. Just before dozing off on an air-mattress, beneath a nylon tent, amid the stench of decaying refuse, they may reflect vaguely on the curious unevenness of their blessings. [5]

We have not quite reached that stage here, but we are well on the way.

Some interpretations of employment policy take it for granted that private enterprise investment should always be given the first claim on resources and public investment should take up the slack. Thus "public works" should be undertaken when private investment appears to be going into a slump and slackened off again when private investment picks up.

It was all very well for Lloyd Geroge and Keynes to advocate clearing the slums and widening the roads purely as a means of giving work, because the official orthodoxy was opposed to doing anything, but now it does not seem to make much sense that we have to wait for a slump to get these jobs done. It is possible to argue that private investment is helpful to exports, that we cannot afford

[5] *The Affluent Society,* pp. 186–7.

to clear the slums until our industry is in better shape, and that exports cannot flourish unless profitable industry as a whole is flourishing. That is a logical argument though not necessarily convincing. But the argument that public investment, however beneficial, must be less eligible from a national point of view than any private investment, merely because it is public, has no logical basis; it is just a hang-over from *laisser-faire* ideology.

To take another example, Keynes maintained (when he allowed his mind to stray over long-run problems) that investment steadily maintained at full-employment levels would soon saturate all useful demands for capital equipment, and require a reduction of the rate of interest to vanishing point. But he did not lament it; he looked forward to it as the beginning of an age of civilized life. The "vulgar Keynesians" took it up in another sense. They turned the prospective drying up of profitable investment opportunities into the "stagnation thesis." The stagnationists, instead of welcoming the prospect of a period when saving would have become unnecessary, high real wages would have reduced the rate of profit to vanishing point, and technical progress could be directed to lightening toil and increasing leisure, regard its approach as a menace. This, of course, is a perfectly reasonable point of view if the aim of economic life is held to be to provide a sphere for making profits. Satiation of material wants is bad for profits. But this does not go very well with the usual claim that the private enterprise system is justified by its power to meet wants.

In practice employment policy is not based on any particular theory but follows the line of least resistance. Public investment is the easiest thing to cut when restriction appears to be called for, and private consumption the pleasantest thing to boost when a stimulus is needed. From the point of view of planning socially beneficial investment it is usually: Heads I win and tails you lose.

Not only is the system distorted by its bias towards investing in what happens to be profitable, but even within that sphere there is no reason to expect the profit motive to lead to a well balanced pattern of investment. This has always been a weak point in the neo-classical system. The doctrine that, under conditions of free competition, given resources are used to yield maximum satisfaction, applies essentially to an equilibrium position. It can be demonstrated only by assuming that an equilibrium exists and showing that a *departure* from it would be harmful (it also has to assume, of course, that the distribution of income is somehow what it ought to be). Walras had the ingenious idea of making the inhabitants of his market "shout" their offers until the equilibrium has been found, and then start actual trading at the equilibrium prices. It is pure effrontery to extend this kind of equilibrium conception to investment; an equilibrium pattern of investment worked out on this system is possible only in a fully planned economy (if there).

Marshall is less fanciful; he assumes that there is a general equilibrium level of profits, and that each particular industry is attracted to invest faster when profits are higher than normal, and so bring down the prices of its products by increasing the supply. But in Vol. I of the *Principles* he assumes general equilibrium conditions and studies departure from equilibrium in one industry at a time. He never got round to writing the volume that would explain how general equilibrium was preserved.

And his own argument shows that it will not be. His own argument shows that a competitive industry will overshoot the equilibrium point under the influence of the prospect of supernormal profits and fall into a period of sub-normal profits thereafter. This arises out of the very nature of competition. Each firm in a seller's market aims to expand its own productive capacity up to the point that would be profitable if the seller's market were to last, but the others are doing the same, and the seller's market will not last. Even a general knowledge that this is likely to be so does not stop the overshoot, for each hopes to be among the lucky ones who will survive while the coming buyer's market drives *others* out of existence.

By the same token, where an industry is in control of a monopoly, wise planning for the future dictates reserve in responding to an increase in demand. Surplus capacity is the great evil to be avoided. The stronger the monopoly, the more cautious it will be, and if, by always remaining in the rear of demand, it can make a seller's market permanent, so much the better.

In a world in which some industries are much easier to enter than others, there is a systematic distortion in the pattern of investment, which is something over and above the general instability that employment policy is designed to control, over and above mistakes in forecasting which are liable to occur in any system, and over and above the misdirection of investment through speculative influences, which Keynes referred to when he said that "When the capital development of a country becomes a by-product of the activities of a Casino, the job is likely to be ill done."[6]

3

All this would be true even if the distribution of income and wealth were accepted as fair and reasonable. In a modern democracy that is far from being the case. Through political channels—the tax system and social services—we are continually pushing against the distribution of income that our economic system throws up.

The pressure is haphazard and often ineffective (the difference between our highly progressive tax system on paper and our highly regressive system of tax avoidance in reality is sufficiently notorious). The effort at redistribution has no particular philosophy behind it and there does not seem to be any rational criterion for the point at which to draw the line; it sways to and fro (though not very far) as the balance of political pressures shifts.

The *utility* economists, according to Wicksell, were committed to a "thoroughly revolutionary programme" precisely on this question of distribution of

[6]*General Theory*, p. 159.

income. Marshall, and to some extent Pigou, got out of the fix that their theory had landed them in by emphasizing the danger to total physical national income that would be associated with an attempt to increase its *utility* by making its distribution more equal. This argument has been spoiled by the Keynesian revolution. If, as Keynes expected, saving is more than sufficient for a satisfactory rate of private investment, to use it for social purpose is not only harmless but actually beneficial to National Income, while if more total saving is needed than would be forthcoming under *laisser faire* it can easily be supplemented by budget surpluses.

Edgworth, . . . and many after him, took refuge in the argument that we do not really know that greater equality would promote greater happiness, because individuals differ in their capacity for happiness, so that, until we have a thoroughly scientific hedonimeter, "the principle 'every man, and every woman, to count for one,' should be very cautiously applied."[7]

Many years ago, this point of view was expressed by Professor Harberler: "How do I know that it hurts you more to have your leg cut off than it hurts me to be pricked by a pin?" It seemed at the time that it would have been more telling if he had put it the other way round.

Such arguments are getting rather dangerous nowadays, for though we shall presumably never have a hedonimeter whose findings would be unambiguous, the scientific measurement of pain is fairly well developed, and it would be very surprising if a national survey of the distribution of susceptibility to pain turned out to have just the same skew as the distribution of income.

If the question is once put: Would a greater contribution to human welfare be made by an investment in capacity to produce knick-knacks that have to be advertised in order to be sold or an investment in improving the health service? it seems to me that the answer would be only too obvious; the best reply that *laisser-faire* ideology can offer is not to ask the question.

It is possible to defend our economic system on the ground that, patched up with Keynesian correctives, it is, as he put it, the "best in sight." Or at any rate that it is not too bad, and change is painful. In short, that our system is the best system that we have got.

Or it is possible to take the tough-minded line that Schumpeter derived from Marx. The system is cruel, unjust, turbulent, but it does deliver the goods, and, damn it all, it's the goods that you want.

Or, conceding its defects, to defend it on political grounds—that democracy as we know it could not have grown up under any other system and cannot survive without it.

What is not possible, at this time of day, is to defend it, in the neo-classical style, as a delicate self-regulating mechanism, that has only to be left to itself to produce the greatest satisfaction for all.

But none of the alternative defences really sounds very well. Nowadays, to support the *status quo*, the best course is just to leave all these awkward problems alone.

[7] *Mathematical Psychics*, p. 81.

4

To descend from questions of universal and of national policy to the internal operation of the system, let us ask what rules of the game are accepted nowadays for various players in an industrial economy.

What about Trade Unions? According to strict *laisser-faire* doctrine they used to be placed on a par with monopolies. The free operation of market forces would secure for each group of workers their marginal net product, and a Trade Union, by forcing the wage above its equilibrium level, would cause unemployment, just as a monopolist restricts sales by keeping up prices.

In some ways the most striking novelty in Keynesian doctrine was that (abstracting from effects on foreign trade) an all-around reduction in wages would not reduce unemployment and (introducing Kalecki's elaboration) would actually be likely to increase it.

At the same time "imperfect competition" had come into fashion and discredited the idea that market forces can be relied upon to establish the equality of wages with the value of marginal products, so that even on its own waters the old orthodoxy could not keep afloat.

Nowadays it is pretty generally agreed that Trade Unions do not introduce an element of monopoly into the system but constitute rather what Professor Galbraith[8] has christened a "countervailing power" to cancel the element of monopoly which inevitably exists on the employer's side of the wage bargain. At the same time the employer's side, at least in big business, has learned to accept the Trade Unions and on the whole, apart from occasional flurries, to co-exist with them fairly amicably.

The new doctrine, however, cuts both ways. A rising tendency of money wage rates is necessary to keep monopoly in check but if it goes too fast it does no good to the workers and is a great nuisance to everyone else.

Experience of the vicious spiral in the years of high employment has demonstrated this clearly enough, as an overall truth. But it remains the duty of each Trade Union individually to look after the interests of its own members. To appeal to any one Union to exercise public spirit and refrain from wage demands is appealing to it to betray its trust. An appeal to organized labour as a whole to exercise restraint is naturally regarded with the deepest suspicion as long as profits are not restrained.

Here there has been a spectacular breakdown in the doctrine that the pursuit of self-interest by each promotes the good of all.

The old theory *assumed* full employment and stable prices. Now history has called its bluff. Where is the mechanism that will establish such a situation? The old rules of the game have become unplayable and badly need to be revised.

What about the other side of the bargain? Is it the proper thing for employers to resist wage demands? Not long ago a lockout in the printing trade reduced the British Press to silence, played havoc with publishing business and

[8] See *American Capitalism.*

ruined a number of small local printers. Afterwards the employers claimed credit for having saved the public, at serious loss to themselves, from the greater rise in wages that they would have had to concede if they had settled without a fight.[9] Do we agree in feeling grateful and congratulating them on their public spirit? or do we regret the loss of production and the general ill-will that followed the dispute? Orthodox doctrine cannot help us.

And what about prices? The old theory that they are settled by competition could not survive the long buyer's market of the inter-war period, and the theories of imperfect and monopolistic competition have left mere chaos in their wake. The business man's theory (which has been taken up by some economists) that prices are governed by costs is no more helpful; it is quite impossible to define the cost, including a proper contribution to overheads, depreciation and "a fair and reasonable profit," for any particular batch of output of any particular commodity. Some formula or other for allocating costs can be found that will justify any price, within reason, that a firm finds it convenient to charge.

The businessman's theory, in any case, is evidently not intended to be taken literally, for, with a few exceptions, they do not show any alacrity in reducing prices when costs fall.

All that orthodox theory tells us is that in conditions of perfect competition prices fall with costs and that in conditions of oligopoly they very likely do not. Does theory tell us that it would be a Good Thing if firms acted *as though* there was perfect competition, and brought prices down? This was the view taken (with some hesitation) in the third report of the Cohen Council.[10] It was greeted by business commentators with some surprise. Surely the proper objective in industry is to make profits? There may be cases where a reduction of price will increase profits, and then it is indicated, but the doctrine that prices ought to fall just because costs have come down seemed very odd. A spokesman of the Federation of British Industries, commenting on the Report remarks—

> *There are ambiguities in its suggestion that industry should reduce prices. It is one thing to reduce prices and thereby expand demand and output; it is another to hold prices below their market level with the object of curbing profits or dividends.*[11]

Then again, there is the question of the durability of commodities, referred to above. Suppose that a manufacturer has discovered a way, without extra cost, to make his products more durable. Should he adopt this method, so as to benefit his customers, or should he rather consider the danger of satisfying their demands and reducing the market for replacements? Would he not be well advised to turn his research workers on to find a less durable material, provided that it can be made to

[9] See *The Times*, 1st September 1959. Letter from J. Brooke-Hunt.
[10] Council on Prices, Productivity and Incomes, 1959.
[11] Report in *The Times*, 7th August 1959.

look as attractive and is not much more costly? Here the doctrine that the most profitable is the most socially beneficial course of conduct hits an awkward snag.

Then again, what about dividend policy? There is a strong propensity in human nature, which has not been explained (perhaps a clue might be found in the instincts of animals that live in packs) for the individual to cotton on to any kind of group of which he finds himself a member, and to develop patriotism for it.

Nation, race, church, city, evoke loyalty. Marx never got round to writing the chapter on class. Class loyalty, in vulgar Marxism, is presented as a form of egoism, but it is not so; it often demands the sacrifice of the immediate interest of an individual.

This tendency of attachment is the foundation for public-school spirit and regimental morale. It also operates strongly for firms; the main cause that has falsified Adam Smith's prediction that joint-stock enterprise would be impossible,[12] and Marshall's dictum that limited liability companies stagnate,[13] is this capacity for managers and boards of directors to project their egos into the organization that they happen to belong to and care for it just as much as if it were a family business.

The entity which evokes this loyalty is the firm as such. The shareholders (apart from those foundation members who are identified with the firm) are regarded more or less on a par with creditors and it is a disagreeable necessity to part with the firm's earnings to satisfy them.

Devotion to the firm as such points to a high rate of self-financing, except in the case of boards of very large companies which want from time to time to make big new issues. They pay out dividends, and seek to keep up the market price of shares, not because they are acting in the interests of the shareholders, but because this is the best way to raise more capital for the firm that they serve.

On this question of distributing profits, what is proper behavior? Some economists are against self-finance because it spoils the marginal theory. Investment goes where profits happen to have been earned and investments of a relatively low marginal productivity may be pushed by old firms while new ones with very high marginal productivity cannot get finance. Much better, they argue, to distribute profits and let all firms go to the market. But of money that has once been paid out, perhaps 10 per cent will be saved and made available for reinvestment, whereas 100 per cent of retained profits are reinvested. Is the superior quality of external finance great enough to outweigh such a large difference in quantity?

Management (for Management with a large M is also an entity with its own point of view) is all against this doctrine and regards reinvestment as the main justification for profits. The idea that the motive for industry is the pursuit of profit is resented as dastardly slander. It is quite the other way around: industry is the motive for the pursuit of profit.

---

[12]*Wealth of Nations*, Vol. I, p. 229.

[13]*Principles*, p. 316.

In a now forgotten manifesto signed by a hundred and twenty businessmen, which was issued during the war, we find this credo set forth: Industry (Industry with a big I)—

> *has a three-fold public responsibility, to the public which consumes its products, to the public which it employs, and to the public which provides the capital by which it operates and develops. . . . The responsibility of those directing Industry is to hold a just balance between the varying interests of the public as consumers, the staff and workmen as employees, and the stockholders as investors, and to make the highest possible contribution to the well-being of the nation as a whole.* [14]

This sounds pompous and arrogant. Who gave these fellows the right to determine the distribution of the National Income and what super-human wisdom do they claim directs them to distribute it aright? Yet there is a great deal of truth in the view that the power to allocate resources and distribute income has in fact been placed in their hands. To the list of interests which they have to balance should be added, first of all, boards of directors, and secondly, in a vague and more diffused way, that solidarity with their colleagues in an industry which nowadays so much softens the edge of competition, and solidarity with Industry as such—that is with the class to which they belong. But the high-mindedness is not all just a publicity stunt to recommend their class to the rest of us. There is a large element, in the patriotism which attaches a manager to his firm, of a desire for a good reputation and a good conscience. Even when it is hypocritical, hypocrisy—the homage which vice pays to virtue—is much to be preferred to cynicism. The modern capitalist is hardly recognizable in Marx's portrait of the ruthless exploiter, squeezing every drop of surplus out of the sweat of the workers.

Keynes in one of his optimistic moods spoke of the tendency of big business to socialize itself. [15] Nowadays Management (the kind with a big M) likes to see itself as a kind of public service.

All this has been much damaged lately by a violent kick-back of old-fashioned profit-seeking capitalism. The legal fiction that firms belong to their shareholders has been taken up to knock high-minded, gentlemanly Management over the head. Once more some economists, clinging to the old orthodoxy, welcome the take-over bidder on the grounds that what is profitable must be right, conceding to the profits of financial manipulations the halo that once belonged to the "reward of Enterprise." Those who hold that the proper purpose of industry is to pay dividends must welcome the pressure being put upon boards of directors to offer counter-bribes to their shareholders.

Which side should we be on? Is the gentlemanly public spirit of Management too often a cloak for gentlemanly ease and long weekends? Will the exaltation

[14] *A National Policy for Industry*, 1942.
[15] *Essays in Persuasion*, p. 314.

of the shareholder make managers cynical and Trade Unions aggressive, and face us once more with sharp questions which have been muffled in the comfortable woolly-mindedness of the Welfare State?

Another question on which orthodoxy has led us into great confusion is monopoly. Generally, in the orthodox scheme, monopoly is a Bad Thing. Professor Knight has been known to attack the U.S. anti-trust laws as an illegitimate interference with the freedom of the individual, but for most economists competition is absolutely essential to the justification of *laisser faire;* it is competition which equates the margins, distributes resources so as to maximize *utility* and generally makes the whole scheme work.

But competition, surely, is the main cause of monopoly? How can it be that to lower prices, expand markets, undersell rivals, is a Good Thing, but that the firm that succeeds in overcoming these difficulties and remains in possession of the field is a wicked monopolist? The objection to restrictive practices, and the main justification for the present campaign against them, is that they restrain competition and keep inefficient producers going. If the campaign succeeds, competition, driving out the inefficient, will create more monopolies. Is that what we want? And if not, what *do* we want? What are the rules of the game?

5

Perhaps all this seems negative and destructive. To some, perhaps, it even recommends the old doctrines, since it offers no "better 'ole" to go to. The contention of this essay is precisely that there is no "better 'ole."

The moral problem is a conflict that can never be settled. Social life will always present mankind with a choice of evils. No metaphysical solution that can ever be formulated will seem satisfactory for long. The solutions offered by economists were no less delusory than those of the theologians that they displaced.

All the same we must not abandon the hope that economics can make an advance towards science, or the faith that enlightenment is not useless. It is necessary to clear the decaying remnants of obsolete metaphysics out of the way before we can go forward.

The first essential for economists, arguing amongst themselves, is to "try very seriously," as Professor Popper says that natural scientists do, "to avoid talking at cross purposes" and, addressing the world, reading their own doctrines aright, to combat, not foster, the ideology which pretends that values which can be measured in terms of money are the only ones that ought to count.

The Corporate Leviathan
●
Robert A. Dahl

Public Authority, Private Rulers

You would be hard put to find a more obvious candidate for testing against the criteria of Personal Choice, Competence, and Economy than the large privately owned business enterprises in the United States—and none whose government is, by these criteria, so lacking in legitimacy. Yet Americans have all but abandoned any serious challenge to the appropriation of public authority by private rulers that is the essence of the giant firm. A recent book on the American corporation by Richard Barber perfectly illustrates the point. Mr. Barber's study is sober, thorough, searching, illuminating, and the author by no means lacks sympathy for his subject. As any honest observer of the corporation must, Mr. Barber establishes that the large corporation is a center of "concentrated private economic power" which neither the market nor the state regulates more than weakly. Yet he does not show us how this power can be tamed.

> For the near future the public may not like the effects of concentrated private power, but there is little it seems able to do about it, given the existing political and economic climate. Power has gravitated to the American corporate giants. They exercise it with some restraint, but realize that their future lies in forming a partnership with a government which need not be greatly feared as a regulatory policeman. [1]

From Robert A. Dahl, *After the Revolution* (New Haven: Yale University Press, 1970), pp. 115–128. Reprinted by permission.

Robert Dahl is Sterling Professor of Political Science at Yale University and author of *Modern Political Analysis* (1963), *A Preface to Democratic Theory* (1956), and other books.

[1]*The American Corporation: Its Power, Its Money, Its Politics* (New York: Dutton, 1970), p. 184.

The problem is rendered even more difficult by the rapid expansion of the international corporation. Until recently the private firm, though long a favorite spook of the orthodox Left and the extreme Right, for the most part played a rather marginal (though not necessarily trivial) role in world affairs, but the flourishing international corporation, typically an oligopoly and typically American-based, is for all practical purposes a new, shadowy, unregulated polity with resources greater than those of most nation-states.[2]

In a society that sought to arrange authority according to the criteria set out in the first part of this book, these new principalities would be an anomaly. Although the power wielded by their rulers can be obfuscated by the dreams of opulence they create, it cannot, I think, be rationally justified. I do not see how the anomaly can persist indefinitely. Unfortunately, when a serious demand arises for changes in the government of the corporation, it will be found that the orthodox alternatives hardly satisfy reasonable criteria better than the existing arrangements.

The Fractured Spectrum

In a rational society guided in all its arrangements for authority by the criteria of Personal Choice, Competence and Economy, how would people look upon economic enterprise? I believe they would see an economic enterprise as a kind of association of all those who are affected by its activities. How such an association might best govern its particular enterprise according to the criteria of Personal Choice, Competence, and Economy would be looked upon as a concrete, practical question to be decided after taking into account the particular circumstances of the enterprise. Depending on these circumstances, the government of an enterprise could take many different forms. Just as people in such a society would think it irrational to believe that one form of democracy is invariably preferable to the others, so they would think it foolish to decide a priori that one form for governing economic enterprise is preferable to others in all circumstances. To debate "capitalism" versus "socialism" would seem as quaint and archaic as to debate whether primary democracy should completely replace polyarchy. In such a society it would seem natural and normal to give serious consideration to the possibility that the steel industry should be turned over to a state-owned corporation and the post office to a quasi-private corporation. Such questions would be thought of as more technical than ideological, problems less of principle than of practical judgment.

Doubtless a few Americans think this way, but overwhelmingly they do not. As everyone knows, in this country the prevailing ideology prescribes "private" enterprise, that is, firms managed by officials who are legally, if not de facto,

[2] "Today the gross sales revenue of the top twenty or so American companies is equal to Britain's GNP. Belgium's budget could be financed from the profits of just America's top four firms." Ibid., p. 257.

responsible to private shareholders. Outside certain functions traditionally reserved to agencies of the state, it is widely taken for granted that the only appropriate form for managing economic enterprise is the privately owned firm. Being more pragmatic in their practices than in their ideology, Americans sometimes resort to other forms, but ordinarily the technical arguments in favor of an alternative must be of enormous weight to overcome the purely ideological bias in favor of the private firm. During the past three decades, for example, the decline in passenger services on American railroads has become scandalous—without, however, creating a scandal. Train after train has been abandoned, equipment has deteriorated, railroad stations have fallen into ruin. A people who settled the West and landed the first man on the moon has been incapable of meeting this challenge. In fact, Americans have accepted it all with astounding passivity, and the idea that the railroads should after all be operated as a truly *public* enterprise has scarcely ever been given serious consideration.

It is as if we were color-blind to half the spectrum. It is as if city planners considered all the alternative ways by which a superhighway might be routed through a city with least damage and greatest benefit, without ever giving thought to the possibility of routing it around the city or not building it at all. It is as if we knew only Rousseau, but not Madison and Jefferson, as if we thought the range of democratic possibilities included committee democracy, primary democracy, and referendum democracy, but not polyarchy or delegated authority.

Why are Americans half color-blind when they look at economic enterprise? An important reason is that our history has left us without a socialist tradition. To be sure, the first labor party in the world appeared in the United States in 1828, and we have had socialist parties as long as any other country. But like many a successor, that first labor party vanished completely in a few years, and the socialist parties never managed to acquire enough of a following to make them a major force in American life. At their peak in 1912 they won 6 percent of the total presidential vote; in the depths of the depression in 1932 the total vote for all socialist parties was less than 4 percent. Why the United States was uniquely able to pass through its industrial stage without generating a major socialist movement is an interesting and complex historical question. I do not wish to search for an explanation here. Let us ignore the causes and consider the consequence.

The consequence is, I think, a serious limit to our capacity for clearheaded public consideration of how economic enterprises should be governed. Because we have no socialist tradition, our debates about economic institutions nearly always leave some major alternatives—chiefly "socialist" alternatives—unexplored.

Not that socialism provides the answers. Socialists often do not even seem to put the right questions. But a socialist tradition helps to fill in some of the missing shades of the spectrum. If Americans were as pragmatic as they are supposed to be, and less ideological than they are in fact, they would not need a socialist tradition to offset their ideological narrowness. But in their present condition, with a patch over one eye and myopia in the other, Americans find it more difficult than they should to see the whole range of possibilities for an economic enterprise.

The Illusion of Private Enterprise

Philosophers point out that if everything in the universe instantaneously multiplied or diminished in size, we should have no way of knowing it. Something like this seems to have happened in this country. A nation of farmers with a sprinkling of merchants became a nation of employees, managers, and owners. The small family enterprise run by its owner became the large enterprise in which operation was separated from ownership. The ideology of the private enterprise of farmer and small merchant was transferred more or less intact to the big corporation. The sanctity of the private property owned by the farmer and small merchant became sanctified in the "private" property of the corporation. Because a nation of farmers had believed in the virtues of private enterprise, a nation of employees continued to accept the virtues of "private" enterprise.

The transfer of the old ideology to the new economy required a vast optical illusion. For nothing could be less appropriate than to consider the giant firm a *private* enterprise. Whatever may be the optimal way of governing the great corporation, surely it is a delusion to consider it a *private* enterprise. General Motors is as much a public enterprise as the U.S. Post Office. With gross receipts approximately equal to Sweden's Gross National Product; with employees and their families about as large as the total population of New Zealand; with outlays larger than those of the central government of France or West Germany, wholly dependent for its survival during every second of its operations on a vast network of laws, protection, services, inducements, constraints, and coercions provided by innumerable governments, federal, state, local, foreign, General Motors is de facto the public's business. It is hardly to be wondered at that the head of General Motors could have believed, and what is more uttered in public, that what is good for General Motors is good for the United States. In the circumstances, to think of General Motors as *private* instead of *public* is an absurdity.

It would be more realistic to think of all economic enterprise as a public service. Thought of in this perspective, a private economy is a contradiction in terms. Every economy is a public or social (not socialist) economy. To think about economic enterprise in this way does not automatically answer the question how an economic enterprise should be governed. But it does compel one to ask the question.

Conventional Nonsolutions

How *should* the large corporation be governed?

In any modern economy, whether you label it capitalist, socialist, mixed, or whatever, an enterprise is subject to three broad kinds of controls. There are the controls exercised by those who directly manage or run the firm. Let me call these *internal* controls. There are the controls exercised by other enterprises and economic entities, suppliers, consumers, rivals. These controls sometimes operate through the complex mechanisms of the market, sometimes through bargaining, collusion, collaboration, and so forth. For convenience, I shall call these *economic* controls. Finally, there are the controls exercised by the various governments of the state, local, provincial, national—*governmental* controls, if you like.

Now it is an arresting fact that the intellectual magicians who manipulated the grand theories about economic enterprises that dominated the public stage for over a century all had a clever way of making one or two of these controls mysteriously disappear. In a magic show, mystification is a good thing, but it is hardly to be commended in an economic program.

The neoclassical economists viewed internal controls, authority within the firm, rather as astronomers regard the gravitational force of the earth. To the astronomer, the earth's gravity is all concentrated at a theoretical point approximately at the center of the globe; from the astronomer's purely professional perspective, all the bustling life, struggle, force, and drama going on at the earth's surface are matters too trivial to be noticed. A revolution, a volcano, a hurricane, an earthquake may destroy his observatory, but *en principe* these things do not matter. In quite the same way, the neoclassical economists reduced the firm to an infinitesimal theoretical point in space where the particularities of Mr. Gradgrind or John D. Rockefeller had no more relevance than the living earth does to the astronomer. The complex government of the firm vanished and reappeared as the single rational entrepreneur pressed on by a lust for profit and an inhuman capacity for responding shrewdly to the impersonal forces of the market. As a classroom exercise this provided an opportunity for the virtuoso of the blackboard, but it told nothing about how General Motors should be governed, or was governed. For that matter, the effects on lung cancer of the "rational" calculations of the cigarette manufacturers are a matter for which a display of fancy cost curves hardly constitutes a satisfactory answer.

Great advocates of the division of labor, the neoclassical economists assumed that the government of a firm was a matter for lawyers to handle. As it happens, lawyers have helped to work out an answer, one that seems to be taken for granted by most Americans. This, the orthodox "private property" view, says that the firm ought to be governed by the people who own it. The lawyer's answer may do for small businesses, the famous corner grocery run by mama and papa. But as an answer to the problem of the large corporation it is barely an improvement on the economists' nonanswer. For who owns the large corporation? The stockholders. And to argue that the large corporation should be governed by the stockholders is highly unpersuasive for two reasons.

In the first place, a moment's thought will show that it is an unreasonable denial of the Principle of Affected Interests. For why should people who own shares be given the privileges of citizenship in the government of the firm when citizenship is denied to other people who also make vital contributions to the firm? The people I have in mind are, of course, employees and customers, without whom the firm could not exist, and the general public, without whose support for (or acquiescence in) the myriad protections and services of the state the firm would instantly disappear. The Principle of Affected Interests gives these people a strong *prima facie* case for citizenship.

That the stockholder has a privileged status in the government of the firm is an anachronistic result of the fact that ownership, authority, and productive work in an enterprise were once united in the same persons. Historically, to own something meant to possess the right to use it as one saw fit under the general protection and regulation of the state. To an America of small farmers and small businessmen, this conception naturally appeared to have great validity. What you owned, it seemed reasonable to suppose, was the product of your own labor. Elementary justice seemed to support your authority over it, your right to do what you pleased with it, subject only to certain legal limits laid down by the state. "In that original state of things, which precedes both the appropriation of land and the accumulation of stock, the whole produce of labor belongs to the laborer." This is not Marx speaking, but Adam Smith in *Wealth of Nations*.[3] The appropriation of land by private owners, and the need of the laborer for capital which he could not himself supply, created claims against "the whole produce of labor," for rent to landlords and for profit to capitalists. So far, Smith and Marx were in perfect accord. What Marx did, however, was nothing more or less than to interpret rent and profit as illegal seizure of the "surplus value" created by labor; because they seized this surplus value, landlord and capitalist were not benefactors but exploiters of labor.

The socialist challenge touched off a lasting debate over the proposition that a person is entitled to own something used by another to furnish the owner a profit. Strictly speaking, the affirmative may not have won the debate. But its proponents won the battle of law and policy, and owners preserved the legal right to claim the profits of an enterprise, which was perhaps all most of them really cared about.

Paradoxically, however, not only Marx but socialists in general helped the defenders of the orthodox view to gain acceptance for one of the great myths of the nineteenth century. This was the myth that ownership, internal control, and legal rights to the profits of an enterprise all *had* to be united in the same persons. The myth obviously served the owners, but it also proved to the satisfaction of socialists that in order to control the firm, and thus acquire the authority to eliminate or otherwise affect profits, ownership has to be shifted to "the public," which in practice means the state.

Neither socialists nor antisocialists seriously challenged the mythology of ownership. Thus one question that had desperately needed to be asked was generally passed over: would it not be possible to split apart the various aspects of "ownership," so that internal control of the firm might be split off from those who claimed the profits? If so, why should citizenship in a firm be linked exclusively to the right to receive the profits of the firm?

By now, the first question has been answered by a resounding and incontrovertible yes. And that yes is the second flaw in the orthodox view. For orthodoxy is flatly belied by the reality of the modern corporation. Even if the owners of a large

[3]*An Inquiry into the Nature and Causes of the Wealth of Nations,* 7th ed. (London: Strahan and Cadell, 1793), p. 96.

firm have the legal right to run it, everyone knows today that they do not and cannot run it. The question that was not asked during the great debate over socialism vs. capitalism has now been answered: ownership has been split off de facto from internal control. Every literate person now rightly takes for granted what Berle and Means established four decades ago in their famous study, *The Modern Corporation and Private Property:* that increasingly in the large corporation ownership is separated from internal control. To be sure, stockholders do retain a nominal right to participate in governing the firm, but they do not and ordinarily cannot exercise that right. The role of the stockholders in the government of the large corporation is rather like that of the British monarch in investing the prime minister with office: the stockholders serve the purely symbolic function of conferring legitimacy and legality on a government that has managed to acquire power by other means. Unlike the British system since 1688, the American corporation occasionally suffers a palace revolution or coup d'etat. As in old-fashioned military coups in Latin America, when one group of rulers is exchanged for another the structure of hierarchic authority under the managers remains unchanged.

Thus the traditional private property view of authority in the corporation denies the right of citizenship in corporate government to all the affected parties except the one group that does not, will not, and probably cannot exercise that right. If property ownership is necessarily attached to the right of internal control, then the modern corporation must be owned de facto not by the stockholders but by the managers. But if property ownership does *not* carry with it the right of internal control, then the stockholders have no special claim to citizenship, and very likely no reasonable claim at all.

If the orthodox private property answer is inadequate, unfortunately the orthodox socialist answer is little better. Over the period of more than a century since the term has come into use, socialism has meant many things, and I do not want to cavil over definitions. One prominent kind of old-fashioned socialism held that a solution to many problems, including the government of the enterprise, was to be found in "public ownership of the means of production." The usual interpretation of this idea was to have the enterprise owned by the state and managed by state officials. What should have been perfectly obvious, but became so only after some industries were nationalized in a number of European countries, is that this solution left the hierarchical structure of authority intact—or strengthened it. The Post Office, after all, is hardly a model of democratic government. Thus the traditional socialist answer ran directly counter to another set of ideas that intersected with socialist thought, the belief in "industrial democracy."

Why socialists were unable to see that "public ownership and operation" might be very different from "industrial democracy" is a fascinating and important chapter in social and intellectual history for which there is no room here. A few aspects, however, are so relevant to the question we are concerned with that they ought to be emphasized. As we have seen, many socialists had, and continue to have, an exaggerated notion of the importance of "property" in the sense of "ownership." The evils they saw in the business firm seemed to flow from the fact that it was privately owned. Ergo: change enterprises from "private" to "public" ownership, and presto! all will be well. But, they asked themselves, how can the "public" own anything except through the state? Hence, they reasoned, public ownership means state ownership. And since they took for granted that "ownership" means, among other things, the right to manage the firm, the state would naturally acquire the right to manage the firm. Having that right, it would use it—in the interests, of course, of the public.

But just as we have learned that the private owners of a large corporation do not govern it, even if they have nominal citizenship rights, so we have learned that government ownership does not necessarily mean that the public, or even that part of the public most affected by the operation of a firm, will have very much to do with governing it. In the USSR, for example, the general "public," as distinct from state officials, has no more to say about the government of enterprises than the general "public" in the U.S. has to say about the government of General Motors; and workers probably have even less say there than in this country.

That socialists who sympathized with industrial democracy ended up by supporting bureaucratic centralization was also a result of their fascination with the nation-state. Among those whom Marx contemptuously labeled utopians, like Fourier and Owen, socialism was envisaged as a decentralized system, for the socialist economy was to consist of a multiplicity of small, autonomous associations. After Marx, the tendency was to lean heavily on the state, not perhaps the bourgeois state, possibly a workers' state, a state that might wither away in some remote future, but in any case the state. In countries like England and Sweden where socialist ideas were not so deeply influenced by Marx, labor-socialist parties nonetheless reflected the general confidence of their fellow citizens that the state was a useful, trustworthy, and effective instrument of rule. Thus socialists were caught up in the centralizing trends of the nineteenth century. Just as liberal reformers turned to the nation-state as the best instrument of reform and regulation, so the socialist leaders placed their hopes, however much their rhetoric sometimes concealed it, in the possibility of using the government of the nation-state to run the economy. Like most reformist liberals, socialists came to see in demands for decentralized institutions of government a mask for privilege and reaction, or the bold, wild face of anarchism, or, like the proposals of Guild Socialists in England, quaint ideas of academic intellectuals. Their prejudice was far from absurd, but whatever their intentions, the upshot was that socialism contributed its own thrust toward bureaucratic centralization and away from "industrial democracy." In politics, as we all know, intentions and consequences are poorly correlated, and idealism has never been a protection against that. . . .

Toward a Pluralist
Commonwealth
●

Gar Alperovitz

Although the concept of socialism involves a broad humanist vision, it has yet to be demonstrated how in advanced industrial settings the abstract ideals might be achieved and sustained *in practice*. While some form of social ownership of capital and the planned use of society's wealth may be necessary to deal adequately with many economic issues, the question remains precisely *what* form? We return to the basic issue: could society ever be organized equitably, cooperatively, humanely, so wealth benefited everyone—without generating a highly centralized, authoritarian system?

A number of traditions have attempted to confront difficulties inherent in the centralizing tendencies of state-socialism; consideration of some of their alternatives suggests an initial approach to defining elements of a positive program:

It is helpful to acknowledge frankly at the very outset that some traditional conservatives (as opposed to rightist demagogues) have long been correct to argue that centralization of both economic and political power leaves the citizen virtually defenseless, without any *institutional* way to control major issues which affect his life. They have objected to state-socialism on the grounds that it destroys individual initiative, responsibility, and freedom—and have urged that privately held property (particularly that of the farmer or small capitalist entrepreneur) at least offers a man some independent ground to stand on in the fight against what they term "statism." Finally, most have held that the competitive market can work to make capitalists responsible to the needs of the community.

Some conservatives have also stressed the concept of "limits," especially limits to state power, and like some new radicals have emphasized the importance

From "Notes Toward a Pluralist Commonwealth (Together with Their Addenda)," by Gar Alperovitz. In *Strategy and Program: Two Essays Toward a New American Socialism* by Staughton Lynd and Gar Alperovitz (Boston: Beacon Press, 1973), pp. 53–69. Copyright 1973 Gar Alperovitz. Reprinted by permission, with minor changes requested by the author.

Gar Alperovitz is a director of the National Center for Economic Alternatives, Washington, D.C.

of voluntary participation and individual, personal responsibility. Karl Hess, Murray Rothbard, and Leonard Liggio, among others of the Libertarian Right, have recently begun to reassert these themes—as against old socialists, liberals, *and* more modern "statist" conservatives like William Buckley, Jr. The conservative sociologist Robert A. Nisbet argues additionally that voluntary associations should serve as intermediate units of community and power between the individual and the state.[1]

Few traditional conservatives or members of the Libertarian Right, however, have recognized the socialist argument that *private property* and the competitive market as sources of independence, power, and responsibility have led historically to other horrendous problems, including exploitation, inequality, ruthless competition, individual alienation, the destruction of community, expansionism, imperialism, war. . . .

A second alternative—also an attempt to organize economic power away from the centralized state—is represented by the Yugoslav argument for workers' self-management. Whereas private property (in principle if not in practice) implies decentralization of economic power to individuals, workers' self-management involves decentralization to the social and organizational unit of those who work in a firm. This alternative may even be thought of as a way to achieve the conservative anti-statist purpose—but to establish different, socially defined priorities over economic resources.

The Yugoslav model of decentralization raises a series of difficult problems: though the Yugoslavs proclaim themselves socialists and urge that the overall industrial system must benefit the entire society, the various workers' groups which actually have direct control of industrial resources are each inevitably only *one part* of society. And as many now see, there is no obvious reason why such (partial) groups will not develop special interests ("workers' capitalism") which run counter to the interests of the broader community.

Indeed, problems very much akin to those of a system based on private property have begun to develop in Yugoslavia. Overreliance on the market has not prevented inequality between communities, and has led to commercialism and exploitation. Both unemployment and inflation also plague Yugoslavia. An ethic of individual gain and profit has often taken precedence over the ideal of cooperation. Worker participation, in many instances, is more theory than practice. Meanwhile, as competitive tendencies emerge between various worker-controlled industries, side by side the need for some central coordination has produced other anomalies: the banks now control many nationwide investment decisions, severely reducing local economic power; the Yugoslav Communist party takes a direct and often arbitrary hand in both national and local decisions. In general, it has been extremely difficult for social units to develop a sense of reciprocal individual responsibility as the basis for an equitable community of mutual obligation.[2]

[1] See especially Nisbet's *Community and Power* (original title, *Quest for Community*, 1953) (New York: Oxford University Press, 1962).

[2] [Footnote deleted.]

The Yugoslav model recalls the historic themes of both guild socialism and syndicalism. It is also closely related to the "participatory economy" alternative recently offered by Jaroslav Vanek, and the model of workers' participation proposed by Robert A. Dahl.[3] All alternatives of this kind, unfortunately, suffer from a major contradiction: it is difficult to see how a political-economy based primarily on the organization of groups by function could ever achieve a just society, since the various structural alternatives seem inherently to tend toward the self-aggrandizement of each functional group—*as against* the rest of the community.

The point may perhaps be most easily understood by imagining workers' control or ownership of the General Motors Corporation in America—an idea close to Dahl's alternative. It should be obvious that: (1) There is no reason to expect white male auto workers easily to admit more blacks, Puerto Ricans, or women into "their" industry when unemployment prevails; (2) No internal dynamic is likely to lead workers automatically or willingly to pay out "their" wages or surpluses to reduce pollution "their" factory chimney might pour onto the community *as a whole*; (3) Above all, the logic of the system militates against going out of "their" business when it becomes clear that the automobile-highway mode of transportation (rather than, say, mass transit)[4] is destructive of the community as a whole though perhaps profitable for "their" industry.

Dahl, for one, is aware of some of these shortcomings; he hopes through interest group representation that somehow an "optimum combination" of worker and general community interests might perhaps be worked out. Clearly, were a planning framework substituted for the capitalist market such problems might in part be alleviated. The Yugoslav experience (where both the commune and the nation have extensive powers), however, teaches that socialism does not automatically resolve either the market's difficulties or the root contradiction inherent in a context which structurally opposes the interests of workers and society as a whole.

Some basic distinctions must be confronted. First, while management by the people who work in a firm should be affirmed, the matter of emphasis is of cardinal importance; "workers' control" should be conceived in the broader context of, and subordinate to, the *entire community.* In order to break down divisions which pose one group against another and to achieve equity, accordingly, the social unit at the heart of any proposed new system should, so far as possible, *be inclusive of all the people*—minorities, the elderly, women, youth—not just the "workers" who have paid "jobs," and who at any one time normally number only some forty percent of the population and sixty percent of the adult citizenry.

A second, perhaps more difficult, point: the only social unit inclusive of *all* the people is one based on geographic contiguity. This, in the context of national geography, is the *general* socialist argument; the requirement of decentralization

[3]See, for instance: Jaroslav Vanek, *The Participatory Economy* (Ithaca: Cornell University Press, 1971); *The General Theory of Labor-Managed Economics* (Ithaca: Cornell University Press, 1970); Robert A. Dahl, *After the Revolution?* (New Haven & London: Yale University Press, 1970); Kenneth Coates and Anthony Topham, *Industrial Democracy in Great Britain* (London: Mac-Gibbon & Kee, 1968).

[4]Or, simply *less* transit—and more planned co-location of functions.

simply reduces its scale. In a territorially defined *local* community, a variety of functional groups must coexist, side by side. Day-to-day communication is possible (indeed, individuals are often members of more than one group); and long-term relationships can be developed. Conflicts must inevitably be mediated directly by people who have to live with the decisions they make. There are, of course, many issues which cannot be dealt with locally, but at least a social unit based on common location proceeds from the assumption of comprehensiveness, and this implies a decision-making context in which the question "How will a given policy affect *all* the community?" is more easily posed.

When small, territorially defined communities control capital or land socially (as, for instance, in the Israeli kibbutz or the Chinese commune), unlike either capitalism or socialism, there is no built-in contradiction between the interests of owners or beneficiaries of industry (capitalist *or* local workers) *as against the community as a whole*. The problem of "externalities," moreover, is in part "internalized" by the structure itself: since the community as a whole controls productive wealth, *it*, for instance, is in a position to decide rationally whether to pay the costs of eliminating the pollution its own industry causes for its own people. The entire community also may decide how to divide work equitably among all its citizens. . . .

Although small scale ownership of capital might resolve some problems it raises others; the likelihood that if workers owned General Motors they might attempt to exploit their position—or oppose changes in the nation's overall transportation system—illuminates a problem which a society based on cooperative communities would also face. So long as the social and economic security of *any* economic unit is not guaranteed, it is likely to function to protect (and, out of insecurity, *extend*) its own special, status quo interests—even when they run counter to the broader interests of the society. The only long-run answer to the basic expansionist tendency of all market systems is to establish some stable larger structural framework to sustain the smaller constituent elements of the political-economy. This poses the issue, of course, of the relative distribution of power between small units and large frameworks, and of precisely which functions can be decentralized and which cannot.

Some of the above questions may perhaps be explored most easily in the context of the alternative to centralization represented by the localized practice of cooperative community socialism in the Israeli kibbutz—an historically agricultural institution which is now rapidly becoming industrialized.[5] The many existing variations of the model suggest numerous alternative ways to make decisions involving not only workers' self-management but community (social) uses of both capital and surpluses. Some approaches have been successful, some obviously mistaken and wasteful. . . .

Within the best communities one major point deserves emphasis: individual responsibility—to act, to take initiative, to build cooperation voluntarily—is

[5] The kibbutzim demonstrate, incidentally, that small industrial units can be highly efficient—contrary to theorists who claim large scale is a technical necessity. The kibbutz movement has continued to grow in Israel, although the proportionate role of this sector has diminished as huge migrations have swelled the capitalist economy since 1948.

a necessary precondition of a community of mutual, reciprocal obligation, and, ultimately, the only real protection against bureaucracy. When the ethic of an equitable, inclusive community is achieved, the efficacy of true "moral incentives" is dramatically revealed: individuals are neither paid nor valued according to their "product," but simply because of their membership in the community. But there are huge problems even in the best settings, not the least of which is that small communities tend easily to become overbearing and ethnocentric. If they are to break out of conformity they must allow a range of free individual initiative—without waiting for majority approval. And they must find ways to achieve flexibility and openness to prevent provincialism and antagonism against outsiders or (all) "others." . . .

The kibbutzim as a group have experimented with confederation, an idea which begins with democratic decentralization as a first premise, and attempts to build a cooperative structure between small units yet remain responsible to them. The confederate framework in part—but only in part—also helps deal with the issue of economic insecurity and the self-aggrandizing expansionist logic of market systems. . . .

The kibbutz experience is of course not transferable directly to advanced industrial society. However, it is highly suggestive as an expression of a final major tradition which attacked centralization: anarchism—a philosophical tendency in which there has historically been a long-standing debate about socialism, about whether it is possible to have individual freedom *without* a framework of state ownership of wealth, about whether it is possible to have it *with* state ownership. The most hopeful attempts to resolve the issue center on abstract formulations like Noam Chomsky's "libertarian socialism," but this idea has not been developed much beyond the level of generalization. Anarchist theory has always been aware of the danger of both a socialist "red bureaucracy" (in Bakunin's term) and *laisser faire* capitalism, but it has no fully developed program. . . .

One may raise objections to practical failings of the existing models or to theoretical aspects of the various traditions, but it is hard to disagree with the judgment that centralization through corporate capitalism, fascism, or state-socialism has destructive implications for local communities—for all the people, that is, except the managing elites (and for them, too, in more subtle, insidious ways). Accordingly, whether one accepts the conservative view that individuals must control capital, or the Yugoslav that workers must, or the radical Israeli or anarcho-communist view that "communities" smaller than the nation state must, we are compelled to come to terms with the general proposition that political power has in some way to be related to decentralized economic power. . . .

A Pluralist Commonwealth?

To review and affirm *both* the cooperative vision *and* the decentralist ideal is to suggest that a basic problem of positive alternative program is how to define community economic institutions which are egalitarian and equitable in the sense of owning and controlling productive resources for the benefit of all, *but* which can prevent centralization of power, *and,* finally, which over time can permit new social relations capable of sustaining an ethic of individual responsibility and group cooperation upon which a larger vision must ultimately be based.

A major challenge of positive program, therefore, is to create "commonwealth" institutions which, through decentralization and cooperation, achieve new ways of organizing economic and political power so that the people (in the local sense of that word) really do have a chance to "decide"—and so that face-to-face relations establish values of central importance to the larger units of society as a whole. . . .

Small units are obviously only part of the answer. My own view is that it is necessary to (1) affirm the principle of collective ownership or control of capital (and democratically planned disposition of surplus), and (2) extend it, at least initially, to local communities, the sub-units of which are sufficiently small so that individuals can, in fact, learn cooperative relationships *in practice.* These, however, should be conceived only as elements of a larger solution—as the natural building blocks of a reconstructed nation of regional commonwealths.

The sketch of a long-term vision might begin with the neighborhood in the city and the county in the countryside (and pose as a research problem which industries—from shoe repair to oil refining—can usefully be decentralized and which cannot, and what scale—say, between 30,000 and 100,000—is appropriate for "communities").[6] Its longer thrust, however, is more complicated: in place of the streamlined socialist planned state which depends upon the assumption of power at the top, I would substitute an organic, diversified vision—a vision of thousands of small communities, each organized cooperatively, each working out its own priorities and methods, each generating broader economic criteria and placing political demands on the larger system out of this experience. The locality should be conceived as a basis for (not an alternative to) a larger framework of regional and national coordinating institutions.

In its local form, such a vision is obviously greatly supportive of the ideal of community proposed by Percival and Paul Goodman in their book *Communitas.*[7] More specifically, a community which owned substantial industry cooperatively and used part of its surplus for its own social services would have important advantages: it could experiment, without waiting for bureaucratic decrees, with new schools, new training approaches, new self-initiated investments (including, perhaps, some small private firms). It could test various worker-management schemes. It would be free for a range of independent social decisions based upon independent control of some community economic resources. It could grapple directly with efforts to humanize technology. It could, through coordination and planning, reorganize the use of time, and also locate jobs, homes, schools so as to maximize community interaction and end the isolated prison aspects of all these presently segregated units of life experience.

[6] With sub-units of still smaller scale . . . .

[7] See especially Scheme II. Percival and Paul Goodman, *Communitas* (Chicago: University of Chicago Press, 1947).

Communities could work out in a thousand diverse localities a variety of new ways to reintegrate a community—to define productive roles for the elderly, for example, or to redefine the role of women in community. They could face squarely the problem of the "tyranny of the majority" (and the concomitant issues of minority rights, and individual privacy), and experiment with new ways to guarantee individual and minority initiative. The anarchist demand for freedom could be faced in the context of a cooperative structure. The issue of legitimate leadership functions might be confronted rather than wished away; and various alternatives, including rotation, recall, apprenticing, etc., might be tested. Communities might even begin to regard themselves as communities—communes, if you like—in the equitable, cooperative, humane sense of that term.

In their larger functions communities would obviously have to work together, for both technological and economic reasons. Modern technology, in fact, permits great decentralization—and new modifications can produce even greater decentralization if that is a conscious objective. In cases where this is not possible or intolerably uneconomical (perhaps, for example, some forms of heavy industry, energy production, transportation) larger confederations of communities in a region or in the integrated unit of the nation state would be appropriate—as they would be for other forms of coordination as well.

The themes of the proposed alternative thus are indicated by the concepts of cooperative community and the Commonwealth of Regions. The program might best be termed "A Pluralist Commonwealth"—"Pluralist," to emphasize decentralization and diversity; "Commonwealth," to focus on the principle that wealth should cooperatively benefit all.

The vision, of course, is utopian, but perhaps in the positive sense of the word, it is a set of ideals to be discussed, a long-range forecast of ultimate objectives. Its purpose is not to blueprint the future but to help define areas for serious inquiry and experimentation, and to facilitate a serious dialogue about the relationship between present action and future consequences. . . .

Staying Alive
●
Nancy Hartsock

Introduction

"Gray is the color of work without purpose or end, and the cancer of hopelessness creeping through the gut." —Marge Piercy, *To Be of Use* (Garden City: Doubleday, 1973), p. 77.

You're there just to filter people and filter telephone calls. . . . You're treated like a piece of equipment, like the telephone. You come in at nine, you open the door, you look at the piece of machinery, you plug in the headpiece. That's how my day begins. You tremble when you hear the first ring. After that, it's sort of downhill. . . . There isn't a ten minute break in the whole day that's quiet. . . . You can't think, you can't even finish a letter. . . . I always dream I'm alone and things are quiet. . . . You know you're not doing anything, not doing a hell of a lot for anyone. Your job doesn't mean anything. Because you're just a little machine. A monkey could do what I do. It's really unfair to ask someone to do that.

I don't know what I'd like to do. That's what hurts the most. That's why I can't quit the job. I really don't know what talents I may have. . . . —Studs Terkel, *Working* (New York: Pantheon, 1972), pp. 29–31.

Whether we work for wages or not, most of us have come to accept that we work because we must. We know that the time we spend on things important to us must somehow be found outside the time we work to stay alive. We have forgotten that work is in fact fundamental to our development as human beings, that it is a

From "Staying Alive" by Nancy Hartsock, *Quest: A Feminist Quarterly*, vol. III, no. 3 (Winter 1976/77), pp. 2–14. Reprinted by permission of the author and publisher.

Nancy Hartsock is an assistant professor of political science at Johns Hopkins University and was a founding editor of *Quest*.

source of our sense of accomplishment, and an important aspect of our sense of self.

Work is an especially important question for feminists since in our capitalist and patriarchal society the work women do goes unrecognized, whether it is done for wages or not. Housework is not defined as work at all, but rather as a "natural" activity, or an expression of love. Only in the last few years have women as a group demanded that housework be recognized as important work. Women who work for wages simply have two jobs—the one, though unimportant and temporary, recognized as work, and the other completely unrecognized.

The liberation of women—and all human beings—depends on understanding that work is essential to our development as individuals and on creating new places in our lives for our work. We must develop a new conception of work itself. To begin this process, we must clarify what is wrong with the capitalist and patriarchal organization of work, and define the requirements of *humane* work. We must critically evaluate the ways we are structuring work in feminist organizations, where we can experiment and invent ways to use our work for our development as human beings.

Estranged Labor

The receptionist has described the way most of us feel about our work— that it is not important, and that the pace is often set by machines or by people who are not involved in the work itself. Work is something we must do, however painful. In our society, work is, almost by definition, something we cannot enjoy. Time at work is time we do not have for ourselves—time when creativity is cut off, time when our activity is structured by rules set down by others. The increasing use of unskilled labor (or more precisely, labor which uses the skills everyone is taught in public schools), and the increasing application of scientific management techniques in manufacturing, the office, and even the home (as home economics) all contribute to the feeling that many jobs could be done by machines, and that people should not have to do them. In these respects, housework does not differ fundamentally from women's wage work. Housewives too experience the isolation described by the receptionist, while the phrase, "just a housewife," expresses the cultural devaluation of housework.

The work most of us do has been described by Marx as estranged labor— time and activity that is taken from us and used against us. Work which should be used for our growth as well-rounded human beings is used instead to diminish us, to make us feel like machines. Estranged labor distorts our lives in a number of ways, most of them illustrated by the receptionist's description of her work.* She expresses what Marx described as our separation from our own activity at work

*All this is more true for working- and lower-class women than for middle-class professional women. Women who are lawyers, for example, have much more control over their work, but the patterns which are so clear for most women (whether we work for wages or not) also structure and limit the ability of any woman to control her own work.

when she says, "the machine dictates. This crummy little machine with buttons on it," so that "you can't think."[1] We are not in control of our actions during the time we work; our time belongs to those who have the money to buy our time. Women's time in particular is not our own but is almost always controlled by men. Our time is not our own even away from work. The rhythms of estranged labor infect our leisure time as well; our work exhausts us and we need time to recover from it. As a result we spend much of our leisure time in passive activities—watching television, listening to the radio, or sleeping.

In addition, Marx pointed out that our work separates us from others, preventing real communication with our fellow workers. Often our work separates us physically from others. Some manufacturers deliberately put working stations too far apart for conversation among employees. But just as often, we are kept from real contact with others not by actual physical barriers but by roles, status differences, and hierarchies. The receptionist points out that although she is surrounded by people, she has little contact with them. Competition on the job also separates us from others. We are forced into situations in which our own promotion or raise means that someone else cannot advance, situations where we can only benefit by another's loss.

Patriarchy too, in giving men more power over women, separates us from real contact with other human beings. And here too, the patterns of our lives at work invade our leisure as well. . . . It carries over. The receptionist says, "The way I talk to people has changed. . . . Now, when I see them, I talk to them like I was talking on the telephone. . . . I don't know what's happened."[2]

Finally, estranged labor prevents us from developing as well-rounded people and keeps us from participating in the life of the community as a whole. Marx argued that rather than participating in community work for joint purposes, our survival as individuals becomes primary for us, and prevents us from recognizing our common interests.[3] Our own activity, especially our actions in our work, separates us from other people and from the people we ourselves could become. We work only because we must earn enough money to satisfy our physical needs. Yet by working only to survive, we are participating in our own destruction as real, social individuals. Worst of all, even though we recognize the dehumanization our work forces on us, we are powerless as individuals to do anything about it. Patriarchy and capitalism work together to define "women's work" as suited only to creatures of limited talent and ambition: the sex-segregation of the labor market ensures that women's work will be especially dehumanizing. The receptionist speaks for most of us when she says she doesn't know what she wants to do. We all have talents we are not developing but we don't really know what they are. . . .

---

[1] Studs Terkel, *Working* (New York: Pantheon, 1972), p. 30.

[2] *Ibid.*

[3] *Karl Marx, Economic and Philosophic Manuscripts of 1844*, ed. Dirk Struik (New York: International Publishers, 1964), pp. 112–113. The account of alienation is taken from pp. 106–119.

Work: The Central Human Activity

Because of the perverted shape of work in a patriarchal, capitalist society, we have forgotten that work is a central human activity, the activity through which the self-creation of human beings is accomplished.[4] Work is a definition of what it is to be human—a striving first to meet physical needs and later to realize all our human potentialities. Marx argues that our practical activity, or work in the largest sense, is so fundamental that social reality itself is made up of human activity (work).[5]

Our work produces both our material existence and our consciousness. Both consciousness and material life grow out of our efforts to satisfy physical needs, a process which leads to the production of new needs. These efforts, however, are more than the simple production of physical existence. They make up a "definite mode of life." "As individuals express their life, so they are. What they are, therefore, coincides with their production, both with *what* they produce and *with how* they produce. The nature of individuals thus depends on the material conditions determining their production."[6] Here individuality must be understood as a social phenomenon, that human existence in all its forms must be seen as the product of human activity—that is, activity and consciousness "both in their content and in their *mode of existence*, are *social: social* activity and *social* mind.[7]

Finally, Marx argued that the realization of all human potential is only possible as and when human beings as a group develop their powers, and that these powers can be realized only through the cooperative action of all people over time.[8] Thus, although it is human work which structures the social world, the structure is imposed not by individuals, but by generations, each building on the work of those who came before. Fully developed individuals, then, are products of human work over the course of history.[9]

However, . . . the fact that a few use the time of a majority for their own profit or their own pleasure makes work into a means to life rather than life itself. The work we do has become estranged labor; and as a result, our humanity itself is diminished. Our work has become a barrier to our self-creation, to the expansion and realization of our potential as human beings. Work in a capitalist and patriarchal society means that in our work and in our leisure we do not affirm but deny ourselves; we are not content but unhappy; we do not develop our own capacities, but destroy our bodies and ruin our minds.[10]

[4]Herbert Marcuse, *Studies in Critical Philosophy*, tr. Joris De Bres (Boston: Beacon Press, 1973), p. 14; Karl Marx, *1844 Manuscripts*, pp. 113, 188.

[5]Karl Marx, *Capital, I* (New York: International Publishers, 1967), pp. 183–184.

[6]Karl Marx and Frederick Engels, *The German Ideology*, ed. C. J. Arthur (New York: International Publishers, 1970), pp. 42, 59.

[7]Karl Marx, *1844 Manuscripts*, p. 137.

[8]*Ibid.*, p. 17.

[9]Marx, *Grundrisse*, tr. Martin Nicolaus (Middlesex, England: Penguin, 1973), p. 162.

[10]Marx, *1844 Manuscripts*, p. 110.

By contrast, creative work could be understood as play, and as an expression of ourselves. "In creative work as well as genuine play, exhaustion is not deadening. . . . When one selects the object of work, determines its method, and creates its configuration, the consciousness of time tends to disappear. While clock-watching is a characteristic disease of those burdened with alienated labor, [when we work creatively], we lose ourselves, and cease to measure our activities in so many units of minutes and hours. . . ."[11]

Alternatives to Estranged Labor

The perversion of our work, then, is the perversion of our lives as a whole. Thus our liberation requires that we recapture our work. Ultimately we can do this only by reordering society as a whole and directing it away from domination, competition, and the isolation of women from each other. What would work be like in such a society? What models can we look to for guidance about ways to reorganize work?

We know that a feminist restructuring of work must avoid the monotonous jobs with little possibility of becoming more creative, and the fragmentation of people through the organization of work into repetitive and unskilled tasks. Although we have some ideas about what such a reorganization of work would look like, the real redefinition of work can occur only in practice. While our alternative institutions cannot fully succeed so long as we live in a society based on private profit rather than public good—a society in which work and human development are polar opposites—feminist organizations provide a framework within which to experiment. The organizations we build are an integral part of the process of creating political change and, in the long run, can perhaps serve as proving grounds for new institutions. . . .

Feminists, in developing new organizational forms, have been concerned with two related factors which structure the estranged labor process in our society—the use of power as domination, both in the workplace and elsewhere, and the separation of mental from manual work. By understanding the ways these two aspects of estranged labor mold the labor process as a whole, we can correct some of the mistakes we have made as a movement and avoid making others in the future.

Power and Political Change

In an article on power, I argued that social theorists have generally conceptualized power as "the ability to compel obedience, or as control and domination."[12] Power must be power over someone—something possessed, a property of

---

[11]Stanley Aronowitz, *False Promises* (New York: McGraw-Hill, 1973), p. 62.

[12]"Political Change: Two Perspectives on Power," *Quest.* I:1 (Summer, 1974), pp. 10–25.

an actor such that he* can alter the will or actions of others in a way which produces results in conformity with his own will. [13] Social theorists have argued that power, like money, is something possessed by an actor which has value in itself as well as being useful for obtaining other valued things.

That power can be compared with money in capitalist society supports Marx's claim that the importance of the market leads to the transformation of all human activity into patterns modeled on monetary transactions. [14] In this society, where human interdependence is fundamentally structured by markets and the exchange of money, power as domination of others (or the use of power to "purchase" certain behavior which diminishes rather than develops us), is what most of us confront in our work.

There are other definitions of power. Berenice Carroll points out that in *Webster's International Dictionary* (1933), power is first defined as "ability, whether physical, mental, or moral, to act; the faculty of doing or performing something," and is synonymous with "strength, vigor, energy, force, and ability." The words "control" and "domination" do not appear as synonyms. [15] In this definition of power, energy and accomplishment are understood to be satisfying in themselves. This understanding of power is much closer to what the Women's Movement has sought, and this aspect of power is denied to all but a few women: the experience described by the receptionist can scarcely be characterized as effective interaction with the environment.

Feminists have rightly rejected the use of power as domination, and as a property analogous to money, but in practice our lack of clarity about the differences between the two concepts of power has led to difficulties about leadership, strength and achievement. In general, feminists have not recognized that power understood as energy, strength, and effectiveness need not be the same as power which requires domination of others.

We must, however, recognize and confront the world of traditional politics in which money and power function in similar ways. For those of us who work in "straight" jobs (whether paid or not) and work part-time in feminist organizations, the confrontation occurs daily. Those of us who work full-time for feminist organizations confront power as domination most often when our organizations try to make changes in the world. Creating political change requires that we set up organizations based on power defined as energy and strength, groups which are structured, not tied to the personality of a single individual and whose structures do not permit the use of power to dominate others in the group. At the same time,

---

*"He" and "men" here refer specifically to men and not women.

[13] See Bertrand Russell, *Power, A New Social Analysis* (N.P., 1936), p. 35, cited by Anthony de Crespigny and Alan Wertheimer, *Contemporary Political Theory* (New York: Atherton Press, 1970), p. 22; Harold Lasswell and Abraham Kaplan, *Power and Society* (New Haven: Yale University Press, 1950), p. 76; Talcott Parsons, "On The Concept of Political Power," in *Political Power*, eds. Roderick Bell, David V. Edwards, and R. Harrison Wagner (New York: Free Press, 1969), p. 256.

[14] Karl Marx, *The Grundrisse*, ed. David McLellan (New York: Harper and Row, 1971), p. 65.

[15] Berenice Carroll, "Peace Research: The Cult of Power," paper presented to the American Sociological Association, Denver, Colorado (Sept., 1971), pp. 6–7.

our organizations must be effective in a society in which power is a means of making others do what they do not wish to do.

Mental and Manual Labor

One of the characteristics of advanced capitalist society is the separation of the conception of work from its execution.[16] This division between mental and manual labor—which also shapes the process of estranged labor—is an expression of the power relations between the rulers and the ruled, and is closely related to the concept of power as domination. Having power and dominating others is commonly associated with conceptual or mental work; subordination, with execution, or with manual (routine) work. Women form a disproportionate number of those who do routine work and rarely are insiders in capitalist rituals and symbols of "know-how."

As the Chinese have recognized, subordination and lack of creativity are not features of routine work itself but rather are aspects of the social relations within which the work takes place.[17] A feminist restructuring of work requires creating a situation in which thinking and doing, planning and routine work, are parts of the work each of us does; it requires creating a work situation in which we can both develop ourselves and transform the external world. Our work itself then would provide us with satisfaction and with the knowledge that we were learning and growing. It would be an expression of our own individuality and power in the world.

The Development of a Feminist Workplace

Specific questions about how to restructure the labor process can be grouped under the two general headings of problems of power and problems about the division between mental and manual labor. Attention to these two factors can provide several specific guidelines. First, overcoming the domination of a few over the majority of workers in an organization requires that we have control over our own time and activity. Second, we need to develop possibilities for cooperative rather than competitive and isolated work; we need to develop ways for people to work together on problems rather than for one (perhaps more experienced) person to give orders to another.

We need to recognize the importance of enabling people to become fully developed rather than one-sided. We need to make sure that women can learn new skills well enough to innovate and improve on what we have been taught. We need to make space for changes in interests and skills over time. We need to include

[16]Harry Braverman, *Labor and Monopoly Capital* (New York: Monthly Review Press), especially pp. 70–121.
[17]See Marilyn Young, "Introduction," *Signs*, II:1 (Autumn, 1976), p. 2, and Mary Sheridan, "Young Women Leaders," *Signs*, II:1 (Autumn, 1976), p. 66.

elements of both mental and manual work, both planning and routine execution, in every job we create. Finally, we must recognize the importance of responsibility as a source of power (energy) for individual members of feminist organizations. To have responsibility for a project means to have the respect of others in the group, and usually means as well that we must develop our capacities to fulfill that responsibility. The lines of responsibility must be clear, and unless the organization is large, they will often end with a single individual. Having responsibility for some parts of the work done by a group allows us not only to see our own accomplishments, but also to expand ourselves by sharing in the accomplishments of others. [18] We are not superwomen, able to do everything. Only by sharing in the different accomplishments of others can we participate in the activities of all women.

Collectives and Cooperatives Work

Given these general guidelines, how should we evaluate one of the most common forms of the organization of work—the collective? Here I am concerned about one type of collective—a group which insists that the work done by each member should be fundamentally the same. This kind of organization is widespread in the women's movement, although not all groups which call themselves collectives function in this way. For example, the Olivia Records collective maintains all lines of individual responsibility for different areas of work. [19]

Just as the Women's Movement erred in its almost universal condemnation of leaders—and its mistaken identification of women who achieved with those that wanted to dominate—we have, through working in collectives, many times simply reacted against the separation of conception from execution. Collective work is our answer to the isolation, competitiveness, and the monotony of the routine work forced on us in capitalist work places. But collectives can at the same time reproduce some of the worst features of estranged labor—the separation of the worker from her own activity, the loss of control over her work, and the separation from real cooperative work—that is, work *with* rather than simply beside others. It can cut us off from real growth as individuals. This happens when collectives reproduce power as domination of others and at the same time reintroduce the division between conception and execution.

Informal rather than formal domination of some members of the collective by others often results from the attempt to avoid hierarchal domination by avoiding formal structure altogether. What is in theory the control of the entire group over its work becomes in fact the domination of some members of the group by others. Some members of the group lose control over their work to those who are more

---

[18] As Marx put it, "I would have been for you the mediator between you and the species and thus been acknowledged and felt by you as a completion of your own essence and a necessary part of yourself and have thus realized that I am confirmed both in your thought and in your love. In my expression of my life I would have fashioned your expression of your life, and thus in my own acitivity have realized my own essence, my human, communal essence," in David McLellan, *The Thought of Karl Marx* (New York: Viking, 1969), p. 32.

[19] Ginny Berson, "Olivia: We Don't Just Process Records," *Sister* VII:2 (December–January, 1976), pp. 8–9.

aggressive, although perhaps not more skilled. Also, informal decision-making, which assumes that every collective member has the same amount to contribute in every area, can result in reducing opportunities for cooperative work, work which recognizes, combines and uses the differing skills and interests of members of the group to create something none could do alone.

In the attempt to make sure that every task is done by every member of the group, those who were less involved in setting up particular tasks are deprived of a sense of accomplishment—a sense that their activity as an individual and unique expression of who they are, a contribution to the group from which the group as a whole can benefit. By rotating all members through the various tasks of the group, and by insisting that every member of a collective do every activity that the group as a whole is engaged in, the collective, in practice, treats its members as interchangeable and equivalent parts. It reproduces the assembly line of the modern factory, but instead of running the work past the people, people are run past the work. . . .

. . . If much of the work done by one member of the collective has been designed and planned by someone else, and accomplishment and creativity involved in designing a system for doing routine work is not possible. . . The separation between conception and execution has not been overcome.

One reply to this criticism is that learning skills is important, and that collectives provide a place to learn new skills. While we can agree that women very much need to learn new skills, it takes time to reach the point where we can be creative with a new skill. We need to *learn* skills rather than simply try out new things. One of the best ways to learn a skill completely is to be entrusted with full responsibility for one or more aspects of the operation. . . .

. . . Thus, learning skills means not only learning the physical operations involved in a particular kind of work, but learning how to organize and set up that work in the best way—from the perspectives both of efficiency and of self-development.

Conclusions: The Fragility of Alternatives

Even if we correctly identify the factors which structure the labor process in our society, the alternatives we construct can only be very tenuous. Work in feminist organizations will exist in the tension between reformism and conformity on the one hand and simple reaction to the capitalist, patriarchal organization of work in our society on the other. Our strategies for change and the internal organization of work must grow out of the tension between using our organizations as instruments for both taking and transforming power in a society structured by power understood only as domination, and using our organizations to build models for a society based on power understood as energy and initiative. Work in feminist organizations must be a way of expressing and sharing with others who we are and what we can do, a means of developing ourselves, as well as a place to contribute to the struggle for liberation.

Economic Justice

Should the state redistribute wealth and income?
What would economic justice require?
What economic rights should citizens in a democracy have?

The Province of Government
●

John Stuart Mill

Of the Grounds and Limits of the *Laisser-Faire* or Non-Interference Principle

1. We have now reached the last part of our undertaking; the discussion, so far as suited to this treatise (that is, so far as it is a question of principle, not detail) of the limits of the province of government: the question, to what objects governmental intervention in the affairs of society may or should extend, over and above those which necessarily appertain to it. . . .

. . . The supporters of interference have been content with asserting a general right and duty on the part of government to intervene, wherever its intervention would be useful: and when those who have been called the *laisser-faire* school have attempted any definite limitation of the province of government, they have usually restricted it to the protection of person and property against force and fraud; a definition to which neither they nor any one else can deliberately adhere, since it excludes . . . some of the most indispensable and unanimously recognised of the duties of government. . . .

We must set out by distinguishing between two kinds of intervention by the government, which, though they may relate to the same subject, differ widely in their nature and effects, and require, for their justification, motives of a very different degree of urgency. The intervention may extend to controlling the free agency of individuals. Government may interdict all persons from doing certain

From John Stuart Mill, *Principles of Political Economy* (1871 edition), Book V, Chap. XI.

John Stuart Mill (1806–1873) was a major English utilitarian philosopher whose influence on the development of political liberalism has remained enormous. Among his other works are *On Liberty, Utilitarianism, Considerations on Representative Government*, and his *Autobiography*.

things; or from doing them without its authorization; or may prescribe to them certain things to be done, or a certain manner of doing things which it is left optional with them to do or to abstain from. This is the *authoritative* interference of government. There is another kind of intervention which is not authoritative: when a government, instead of issuing a command and enforcing it by penalties, adopts the course so seldom resorted to by governments, and of which such important use might be made, that of giving advice, and promulgating information; or when, leaving individuals free to use their own means of pursuing any object of general interest, the government, not meddling with them, but not trusting the object solely to their care, establishes, side by side with their arrangements, an agency of its own for a like purpose. . . . There might be a national bank, or a government manufactory, without any monopoly against private banks and manufactories. There might be a post-office, without penalties against the conveyance of letters by other means. There may be a corps of government engineers for civil purposes, while the profession of a civil engineer is free to be adopted by every one. There may be public hospitals, without any restriction upon private medical or surgical practice.

2. It is evident, even at first sight, that the authoritative form of government intervention has a much more limited sphere of legitimate action than the other. It requires a much stronger necessity to justify it in any case; while there are large departments of human life from which it must be unreservedly and imperiously excluded. Whatever theory we adopt respecting the foundation of the social union, and under whatever political institutions we live, there is a circle around every individual human being, which no government, be it that of one, of a few, or of the many, ought to be permitted to overstep: there is a part of the life of every person who has come to years of discretion, within which the individuality of that person ought to reign uncontrolled either by any other individual or by the public collectively. That there is, or ought to be, some space in human existence thus entrenched [around], and sacred from authoritative intrusion, no one who professes the smallest regard to human freedom or dignity will call in question: the point to be determined is, where the limit should be placed; how large a province of human life this reserved territory should include. I apprehend that it ought to include all that part which concerns only the life, whether inward or outward, of the individual, and does not affect the interests of others, or affects them only through the moral influence of example. . . .

Even in those portions of conduct which do affect the interest of others, the onus of making out a case always lies on the defenders of legal prohibitions. It is not a merely constructive or presumptive injury to others, which will justify the interference of law with individual freedom. To be prevented from doing what one is inclined to, or from acting according to one's own judgment of what is desirable, is not only always irksome, but always tends, *pro tanto*, to starve the development of some portion of the bodily or mental faculties, either sensitive or active; and unless the conscience of the individual goes freely with the legal restraint, it partakes, either in a great or in a small degree, of the degradation of slavery. Scarcely any degree of utility, short of absolute necessity, will justify a prohibitory regulation, unless it can also be made to recommend itself to the general conscience; unless persons of ordinary good intentions either believe already, or can be induced to believe, that the thing prohibited is a thing which they ought not to wish to do.

It is otherwise with governmental interferences which do not restrain individual free agency. When a government provides means for fulfilling a certain end, leaving individuals free to avail themselves of different means if in their opinion preferable, there is no infringement of liberty, no irksome or degrading restraint. One of the principal objections to government interference is then absent. There is, however, in almost all forms of government agency, one thing which is compulsory; the provision of the pecuniary means. . . .

7. . . . *Laisser-faire*, in short, should be the general practice: every departure from it, unless required by some great good, is a certain evil. . . .

. . . As a general rule, the business of life is better performed when those who have an immediate interest in it are left to take their own course, uncontrolled either by the mandate of the law or by the meddling of any public functionary. The persons, or some of the persons, who do the work, are likely to be better judges than the government, of the means of attaining the particular end at which they aim. Were we to suppose, what is not very probable, that the government has possessed itself of the best knowledge which had been acquired up to a given time by the persons most skilled in the occupation; even then, the individual agents have so much stronger and more direct an interest in the result, that the means are far more likely to be improved and perfected if left to their uncontrolled choice. But if the workman is generally the best selector of means, can it be affirmed with the same universality, that the consumer, or person served, is the most competent judge of the end? Is the buyer always qualified to judge of the commodity? If not, the presumption in favour of the competition of the market does not apply to the case; and if the commodity be one, in the quality of which society has much at stake, the balance of advantages may be in favour of some mode and degree of intervention, by the authorized representatives of the collective interest of the state.

8. Now, the proposition that the consumer is a competent judge of the commodity, can be admitted only with numerous abatements and exceptions. He is generally the best judge (though even this is not true universally) of the material objects produced for his use. These are destined to supply some physical want, or gratify some taste or inclination, respecting which wants or inclinations there is no appeal from the person who feels them; or they are the means and appliances of some occupation, for the use of the persons engaged in it, who may be presumed to be judges of the things required in their own habitual employment. But there are other things, of the worth of which the demand of the market is by no means a test; things of which the utility does not consist in ministering to inclinations, nor in serving the daily uses of life, and the want of which is least felt where the need is greatest. This is peculiarly true of those things which are chiefly useful as tending

to raise the character of human beings. . . . Now any well-intentioned and tolerably civilized government may think, without presumption, that it does or ought to possess a degree of cultivation above the average of the community which it rules, and that it should therefore be capable of offering better education and better instruction to the people, than the greater number of them would spontaneously demand. Education, therefore, is one of those things which it is admissible in principle that a government should provide for the people. . . .

With regard to elementary education, the exception to ordinary rules may, I conceive, justifiably be carried still further. There are certain primary elements and means of knowledge, which it is in the highest degree desirable that all human beings born into the community should acquire during childhood. If their parents, or those on whom they depend, have the power of obtaining for them this instruction, and fail to do it, they commit a double breach of duty, towards the children themselves, and towards the members of the community generally, who are all liable to suffer seriously from the consequences of ignorance and want of education in their fellow-citizens. It is therefore an allowable exercise of the powers of government, to impose on parents the legal obligation of giving elementary instruction to children. This, however, cannot fairly be done, without taking measures to insure that such instruction shall be always accessible to them, either gratuitously or at a trifling expense. . . .

. . . Instruction, when it is really such, does not enervate, but strengthens as well as enlarges the active faculties: in whatever manner acquired, its effect on the mind is favourable to the spirit of independence: and when, unless had gratuitously, it would not be had at all, help in this form has the opposite tendency to that which in so many other cases makes it objectionable; it is help towards doing without help. . . .

One thing must be strenuously insisted on; that the government must claim no monopoly for its education, either in the lower or in the higher branches; must exert neither authority nor influence to induce the people to resort to its teachers in preference to others, and must confer no peculiar advantages on those who have been instructed by them. . . . A government which can mould the opinions and sentiments of the people from their youth upwards, can do with them whatever it pleases. Though a government, therefore, may, and in many cases ought to, establish schools and colleges, it must neither compel nor bribe any person to come to them; nor ought the power of individuals to set up rival establishments to depend in any degree upon its authorization. It would be justified in requiring from all the people that they shall possess instruction in certain things, but not in prescribing to them how or from whom they shall obtain it.

9. . . . Most persons take a juster and more intelligent view of their own interest, and of the means of promoting it, than can either be prescribed to them by a general enactment of the legislature, or pointed out in the particular case by a public functionary. The maxim is unquestionably sound as a general rule; but there is no difficulty in perceiving some very large and conspicuous exceptions to it. These may be classed under several heads.

First:—The individual who is presumed to be the best judge of his own interests may be incapable of judging or acting for himself; may be a lunatic, or idiot, an infant: or though not wholly incapable, may be of immature years and judgment. In this case the foundation of the *laisser-faire* principle breaks down entirely. The person most interested is not the best judge of the matter, nor a competent judge at all. Insane persons are everywhere regarded as proper objects of the care of the state. In the case of children and young persons, it is common to say, that though they cannot judge for themselves, they have their parents or other relatives to judge for them. But this removes the question into a different category; making it no longer a question whether the government should interfere with individuals in the direction of their own conduct and interests, but whether it should leave absolutely in their power the conduct and interests of somebody else. Parental power is as susceptible of abuse as any other power, and is, as a matter of fact, constantly abused. . . . Whatever it can be clearly seen that parents ought to do or forbear for the interest of children, the law is warranted, if it is able, in compelling to be done or forborne, and is generally bound to do so. To take an example from the peculiar province of political economy; it is right that children, and young persons not yet arrived at maturity, should be protected, so far as the eye and hand of the state can reach, from being over-worked. Labouring for too many hours in the day, or on work beyond their strength, should not be permitted to them, for if permitted it may always be compelled. Freedom of contract, in the case of children, is but another word for freedom of coercion. Education also, the best which circumstances admit of their receiving, is not a thing which parents or relatives, from indifference, jealousy, or avarice, should have it in their power to withhold. . . .

Among these members of the community whose freedom of contract ought to be controlled by the legislature for their own protection, on account (it is said) of their dependent position, it is frequently proposed to include women: and in the existing Factory Acts, their labour, in common with that of young persons, has been placed under peculiar restrictions. But the classing together, for this and other purposes, of women and children, appears to me both indefensible in principle and mischievous in practice. Children below a certain age *cannot* judge or act for themselves; up to a considerably greater age they are inevitably more or less disqualified for doing so; but women are as capable as men of appreciating and managing their own concerns, and the only hindrance to their doing so arises from the injustice of their present social position. When the law makes everything which the wife acquires, the property of the husband, while by compelling her to live with him it forces her to submit to almost any amount of moral and even physical tyranny which he may choose to inflict, there is some ground for regarding every act done by her as done under coercion: but it is the great error of reformers and philanthropists in our time, to nibble at the consequences of unjust power, instead of redressing the injustice itself. . . .

11. [Another] exception which I shall notice, to the doctrine that government cannot manage the affairs of individuals as well as the individuals themselves, has reference to the great class of cases in which the individuals can only

manage the concern by delegated agency, and in which the so-called private management is, in point of fact, hardly better entitled to be called management by the persons interested, than administration by a public officer. Whatever, if left to spontaneous agency, can only be done by joint-stock associations, will often be as well, and sometimes better done, as far as the actual work is concerned, by the state. Government management is, indeed, proverbially jobbing, careless, and ineffective, but so likewise has generally been joint-stock management. The directors of a joint-stock company, it is true, are always shareholders; but also the members of a government are invariably taxpayers; and in the case of directors, no more than in that of governments, is their proportional share of the benefits of good management, equal to the interest they may possibly have in mismanagement, even without reckoning the interest of their ease. It may be objected, that the shareholders, in their collective character, exercise a certain control over the directors, and have almost always full power to remove them from office. Practically, however, the difficulty of exercising this power is found to be so great, that it is hardly ever exercised except in cases of such flagrantly unskillful, or, at least, unsuccessful management, as would generally produce the ejection from office of managers appointed by the government. Against the very ineffectual security afforded by meetings of shareholders, and by their individual inspection and inquiries, may be placed the greater publicity and more active discussion and comment, to be expected in free countries with regard to affairs in which the general government takes part. The defects, therefore, of government management, do not seem to be necessarily much greater, if necessarily greater at all, than those of management by joint-stock. . . .

. . . There are many cases in which the agency, of whatever nature, by which a service is performed, is certain, from the nature of the case, to be virtually single; in which a practical monopoly, with all the power it confers of taxing the community, cannot be prevented from existing. I have already more than once adverted to the case of the gas and water companies, among which, though perfect freedom is allowed to competition, none really takes place, and practically they are found to be even more irresponsible, and unapproachable by individual complaints, than the government. . . . In the case of these particular services, the reasons preponderate in favour of their being performed, like the paving and cleansing of the streets, not certainly by the general government of the state, but by the municipal authorities of the town, and the expense defrayed, as even now it in fact is, by a local rate. But in the many analogous cases which it is best to resign to voluntary agency, the community needs some other security for the fit performance of the service than the interest of the managers; and it is the part of government, either to subject the business to reasonable conditions for the general advantage, or to retain such power over it, that the profits of the monopoly may at least be obtained for the public. This applies to the case of a road, a canal, or a railway. These are always, in a great degree, practical monopolies; and a government which concedes such monopoly unreservedly to a private company, does much the same thing as if it allowed an individual or an association to levy any tax they chose, for their own benefit, on all the malt produced in the country, or on all the cotton imported into it. . . .

12. . . . There are matters in which the interference of law is required, not to overrule the judgment of individuals respecting their own interest, but to give effect to that judgment: they being unable to give effect to it except by concert, which concert again cannot be effectual unless it receives validity and sanction from the law. For illustration, and without prejudging the particular point, I may advert to the question of diminishing the hours of labour. Let us suppose, what is at least supposable, whether it be the fact or not—that a general reduction of the hours of factory labour, say from ten to nine, would be for the advantage of the work-people: that they would receive as high wages, or nearly as high, for nine hours' labour as they receive for ten. If this would be the result, and if the operatives generally are convinced that it would, the limitation, some may say, will be adopted spontaneously. I answer, that it will not be adopted unless the body of operatives bind themselves to one another to abide by it. A workman who refused to work more than nine hours while there were others who worked ten, would either not be employed at all, or if employed, must submit to lose one-tenth of his wages. However convinced, therefore, he may be that it is the interest of the class to work short time, it is contrary to his own interest to set the example, unless he is well assured that all or most others will follow it. But suppose a general agreement of the whole class: might not this be effectual without the sanction of law? Not unless enforced by opinion with a rigour practically equal to that of law. For however beneficial the observance of the regulation might be to the class collectively, the immediate interest of every individual would lie in violating it: and the more numerous those were who adhered to the rule, the more would individuals gain by departing from it. If nearly all restricted themselves to nine hours, those who chose to work for ten would gain all the advantages of the restriction, together with the profit of infringing it; they would get ten hours' wages for nine hours' work, and an hour's wages besides. I grant that if a large majority adhered to the nine hours, there would be no harm done: the benefit would be, in the main, secured to the class, while those individuals who preferred to work harder and earn more, would have an opportunity of doing so. . . . Probably, however, so many would prefer the ten hours' work on the improved terms, that the limitation could not be maintained as a general practice: what some did from choice, others would soon be obliged to do from necessity, and those who had chosen long hours for the sake of increased wages, would be forced in the end to work long hours for no greater wages than before. Assuming then that it really would be the interest of each to work only nine hours if he could be assured that all others would do the same, there might be no means of their attaining this object but by converting their supposed mutual agreement into an engagement under penalty, by consenting to have it enforced by law. I am not expressing any opinion in favour of such an enactment, which has never in this country been demanded, and which I certainly should not, in present circumstances, recommend: but it serves to exemplify the manner in which classes of persons may need the assistance of law, to give effect to their deliberate collective opinion of their own interest, by affording to every individual a guarantee that his competitors will pursue the same course, without which he cannot safely adopt it himself. . . .

. . . It is the interest of each to do what is good for all, but only if others will do likewise. . . .

13. . . . Though individuals should, in general, be left to do for themselves whatever it can reasonably be expected that they should be capable of doing, yet when they are at any rate not to be left to themselves, but to be helped by other people, the question arises whether it is better that they should receive this help exclusively from individuals, and therefore uncertainly and casually, or by systematic arrangements, in which society acts through its organ, the state. . . .

Apart from any metaphysical considerations respecting the foundation of morals or of the social union, it will be admitted to be right that human beings should help one another; and the more so, in proportion to the urgency of the need: and none needs help so urgently as one who is starving. The claim to help, therefore, created by destitution, is one of the strongest which can exist; and there is *primâ facie* the amplest reason for making the relief of so extreme an exigency as certain to those who require it, as by any arrangements of society it can be made.

On the other hand, in all cases of helping, there are two sets of consequences to be considered; the consequences of the assistance itself, and the consequences of relying on the assistance. The former are generally beneficial, but the latter, for the most part, injurious; so much so, in many cases, as greatly to outweigh the value of the benefit. And this is never more likely to happen than in the very cases where the need of help is the most intense. . . . The problem to be solved is therefore one of peculiar nicety as well as importance; how to give the greatest amount of needful help, with the smallest encouragement to undue reliance on it.

Energy and self-dependence are, however, liable to be impaired by the absence of help, as well as by its excess. It is even more fatal to exertion to have no hope of succeeding by it, than to be assured of succeeding without it. When the condition of any one is so disastrous that his energies are paralyzed by discouragement, assistance is a tonic, not a sedative: it braces instead of deadening the active faculties: always provided that the assistance is not such as to dispense with self-help, by substituting itself for the person's own labour, skill, and prudence, but is limited to affording him a better hope of attaining success by those legitimate means. . . .

15. The same principle . . . extends also to a variety of cases, in which important public services are to be performed, while yet there is no individual specially interested in performing them, nor would any adequate remuneration naturally or spontaneously attend their performance. Take for instance a voyage of geographical or scientific exploration. The information sought may be of great public value, yet no individual would derive any benefit from it which would repay the expense of fitting out the expedition; and there is no mode of intercepting the benefit on its way to those who profit by it, in order to levy a toll for the remuneration of its authors. . . . Again, it is a proper office of government to build and maintain lighthouses, establish buoys, &c. for the security of navigation: for since it is impossible that the ships at sea which are benefited by a lighthouse, should be

made to pay a toll on the occasion of its use, no one would build lighthouses from motives of personal interest, unless indemnified and rewarded from a compulsory levy made by the state. There are many scientific researches, of great value to a nation and to mankind, requiring assiduous devotion of time and labour, and not unfrequently great expense, by persons who can obtain a high price for their services in other ways. If the government had no power to grant indemnity for expense, and remuneration for time and labour thus employed, such researches could only be undertaken by the very few persons who, with an independent fortune, unite technical knowledge, laborious habits, and either great public spirit, or an ardent desire of scientific celebrity.

Connected with this subject is the question of providing, by means of endowments or salaries, for the maintenance of what has been called a learned class. The cultivation of speculative knowledge, though one of the most useful of all employments, is a service rendered to a community collectively, not individually, and one consequently for which it is, *primâ facie*, reasonable that the community collectively should pay; since it gives no claim on any individual for a pecuniary remuneration; and unless a provision is made for such services from some public fund, there is not only no encouragement to them, but there is as much discouragement as is implied in the impossibility of gaining a living by such pursuits, and the necessity consequently imposed on most of those who would be capable of them, to employ the greatest part of their time in gaining a subsistence. . . . It is highly desirable, therefore, that there should be a mode of insuring to the public the services of scientific discoverers, and perhaps of some other classes of savants, by affording them the means of support consistently with devoting a sufficient portion of time to their peculiar pursuits. The fellowships of the Universities are an institution excellently adapted for such a purpose. . . . In some countries, Academies of science, antiquities, history, &c., have been formed, with emoluments annexed. The most effectual plan, and at the same time least liable to abuse, seems to be that of conferring Professorships, with duties of instruction attached to them. . . . The greatest advances which have been made in the various sciences, both moral and physical, have originated with those who were public teachers of them; from Plato and Aristotle to the great names of the Scotch, French, and German Universities. . . .

It may be said generally, that anything which it is desirable should be done for the general interests of mankind or of future generations, or for the present interests of those members of the community who require external aid, but which is not of a nature to remunerate individuals or associations for undertaking it, is in itself a suitable thing to be undertaken by government: though, before making the work their own, governments ought always to consider if there be any rational probability of its being done on what is called the voluntary principle, and if so, whether it is likely to be done in a better or more effectual manner by government agency, than by the zeal and liberality of individuals.

16. . . . The intervention of government cannot always practically stop short at the limit which defines the cases intrinsically suitable for it. In the particular

circumstances of a given age or nation, there is scarcely anything really important to the general interest, which it may not be desirable, or even necessary, that the government should take upon itself, not because private individuals cannot effectually perform it, but because they will not. At some times and places, there will be no roads, docks, harbours, canals, works of irrigation, hospitals, schools, colleges, printing-presses, unless the government establishes them; the public being either too poor to command the necessary resources, or too little advanced in intelligence to appreciate the ends, or not sufficiently practised in joint action to be capable of the means. This is true, more or less, of all countries inured to despotism, and particularly of those in which there is a very wide distance in civilization between the people and the government: as in those which have been conquered and are retained in subjection by a more energetic and more cultivated people. In many parts of the world, the people can do nothing for themselves which requires large means and combined action: all such things are left undone, unless done by the state. In these cases, the mode in which the government can most surely demonstrate the sincerity with which it intends the greatest good of its subjects, is by doing the things which are made incumbent on it by the helplessness of the public, in such a manner as shall tend not to increase and perpetuate, but to correct, that helplessness. A good government will give all its aid in such a shape, as to encourage and nurture any rudiments it may find of a spirit of individual exertion. . . .

The Nature of the State
•

John Hospers

Most academicians, somewhat isolated from the marketplace which ultimately pays their salaries, still appear to think of the State as a benevolent agent
which may have gone wrong in this way or that, but still to be trusted and admired
(and in any case, used by them). My own attitude toward the State, based on its
workings and the experience of myself and many others with its representatives, is
very different.

It is difficult to communicate briefly an attitude toward the State which
took many years of reading and reflection to develop. I shall begin with the thesis of
Franz Oppenheimer's book *The State* (1908). There are, he said, two ways of obtaining the things one needs and wants: the first method is production and
exchange—to produce something out of nature's raw materials or transform them
into a product (or service) desired by others, and to take the surplus of one's own
production of one thing and exchange it for another kind of surplus from the
production of others. This method of survival, production and exchange, he called
the *economic* means. But there is also a second means: not to produce anything at all
but to seize by force the things that others have produced—the method of plunder.
This he called the *political* means.

Not everyone, of course, can use the second means, since one cannot seize
from others something they have not already created or produced. But some people
can and do, siphoning off the fruits of other people's labor for themselves. In the
end, the supply is destroyed if this means is used too extensively, since it does not
add to but rather subtracts from the totality of production: the more that is used up
by the predator, the more must be created by others to replenish the supply. And of
course the systematic plunder of the goods that someone has produced considerably reduces his motivation for producing any more.

Now the State, said Oppenheimer, is *the organization of the political means.* It
is the systematic use of the predatory process over a given territory. Crimes com-

From John Hospers, "The Nature of the State," *The Personalist* 59, no. 4 (October 1978):
398–404. Reprinted by permission.

    John Hospers is professor of philosophy at the University of Southern California
and editor of *The Personalist*.

mitted by individuals, e.g. murder and theft, are sporadic and uncertain in their outcome: the victims may resist and even win. But the State provides a legal, orderly, systematic channel for the seizure of the fruits of other men's labor, and through the use of force it renders secure the parasitic caste in society.

> *The classic paradigm was a conquering tribe pausing in its time-honored method of looting and murdering a conquered tribe, to realize that the time-span of plunder would be longer and more secure, and the situation more pleasant, if the conquered tribe were allowed to live and produce, with the conquerors settling among them as the rulers exacting a steady annual tribute. One method of the birth of a State may be illustrated as follows: in the hills of southern Ruritania, a bandit group manages to obtain physical control over the territory, and finally the bandit chieftain proclaims himself "King of the sovereign and independent government of South Ruritania"; and, if he and his men have the force to maintain this rule for a while, lo and behold! a new State has joined the "family of nations," and the former bandit leaders have been transformed into the lawful nobility of the realm.* [1]

The State cannot keep the process of extortion going indefinitely unless it also confers some benefits (people might sooner or later revolt). One such benefit is protection—protection against other tribes, and protection against aggressors within the tribe. The State seldom manages this efficiently (what *does* it do efficiently?)—e.g. it protects only heads of state, and with everyone else it punishes (if at all) only after the aggression has been committed. And of course it increases its levy on all citizens to pay for this protection. But the State well knows that people also desire other benefits, specifically economic benefits. And these the State endeavors to supply, if for no other reason than to keep them peaceful, and, in the case of a democracy, to win their votes.

But this presents a problem, for the State has no resources of its own with which to confer these benefits. It can give to one person only by first seizing it from another; if one person gets something for nothing, another must get nothing for something. But the citizen-voter's attention is so centered on the attractiveness of the things being promised that he forgets that the politician making the promises doesn't have any of these things to give—and that he will have none of them after he gets into office; he will seize the earnings of one special interest group and distribute those earnings to another such group (minus the government's 40% handling fee, of course). And thus

> *. . . the promisees continue to give their votes to the candidate making the biggest promises. One candidate promises to get sufficient federal*

---

[1] Murray Rothbard, *Egalitarianism and Other Essays* (New York: Laissez Faire Press, 1973), p. 37. See also the opening pages of Richard Taylor, *Freedom, Anarchy and the Law* (Prentice-Hall, 1973).

funds for urban transportation to maintain the artificially low-priced subway ride in New York City. Another promises sufficient funds to guarantee Kansas wheat farmers more income for less wheat than the open market gives. Both candidates win. They meet in the cloak room on Capitol Hill, confess their sins to each other, and each one pledges to help the other deliver on his promise.

As the farmer collects the higher price for his wheat and the New Yorker enjoys his subsidized subway ride, each of them takes pride in the fine representative he has in Washington. As the farmer and the subway rider see it, each representative has just demonstrated that free servants are available, and that the honest citizen can get something for nothing if he will vote for the right candidate. The New Yorker fails to see that his own taxes have been increased in order to pay the Kansas farmer to cut down on his wheat production so the farmer can get a higher price for what he sells; so the New Yorker will have to pay a higher price for his bread. In like manner, the farmer doesn't seem to realize that his taxes have been increased in order to subsidize the urban transportation system, so the city dweller can enjoy a higher standard of living while lowering his own level of production; so the farmer will have the dubious privilege of paying the higher prices for the tools and machinery he has to buy. The farmer and the subway rider are expropriating each other's productive capacity and paying a handsome royalty to an unruly bureaucracy for the privilege of doing it. In the marketplace that would be called plundering. In the political arena it is known as social progress.[2]

Particularly profitable for the State is the "discovery" of scapegoats, those whose earnings it can systematically loot, and gain public approval for doing so through an incessant barrage of propaganda against them. Such scapegoats are not difficult to find: any person who wishes to be independent of the State; anyone who is a "self-made man," and most of all anyone who has produced and marketed something and attained wealth. Those who have not succeeded in open competition tend to envy those who have, and the State fans this envy.[3] Thus the majority of the population actually come to applaud the State for taking it away from those who have been more successful than they. Like those that killed the goose that laid the golden egg, they do not see ahead to the time when there will be no more eggs forthcoming. There will be little incentive to produce if years of effort are confiscated by the State, and many people who were employed before will now find themselves without work. The general standard of living of course will decline—most citizens do not see the inevitability of this, and some politicians do but don't mind, preferring to have a subservient and poverty-stricken population. In some States the process goes so far that the State itself becomes the sole owner of land, the sole employer of everyone (e.g., the Soviet Union); determining the profession

[2]Bertel Sparks, "How Many Servants Can You Afford?" *The Freeman*, October 1976, p. 593.
[3]See Helmut Schoeck, *Envy*.

and salary of every worker; and anyone who tries to save anything for himself, or earn anything other than through the State, is subject to interrogation, torture, and death by shooting or exile to the Gulag. Yet so successful, often, is the propaganda of the State on its own behalf, that even with this ultimate control over the life of every citizen, some people applaud the State as their protector and security ("the sanction of the victim"). As if the State could supply security, instead of (as it does) taking away from its subjects that much chance of ever taking steps to achieve their own security! But the process continues:

> As the competition for votes increases, each candidate finds it necessary to broaden his base. He must make more promises to more people. As these promises are fulfilled, more and more people find it advantageous to lower their own level of production so they can qualify for larger appropriations from the public till. Direct payments to farmers for producing less is an example of this. So are rent subsidies and food stamps for the lower income groups . . . [And] some of the less skilled members of society learn that it is more profitable to them to cease production altogether and rely upon the relief rolls for everything. . . . [Increasingly] the expectations of some special interest group have not been met, and the government is called upon to supply the shortage. That is to say, the government is called upon to supply some "free" services. Unfortunately, the government has nothing to give any special group except what it expropriates through taxation or otherwise from some other group.
>
> The contest becomes a contest between producers and non-producers, with the government aligned on the side of the non-producers. This result has nothing to do with whether government officials are honest or dishonest, wise or stupid. They are mere agents administering a system which the citizens, acting in their capacity as voters, have demanded. It is a system that includes in its own mechanism the seeds of its own destruction. The marginal producer, whether he is a laborer or a manager, cannot avoid seeing the advantages of allowing himself to fall below the survival line, cease his contributions to those who are still further below, and qualify for a claim upon his government, and through his government upon more successful competitors, for his own support. And each individual or business enterprise that takes that step will automatically draw the producer who is only slightly higher on the economic scale just a little closer to that same survival line. Eventually all are pulled below it and are faced with the necessity of beginning over again without any prosperous neighbors upon whom they can call for help, and without any backlog of capital they can use as a starting point. [4]

And thus does the State, once it goes into the business of conferring economic benefits, cause a state of splendidly equalized destitution for everyone. The State

[4] Bertel Sparks, *op. cit.*, pp. 593–5.

itself rises from the ashes more powerful than ever: with every economic crisis a new emergency is declared, giving the State more power with the full approval of the majority of its citizens ("only for the duration of the emergency"—whose end is never in sight), until it ends up in total control of everything and everyone—which of course is just what the State wanted all along. But by that time it is too late for anyone to object.

The full story is far too long even to outline here. I shall mention only a few chapter headings in the saga of The State:

1. *Taxation.* It can usually be relied upon to increase until the point of total collapse ("take till there's nothing left to be taken").

2. *Inflation.* Even high taxation is not enough to pay for what the politicians have promised the voters, so the State increases the money supply to meet the deficit. This of course decreases the value of each dollar saved, and ultimately destroys savings, penalizes thrift, wrecks incentive, bankrupts business enterprises and creates huge unemployment. But this is only the beginning:

3. *Dictatorship.* As prices rise out of sight, demand for price controls increases. Price controls create shortages (men cannot continue to produce at a loss). Shortages create strikes, hunger riots, civil commotion as the shortages spread. From this arises a Caesar, to "take a firm hand" and "restore law and order." The economy is now totally controlled from the center (with all the inefficiency and waste that this implies), and each individual, including his wages and conditions of work (and what he may work at), is thoroughly regimented. Liberty has now been lost. Most of this scenario is probably inevitable for the U.S. in the next two decades. [5]

Other chapter headings along the way would include: (4) Depressions. The State, through its interventionist policies, is solely responsible for economic depressions. [6] (5) Poverty. The State is the cause of most of the poverty that there is in this country. If you want to eliminate poverty, eliminate State intervention in the marketplace. [7]—There are others, but the point is aptly summarized by Rose Wilder Lane, commenting on the slogan "Government should do for people what people can not do for themselves":

> *Would persons who adopt such resolutions (and say the same thing again and again, all the time, everywhere) put that idea in realistic terms and say, "Government should do nothing but compel other persons, by force, to do what those persons do not want to do?" Because, obviously, if those*

[5]See Irwin Schiff, *The Biggest Con* (Arlington House, 1976), C. V. Myers, *The Coming Deflation* (Arlington House, 1976), Clarence B. Carson, *The War on the Poor* (Arlington House, 1970), and others.
[6]See, for example, Lionel Robbins, *The Great Depression,* and Murray Rothbard, *The Great Depression.*
[7]See, e.g., Clarence B. Carson, *The War on the Poor,* and Shirley Scheibla, *Poverty Is Where the Money Is.*

> *other persons* want *to do it, they* will *do it, if it can possibly be done; so it will be done, if it can be—if they're simply let alone.*
>
> *"The people" have in fact done everything that is done; they built the houses and roads and railroads and telephones and planes, they organized the oil companies, the banks, the postal services, the schools— what didn't "the people" do? What happens is that, after they do it, the Government takes it. The government takes the roads, the postal service, the systems of communications, the banks, the markets, the stock exchange, insurance companies, schools, building trades, telegraphs and telephones, after "the people" have done all these things for themselves.*[8]

Small children are prolific with their spending proposals because their eyes are on the goodies to be attained, and they do not see the labor, the cost, the hardship and deprivation which their spending schemes would entail. Social planners are as a whole in the same category; they see the end but not the means.

These views have often been accused of being un-humanitarian. (Though President Ford is also among the big spenders—what else would you call a hundred billion dollar deficit in one year? which is more than all the profits of all American corporations put together—he occasionally vetoes a particularly virulent piece of legislation, and is accused of being un-humanitarian.) What is humanitarian about seizing other people's earnings and using them for purposes which *you* think they should be used for? While others think of the "great social gains" to be achieved (which will not occur anyway, since the State employees waste most of it—what poverty has been ended by poverty programs?), I think of the corner shopkeeper, already forced to the wall by confiscatory taxation, government inflation, and endless government regulation, trying to keep his head above water, and the effect of one government scheme after another to spend his money—what will be the effect of all this on him and others like him? Much more humanitarian are the words of the great French economist Frederic Bastiat, written in 1848:

> *How is legal plunder to be identified? Quite simply. See if the law takes from some persons what belongs to them, and gives it to the other persons to whom it does not belong. See if the law benefits one citizen at the expense of another by doing what the citizen himself cannot do without committing a crime.*[9]

The State, implemented by all the channels of communications which it controls, will use all its powers to resist such advice; and every economic incentive (and threat of deprivation) at its command will be used as well. But this in no way alters the fact that

[8]Rose Wilder Lane, in Roger L. MacBride (ed.), *The Lady and the Tycoon* (Caxton Press, 1973), pp. 332–3.
[9]Frederic Bastiat, *The Law* (Foundation for Economic Education edition, p. 21).

> . . . *The State is no proper agency for social welfare, and never will be,*
> *for exactly the same reason that an ivory paperknife is nothing to shave*
> *with. The interests of society and of the State do not coincide; any*
> *pretense that they can be made to coincide is sheer nonsense. Society gets*
> *on best when people are most happy and contented, which they are when*
> *freest to do as they please and what they please; hence society's interest is*
> *in having as little government as possible, and in keeping it as decen-*
> *tralized as possible. The State, on the other hand, is administered by*
> *job-holders; hence its interest is in having as much government as possi-*
> *ble. It is hard to imagine two sets of interests more directly opposed than*
> *these.* [10]

Those who ignore these remarks, and seek to use the coercive power of the State to impose their ideas of welfare or utopia on others, must bear a heavy moral burden—the burden of the suffering they impose (however inadvertently) on others by their actions, of the incalculable loss in human well-being.

According to Rawls, man's primary social goods are "rights and liberties, opportunities and powers, income and wealth." [11] But some of these, when put into practice, would negate others. Rawls advocates (to take one example among many) government ownership of the means of production (though not necessarily all of them). This entails not only the inefficiency and waste and corruption that regularly characterize enterprises handled by the State, from the post office on down (or up?), but the huge bureaucracy required to administer it, which always seeks to increase its own numbers and power, and over which the citizen has no direct control. [12] When one spells out the full implications of all of this, very little is left of liberty; and the ostensible reason for placing such things in the hands of government—"so that everyone can have it"—ends up as its very opposite, "there's nothing left to distribute." Any resemblance between Rawls' theory and justice is strictly coincidental.

Dr. Burrill, like most of his colleagues, considers some ends so important that he would use the coercive apparatus of the State to enforce his ideals on everyone. He concludes that the marketplace is in need of improvement through State intervention (presumably along the lines of his own ideals), and that we need "a general justification of the entrepreneurial system as it stands." As it stands! As if there were anything left of the entrepreneurial system in this country but a mangled hulk, with a few crumbs thrown out by omnipotent government to produce and make money so that the State could confiscate it! as if this country still had a live and functioning "entrepreneurial system" instead of what we have now, a fascist-type State in which the State has a life-and-death stranglehold on every industry, every trade, every farm, every enterprise that exists! Is this battered ruin

[10] Albert Jay Nock, *Cogitations*, p. 40.

[11] John Rawls, *A Theory of Justice* (Harvard University Press, 1971), p. 91.

[12] For many examples of this, in the context of American history, see William Wooldridge, *Uncle Sam the Monopoly Man* (Arlington House, 1970).

to be "improved" by still further interventions by the State? And what justifies one person in imposing *his* ideals on *everyone* through the coercive machinery of the State?"[13]

It matters little whether Oppenheimer's account of the origins of the State is correct. (It surely is in most cases, but there are very significant differences in the case of the origin of the U.S.A.) It matters much more what the State is doing *now*. Whether the State was conceived and born in sin is less important than whether it is involved in sin now. And there is little doubt that, whatever its origin, sinning is currently its principal activity.

In a remarkably prescient letter to one H. S. Randall of New York, the British historian Thomas Macaulay wrote (May 23, 1857):

> *The day will come when . . . a multitude of people will choose the legislature. Is it possible to doubt what sort of legislature will be chosen? On the one side is a statesman preaching patience, respect for rights, strict observance of the public faith. On the other is the demagogue ranting about the tyranny of capitalism . . . Which of the Candidates is likely to be preferred. . . ? I seriously apprehend that you will, in some season of adversity, do things which will prevent prosperity from returning; that you will act like some people in a year of scarcity: devour all the seed corn and thus make next year a year, not of scarcity but of absolute failure. There will be, I fear, spoliation. This spoliation will increase distress. The distress will produce fresh spoliation. There is nothing to stay you. Your Constitution is all sail and no anchor. When Society has entered on this downward progress, either civilization or liberty must perish. Either some Caesar or Napolean will seize the reins of government with a strong hand, or your Republic will be as fearfully plundered and laid waste by barbarians in the twentieth century as the Roman Empire in the fifth: with this difference, that the Huns and Vandals who ravaged the Roman Empire came from without, and that your Huns and Vandals will have been engendered within your country, by your own institutions.*[14]

The State, says Robert Paul Wolff in his *In Defense of Anarchism,* wields great *power* over us—but whence derives its *authority* (the moral right to wield that power)? In a telling exposition of the distinction, he finds no basis for any such authority; nor does he succeed in solving this problem in the later (more pragmatic) sections of the book. (Even if a contract theory would help—and as Hume cogently argued, it wouldn't—there was in fact no such contract. Unlike other organizations such as churches and clubs, no one contracted to be ruled by the State.)

[13] See John Hospers, *Libertarianism* (Nash, 1971); also Robert Nozick, *Anarchy, State, and Utopia* (Basic Books, 1975); Frederic Bastiat, *The Law*; Henry Hazlitt, *Economics in One Lesson* (Harper, 1946); Ludwig von Mises' books *Socialism; Bureaucracy;* and *Omnipotent Government* (all Yale University Press).

[14] For similar predictions, see Alexis de Toqueville, *Democracy in America,* 1840.

In all existing States, some individuals (through their representatives) get hold of the State apparatus to enforce their ideas of a good society on others, including those who find it useless, repellent, or immoral. A would like to impose his plan on B and C (they would be pawns on *his* chessboard); B would impose his plan on A and C; and so on. But, observed Bastiat,

> . . . *by what right does the law force me to conform to the social plan of Mr. A or Mr. B or Mr. C? If the law has a moral right to do this, why does it not, then, force these gentlemen to submit to* my *plans? Is it logical to suppose that nature has not given* me *sufficient imagination to dream up a utopia also? Should the law choose one fantasy among many, and put the organized force of government at its service only?* [15]

Am I then committed to anarchism? Not necessarily, though as it has been worked out in detail by numerous writers, with provisions for a system of private defense and courts, I consider it greatly preferable to the leviathan we have today. [16] One of the greatest and least appreciated of political philosophers, Herbert Spencer, was not an anarchist. [17] He set forth "The Law of Equal Freedom": "Each man should be free to act as he chooses, provided he trenches not on the equal freedom of each other man to act as he chooses." Then he attempted to resolve the "problem of political authority" as follows, in the chapter "The Right to Ignore the State" (omitted from most subsequent editions) of his book *Social Statics:*

> . . . *we can not choose but admit the right of the citizen to adopt a condition of* voluntary outlawry. *If every man has freedom to do all that he wills, provided he infringes not on the equal freedom of any others, then he is free to* drop connection with the State—*to relinquish its protection and to refuse paying toward its support. It is self-evident that in so behaving he in no way trenches upon the liberty of others, for his position is a passive one, and while passive he cannot become an aggressor* . . . *He cannot be compelled to continue one of a political corporation without a breach of the moral law, seeing that citizenship involves payment of taxes; and the taking away of a man's property against his will is an infringement of his rights.* Government being simply an agent employed in common by a number of individuals to secure to them certain advantages, the very nature of the connection implies that it is for each to say whether he will employ such an agent or not. *If any one of them determines to ignore this mutual-safety*

[15] Bastiat, *The Law,* p. 71.

[16] See, for example, Morris and Linda Tannehill, *The Market for Liberty,* 1970; David Friedman, *The Machinery of Freedom* (Anchor Doubleday, 1973); Leonard Krimerman and Lewis Perry (ed.), *Patterns of Anarchy* (Anchor Doubleday, 1966); Lysander Spooner, *The Constitution of No Authority;* James J. Martin (ed.), *Men against the State* (De Kalb, Ill.: Adrian Allen Associates, 1953); also Chapter 11 of J. Hospers, *Libertarianism* (Nash, 1971).

[17] See his monumental work, *The Man versus the State* (1884; reprinted by Caxton Press, 1940).

confederation, nothing can be said except that he loses all claim to its
good offices and exposes himself to the danger of maltreatment—a thing
he is quite at liberty to do if he likes. He cannot be coerced into political
combination without breach of the Law of Equal Freedom; he can with-
draw from it without committing any such breach, and he has therefore a
right so to withdraw. [18]

These words of Spencer seem to me to contain the core of any political philosophy worthy of the name. No other provides sufficiently for voluntary consent and human liberty (or as Wolff says, autonomy), not to mention such other human values as individuality, enduring prosperity, creative opportunity, and peace.

[18] Herbert Spencer, *Social Statics*, 1845, p. 185. Italics mine.

A Kantian Conception of
Equality*
•

John Rawls

My aim in these remarks is to give a brief account of the conception of equality that underlies the view expressed in *A Theory of Justice* and the principles considered there. I hope to state the fundamental intuitive idea simply and informally; and so I make no attempt to sketch the argument from the original position.[1] In fact, this construction is not mentioned until the end and then only to indicate its role in giving a Kantian interpretation to the conception of equality already presented.

I

When fully articulated, any conception of justice expresses a conception of the person, of the relations between persons, and of the general structure and ends of social cooperation. To accept the principles that represent a conception of justice

John Rawls, "A Kantian Conception of Equality," *Cambridge Review*, February 1975, pp. 94–99. Reprinted in its entirety, by permission, with an addition suggested by the author.

John Rawls is James Bryant Conant University Professor of philosophy at Harvard University. He is the author of many papers in political and moral philosophy in addition to his major and influential work, *A Theory of Justice* (1971).

*Sections I, III and IV of this discussion draw upon sections I and III of "Reply to Alexander and Musgrave," *Quarterly Journal of Economics*, November, 1974. Sections II, V and VI of that paper take up some questions about the argument from the original position.

[1]The argument in *A Theory of Justice* was likewise informal in that I argued for the principles of justice by considering the balance of reasons in their favor given a short list of traditional philosophical conceptions. It appears, however, that formal arguments may be possible. Steven Strasnick has found a proof that certain familiar conditions on social choice functions (which it seems natural to associate with the original position), when conjoined with a principle of preference priority, entail the difference principle. He has also shown that a form of the difference principle follows once Arrow's independence condition (used in the proof of the impossibility theorem) is modified to accommodate the notion of preference priority. See Steven Strasnick, "The Problem of Social Choice: Arrow to Rawls," *Philosophy and Public Affairs* 5, no. 3 (Spring 1976).

is at the same time to accept an ideal of the person; and in acting from these principles we realise such an ideal. Let us begin, then, by trying to describe the kind of person we might want to be and the form of society we might wish to live in and to shape our interests and character. In this way we arrive at the notion of a well-ordered society. I shall first describe this notion and then use it to explain a Kantian conception of equality.

First of all, a well-ordered society is effectively regulated by a public conception of justice. That is, it is a society all of whose members accept, and know that the others accept, the same principles (the same conception) of justice. It is also the case that basic social institutions and their arrangement into one scheme (the basic structure) actually satisfy, and are on good grounds believed by everyone to satisfy, these principles. Finally, publicity also implies that the public conception is founded on reasonable beliefs that have been established by generally accepted methods of inquiry; and the same is true of the application of its principles to basic social arrangements. This last aspect of publicity does not mean that everyone holds the same religious, moral, and theoretical beliefs; on the contrary, there are assumed to be sharp and indeed irreconcilable differences on such questions. But at the same time there is a shared understanding that the principles of justice, and their application to the basic structure of society, should be determined by considerations and evidence that are supported by rational procedures commonly recognised.

Secondly, I suppose that the members of a well-ordered society are, and view themselves as, free and equal moral persons. They are moral persons in that, once they have reached the age of reason, each has, and views the others as having, a realised sense of justice; and this sentiment informs their conduct for the most part. That they are equal is expressed by the supposition that they each have, and view themselves as having, a right to equal respect and consideration in determining the principles by which the basic arrangements of their society are to be regulated. Finally, we express their being free by stipulating that they each have, and view themselves as having, fundamental aims and higher-order interests (a conception of their good) in the name of which it is legitimate to make claims on one another in the design of their institutions. At the same time, as free persons they do not think of themselves as inevitably bound to, or as identical with, the pursuit of any particular array of fundamental interests that they may have at any given time; instead, they conceive of themselves as capable of revising and altering these final ends and they give priority to preserving their liberty in this regard.

In addition, I assume that a well-ordered society is stable relative to its conception of justice. This means that social institutions generate an effective supporting sense of justice. Regarding society as a going concern, its members acquire as they grow up an allegiance to the public conception and this allegiance usually overcomes the temptations and strains of social life.

Now we are here concerned with a conception of justice and the idea of equality that belongs to it. Thus, let us suppose that a well-ordered society exists under circumstances of justice. These necessitate some conception of justice and give point to its special role. First, moderate scarcity obtains. This means that although social cooperation is productive and mutually advantageous (one person's or group's gain need not be another's loss), natural resources and the state of technology are such that the fruits of joint efforts fall short of the claims that people make. And second, persons and associations have contrary conceptions of the good that lead them to make conflicting claims on one another; and they also hold opposing religious, philosophical, and moral convictions (on matters the public conception leaves open) as well as different ways of evaluating arguments and evidence in many important cases. Given these circumstances, the members of a well-ordered society are not indifferent as to how the benefits produced by their cooperation are distributed. A set of principles is required to judge between social arrangements that shape this division of advantages. Thus the role of the principles of justice is to assign rights and duties in the basic structure of society and to specify the manner in which institutions are to influence the overall distribution of the returns from social cooperation. The basic structure is the primary subject of justice and that to which the principles of justice in the first instance apply.

It is perhaps useful to observe that the notion of a well-ordered society is an extension of the idea of religious toleration. Consider a pluralistic society, divided along religious, ethnic, or cultural, lines in which the various groups have reached a firm understanding on the scheme of principles to regulate their fundamental institutions. While they have deep differences about other things, there is public agreement on this framework of principles and citizens are attached to it. A well-ordered society has not attained social harmony in all things, if indeed that would be desirable; but it has achieved a large measure of justice and established a basis for civic friendship, which makes people's secure association together possible.

II

The notion of a well-ordered society assumes that the basic structure, the fundamental social institutions and their arrangement into one scheme, is the primary subject of justice. What is the reason for this assumption? First of all, any discussion of social justice must take the nature of the basic structure into account. Suppose we begin with the initially attractive idea that the social process should be allowed to develop over time as free agreements fairly arrived at and fully honored require. Straightaway we need an account of when agreements are free and the conditions under which they are reached are fair. In addition, while these conditions may be satisfied at an earlier time, the accumulated results of agreements in conjunction with social and historical contingencies are likely to change institutions and opportunities so that the conditions for free and fair agreements no longer hold. The basic structure specifies the background conditions against which the actions of individuals, groups, and associations take place. Unless this structure is regulated and corrected so as to be just over time, the social process with its procedures and outcomes is no longer just, however free and fair particular transactions may look to us when viewed by themselves. We recognise this principle when we say that the distribution resulting from voluntary market transactions will not in general be fair unless the antecedent distribution of income and wealth and the structure of the market is fair. Thus we seem forced to start with an account of a just basic structure. It's as if the most important agreement is that which establishes the principles to govern this structure. Moreover, these principles must be acknowledged ahead of time, as it were. To agree to them now, when everyone knows their present situation, would enable some to take unfair advantage of social and natural contingencies, and of the results of historical accidents and accumulations.

Other considerations also support taking the basic structure as the primary subject of justice. It has always been recognised that the social system shapes the desires and aspirations of its members; it determines in large part the kind of persons they want to be as well as the kind of persons they are. Thus an economic system is not only an institutional device for satisfying existing wants and desires but a way of fashioning wants and desires in the future. By what principles are we to regulate a scheme of institutions that has such fundamental consequences for our view of ourselves and for our interests and aims? This question becomes all the more crucial when we consider that the basic structure contains social and economic inequalities. I assume that these are necessary, or highly advantageous, for various reasons: they are required to maintain and to run social arrangements, or to serve as incentives; or perhaps they are a way to put resources in the hands of those who can make the best social use of them; and so on. In any case, given these inequalities, individuals' life-prospects are bound to be importantly affected by their family and class origins, by their natural endowments and the chance contingencies of their (particularly early) development, and by other accidents over the course of their lives. The social structure, therefore, limits people's ambitions and hopes in different ways, for they will with reason view themselves in part according to their place in it and take into account the means and opportunities they can realistically expect.

The justice of the basic structure is, then, of predominant importance. The first problem of justice is to determine the principles to regulate inequalities and to adjust the profound and long-lasting effects of social, natural, and historical contingencies, particularly since these contingencies combined with inequalities generate tendencies that, when left to themselves, are sharply at odds with the freedom and equality appropriate for a well-ordered society. In view of the special role of the basic structure, we cannot assume that the principles suitable to it are natural applications, or even extensions, of the familiar principles governing the actions of individuals and associations in everyday life which take place within its framework. Most likely we shall have to loosen ourselves from our ordinary perspective and take a more comprehensive viewpoint.

III

I shall now state and explain two principles of justice, and then discuss the appropriateness of these principles for a well-ordered society. They read as follows:

1. Each person has an equal right to the most extensive scheme of equal basic liberties compatible with a similar scheme of liberties for all.

2. Social and economic inequalities are to meet two conditions: they must be (a) to the greatest expected benefit of the least advantaged; and (b) attached to offices and positions open to all under conditions of fair opportunity.

The first of these principles is to take priority over the second; and the measure of benefit to the least advantaged is specified in terms of an index of social primary goods. These goods I define as rights, liberties, and opportunities, income and wealth, and the social bases of self-respect. Individuals are assumed to want these goods whatever else they want, or whatever their final ends, 'The least advantaged are defined, very roughly, as the overlap between those who are least favored by each of the three main kinds of contingencies. Thus this group includes persons whose family and class origins are more disadvantaged than others, whose natural endowments have permitted them to fare less well, and whose fortune and luck have been relatively less favourable, all within the normal range (as noted below) and with the relevant measures based on social primary goods. Various refinements are no doubt necessary, but this definition of the least advantaged suitably expresses the link with the problem of contingency and should suffice for our purposes here.

I also suppose that everyone has physical needs and psychological capacities within the normal range, so that the problems of special health care and of how to treat the mentally defective do not arise. Besides prematurely introducing difficult questions that may take us beyond the theory of justice, the consideration of these hard cases can distract our moral perception by leading us to think of people distant from us whose fate arouses pity and anxiety. Whereas the first problem of justice concerns the relations among those who in the normal course of things are full and active participants in society and directly or indirectly associated together over the whole course of their life.

Now the members of a well-ordered society are free and equal; so let us first consider the fittingness of the two principles to their freedom, and then to their equality. These principles reflect two aspects of their freedom, namely, liberty and responsibility, which I take up in turn. In regard to liberty, recall that people in a well-ordered society view themselves as having fundamental aims and interests which they must protect, if this is possible. It is partly in the name of these interests that they have a right to equal consideration and respect in the design of their society. A familiar historical example is the religious interest; the interest in the integrity of the person, freedom from psychological oppression and from physical assault and dismemberment is another. The notion of a well-ordered society leaves open what particular expression these interests take; only their general form is specified. But individuals do have interests of the requisite kind and the basic liberties necessary for their protection are guaranteed by the first principle.

It is essential to observe that these liberties are given by a list of liberties; important among these are freedom of thought and liberty of conscience, freedom of the person and political liberty. These liberties have a central range of application within which they can be limited and compromised only when they conflict with other basic liberties. Since they may be limited when they clash with one another, none of these liberties is absolute; but however they are adjusted to form one system, this system is to be the same for all. It is difficult, perhaps impossible, to give a complete definition of these liberties independently from the particular circumstances, social, economic, and technological, of a given well-ordered society. Yet the hypothesis is that the general form of such a list could be devised with sufficient exactness to sustain this conception of justice. Of course, liberties not on the list, for example, the right to own certain kinds of property (e.g., means of production), and freedom of contract as understood by the doctrine of laissez-faire, are not basic; and so they are not protected by the priority of the first principle.[2]

One reason, then, for holding the two principles suitable for a well-ordered society is that they assure the protection of the fundamental interests that members of such a society are presumed to have. Further reasons for this conclusion can be given by describing in more detail the notion of a free person. Thus we may suppose that such persons regard themselves as having a highest-order interest in how all their other interests, including even their fundamental ones, are shaped and regulated by social institutions. As I noted earlier, they do not think of themselves as unavoidably tied to any particular array of fundamental interests; instead they view themselves as capable of revising and changing these final ends. They wish, therefore, to give priority to their liberty to do this, and so their original allegiance and continued devotion to their ends are to be formed and affirmed under conditions that are free. Or, expressed another way, members of a well-ordered society are viewed as responsible for their fundamental interests and ends. While as members of particular associations some may decide in practice to yield much of this responsibility to others, the basic structure cannot be arranged so as to prevent people from developing their capacity to be responsible, or to obstruct their exercise of it once they attain it. Social arrangements must respect their autonomy and this points to the appropriateness of the two principles.

IV

These last remarks about responsibility may be elaborated further in connection with the role of social primary goods. As already stated, these are things that people in a well-ordered society may be presumed to want, whatever their final ends. And the two principles assess the basic structure in terms of certain of these goods: rights, liberties, and opportunities, income and wealth, and the social bases of self-respect. The latter are features of the basic structure that may reasonably be expected to affect people's self-respect and self-esteem (these are not the same) in important ways.[3] Part (a) of the second principle (the difference principle, or as economists prefer to say, the maximin criterion) uses an index of these goods to determine the least advantaged. Now certainly there are difficulties in working

[2]This paragraph confirms H. L. A. Hart's interpretation. See his discussion of liberty and its priority, *Chicago Law Review*, April, 1973, pp. 536–40.

[3]I discuss certain problems in interpreting the account of primary goods in "Fairness to Goodness," *Philosophical Review* 84 (October 1975): 536–54.

out a satisfactory index, but I shall leave these aside. Two points are particularly relevant here: first, social primary goods are certain objective characteristics of social institutions and of people's situation with respect of them; and second, the same index of these goods is used to compare everyone's social circumstances. It is clear, then, that although the index provides a basis for interpersonal comparisons for the purposes of justice, it is not a measure of individuals' overall satisfaction or dissatisfaction. Of course, the precise weights adopted in such an index cannot be laid down ahead of time, for these should be adjusted, to some degree at least, in view of social conditions. What can be settled initially is certain constraints on these weights, as illustrated by the priority of the first principle.

Now, that the responsibility of free persons is implicit in the use of primary goods can be seen in the following way. We are assuming that people are able to control and to revise their wants and desires in the light of circumstances and that they are to have responsibility for doing so, provided that the principles of justice are fulfilled, as they are in a well-ordered society. Persons do not take their wants and desires as determined by happenings beyond their control. We are not, so to speak, assailed by them, as we are perhaps by disease and illness so that wants and desires fail to support claims to the means of satisfaction in the way that disease and illness support claims to medicine and treatment.

Of course, it is not suggested that people must modify their desires and ends whatever their circumstances. The doctrine of primary goods does not demand the stoic virtues. Society for its part bears the responsibility for upholding the principles of justice and securing for everyone a fair share of primary goods (as determined by the difference principle) within a framework of equal liberty and fair equality of opportunity. It is within the limits of this division of responsibility that individuals and associations are expected to form and moderate their aims and wants. Thus among the members of a well-ordered society there is an understanding that as citizens they will press claims for only certain kinds of things, as allowed for by the principles of justice. Passionate convictions and zealous aspirations do not, as such, give anyone a claim upon social resources or the design of social institutions. For the purposes of justice, the appropriate basis of interpersonal comparisons is the index of primary goods and not strength of feeling or intensity of desire. The theory of primary goods is an extension of the notion of needs, which are distinct from aspirations and desires. One might say, then, that as citizens the members of a well-ordered society collectively take responsibility for dealing justly with one another founded on a public and objective measure of (extended) needs, while as individuals and members of associations they take responsibility for their preferences and devotions.

V

I now take up the appropriateness of the two principles in view of the equality of the members of a well-ordered society. The principles of equal liberty and fair opportunity (part (b) of the second principle) are a natural expression of this equality; and I assume, therefore, that such a society is one in which some form of democracy exists. Thus our question is: by what principle can members of a democratic society permit the tendencies of the basic structure to be deeply affected by social chance, and natural and historical contingencies?

Now since we are regarding citizens as free and equal moral persons (the priority of the first principle of equal liberty gives institutional expression to this), the obvious starting point is to suppose that all other social primary goods, and in particular income and wealth, should be equal: everyone should have an equal share. But society must take organizational requirements and economic efficiency into account. So it is unreasonable to stop at equal division. The basic structure should allow inequalities so long as these improve everyone's situation, including that of the least advantaged, provided these inequalities are consistent with equal liberty and fair opportunity. Because we start from equal shares, those who benefit least have, so to speak, a veto; and thus we arrive at the difference principle. Taking equality as the basis of comparison those who have gained more must do so on terms that are justifiable to those who have gained the least.

In explaining this principle, several matters should be kept in mind. First of all, it applies in the first instance to the main public principles and policies that regulate social and economic inequalities. It is used to adjust the system of entitlements and rewards, and the standards and precepts that this system employs. Thus the difference principle holds, for example, for income and property taxation, for fiscal and economic policy; it does not apply to particular transactions or distributions, nor, in general, to small scale and local decisions, but rather to the background against which these take place. No observable pattern is required of actual distributions, nor even any measure of the degree of equality (such as the Gini coefficient) that might be computed from these.[4] What is enjoined is that the inequalities make a functional contribution to those least favoured. Finally, the aim is not to eliminate the various contingencies, for some such contingencies seem inevitable. Thus even if an equal distribution of natural assets seemed more in keeping with the equality of free persons, the question of redistributing these assets (were this conceivable) does not arise, since it is incompatible with the integrity of the person. Nor need we make any specific assumptions about how great these variations are; we only suppose that, as realized in later life, they are influenced by all three kinds of contingencies. The question, then, is by what criterion a democratic society is to organize cooperation and arrange the system of entitlements that encourages and rewards productive efforts? We have a right to our natural abilities and a right to whatever we become entitled to by taking part in a fair social process. The problem is to characterise this process.[5]

At first sight, it may appear that the difference principle is arbitrarily biased towards the least favoured. But suppose, for simplicity, that there are only two groups, one significantly more fortunate than the other. Society could

[4]For a discussion of such measures, see A. K. Sen, *On Economic Inequality* (Oxford, 1973), chap. 2.
[5]The last part of this paragraph alludes to some objections raised by Robert Nozick in his *Anarchy, State, and Utopia* (New York, 1974), esp. pp. 213, 229.

maximise the expectations of either group but not both, since we can maximise with respect to only one aim at a time. It seems plain that society should not do the best it can for those initially more advantaged; so if we reject the difference principle, we must prefer maximising some weighted mean of the two expectations. But how should this weighted mean be specified? Should society proceed as if we had an equal chance of being in either group (in proportion to their size) and determine the mean that maximises this purely hypothetical expectation? Now it is true that we sometimes agree to draw lots but normally only to things that cannot be appropriately divided or else cannot be enjoyed or suffered in common.[6] And we are willing to use the lottery principle even in matters of lasting importance if there is no other way out. (Consider the example of conscription.) But to appeal to it in regulating the basic structure itself would be extraordinary. There is no necessity for society as an enduring system to invoke the lottery principle in this case; nor is there any reason for free and equal persons to allow their relations over the whole course of their life to be significantly affected by contingencies to the greater advantage of those already favored by these accidents. No one had an antecedent claim to be benefited in this way; and so to maximise a weighted mean is, so to speak, to favour the more fortunate twice over. Society can, however, adopt the difference principle to arrange inequalities so that social and natural contingencies are efficiently used to the benefit of all, taking equal division as a benchmark. So while natural assets cannot be divided evenly, or directly enjoyed or suffered in common, the results of their productive efforts can be allocated in ways consistent with an initial equality. Those favoured by social and natural contingencies regard themselves as already compensated, as it were, by advantages to which no one (including themselves) had a prior claim. Thus they think the difference principle appropriate for regulating the system of entitlements and inequalities.

VI

The conception of equality contained in the principles of justice I have described as Kantian. I shall conclude by mentioning very briefly the reasons for this description. Of course, I do not mean that this conception is literally Kant's conception, but rather that it is one of no doubt several conceptions sufficiently similar to essential parts of his doctrine to make the adjective appropriate. Much depends on what one counts as essential. Kant's view is marked by a number of dualisms, in particular, the dualisms between the necessary and the contingent, form and content, reason and desire, and noumena and phenomena. To abandon these dualisms as he meant them is, for many, to abandon what is distinctive in his theory. I believe otherwise. His moral conception has a characteristic structure that is more clearly discernible when these dualisms are not taken in the sense he gave them but reinterpreted and their moral force reformulated within the scope of an empirical theory. One of the aims of A Theory of Justice was to indicate how this might be done.

[6]At this point I adapt some remarks of Hobbes. See The Leviathan, Ch. 15, under the thirteenth and fourteenth laws of nature.

To suggest the main idea, think of the notion of a well-ordered society as an interpretation of the idea of a kingdom of ends thought of as a human society under circumstances of justice. Now the members of such a society are free and equal and so our problem is to find a rendering of freedom and equality that it is natural to describe as Kantian; and since Kant distinguished between positive and negative freedom, we must make room for this contrast. At this point I resorted to the idea of the original position: I supposed that the conception of justice suitable for a well-ordered society is the one that would be agreed to in a hypothetical situation that is fair between individuals conceived as free and equal moral persons, that is, as members of such a society. Fairness of the circumstances under which agreement is reached transfers to the fairness of the principles agreed to. The original position was designed so that the conception of justice that resulted would be appropriate.

Particularly important among the features of the original position for the interpretation of negative freedom are the limits on information, which I called the veil of ignorance. Now there is a stronger and a weaker form of these limits. The weaker supposes that we begin with full information, or else that which we possess in everyday life, and then proceed to eliminate only the information that would lead to partiality and bias. The stronger form has a Kantian explanation: we start from no information at all; for by negative freedom Kant means being able to act independently from the determination of alien causes; to act from natural necessity is to subject oneself to the heteronomy of nature. We interpret this as requiring that the conception of justice that regulates the basic structure, with its deep and long-lasting effects on our common life, should not be adopted on grounds that rest on a knowledge of the various contingencies. Thus when this conception is agreed to, knowledge of our social position, our peculiar desires and interests, or of the various outcomes and configurations of natural and historical accident is excluded. One allows only that information required for a rational agreement. This means that, so far as possible, only the general laws of nature are known together with such particular facts as are implied by the circumstances of justice.

Of course, we must endow the parties with some motivation, otherwise no acknowledgement would be forthcoming. Kant's discussion in the *Groundwork* of the second pair of examples indicates, I believe, that in applying the procedure of the categorical imperative he tacitly relied upon some account of primary goods. In any case, if the two principles would be adopted in the original position with its limits on information, the conception of equality they contain would be Kantian in the sense that by acting from this conception the members of a well-ordered society would express their negative freedom. They would have succeeded in regulating the basic structure and its profound consequences on their persons and mutual relationships by principles the grounds for which are suitably independent from chance and contingency.

In order to provide an interpretation of positive freedom, two things are necessary: first, that the parties are conceived as free and equal moral persons must play a decisive part in their adoption of the conception of justice; and second, the principles of this conception must have a content appropriate to express this determining view of persons and must apply to the controlling institutional subject.

Now if correct, the argument from the original position seems to meet these conditions. The assumption that the parties are free and equal moral persons does have an essential role in this argument; and as regards content and application, these principles express, on their public face as it were, the conception of the person that is realised in a well-ordered society. They give priority to the basic liberties, regard individuals as free and responsible masters of their aims and desires, and all are to share equally in the means for the attainment of ends unless the situation of everyone can be improved, taking equal division as the starting point. A society that realized these principles would attain positive freedom, for these principles reflect the features of persons that determined their selection and so express a conception they give to themselves.

A Political Theory of Property

•

C. B. Macpherson

. . . The weakness of the "traditional" liberal-democratic theory has been traced to its retention of the concept of man as infinite consumer and infinite appropriator: that concept of man is clearly inextricable from a concept of property. Alternatively, the failure of the traditional theory of Mill and Green has been traced to their failure to recognize that the individual property right on which they insisted meant a denial to most men of equitable access to the means of life and the means of labour, without which access men could not hope to realize their human potential: here again the concept of property is crucial.

The shortcomings of what I have called revisionist liberalism could be restated in much the same terms. So could the deficiencies of those twentieth-century political theories which have in their various ways reduced democracy to a market phenomenon. And so could the illogic of extreme neo-liberals.

The central importance of access to the means of life and the means of labour has been seen in other contexts as well. Denial or limitation of access is a means of maintaining class-divided societies, with a class domination which thwarts the humanity of the subordinate and perverts that of the dominant class; this is a condition which neither any amount of "consumers' sovereignty," nor the fairest system of distributive justice, can offset or remedy. And one main constituent of liberty itself, both "negative" and "positive," is, I have argued, this same access to the means of life and labour. The extent and distribution of that access is set by the institution of property.

Again, the dangerous flaw in liberal-democratic theory has been presented as the conflict within it between developmental power and extractive power. Progress towards the democratic goal of maximizing men's developmental powers

From *Democratic Theory: Essays in Retrieval* by C. B. Macpherson, Essay VI, "A Political Theory of Property" (Oxford: Claredon Press, 1973), pp. 120–23, 131–40. © Oxford University Press, 1973. Reprinted by permission of the author and Oxford University Press.

C. B. Macpherson is professor of political science at the University of Toronto and the author of *The Political Theory of Possessive Individualism: Hobbes to Locke* (1962) and other books.

has been seen to be impeded by the market society's retention of individual and corporate extractive powers. And extractive powers, which are the obverse of access, are maintained by an institution of property. Property in capital, which is the accumulation of extractive power, has become the measure of man. I have argued that genuine democracy, and genuine liberty, both require the absence of extractive powers. But this does not mean the absence of any institution of property. A society in which extractive powers were absent would of course also need an institution of property, if only to prevent a recurrence of types of property which support extractive powers.[1] But it would clearly need to be a very different institution of property.

So all roads lead to property. The retrieval of a genuine democratic theory, the attainment of an adequate theory of liberty, and the realization of both in practice, all require a fresh look at the theory and practice of property. How need that theory and practice change, to yield a genuinely democratic and genuinely liberal society? And what are the chances of their so changing? This will depend partly on the relation we find between the theory and the practice of property. We cannot undertake here a whole social history of property. But we can perhaps sufficiently point to an interdependence between the theory and practice to allow us to presume that an inquiry which focuses on the theory may take us to the heart of the matter.

Briefly it may be said that the theory and practice, or the concept and the institution, of property are interdependent, in that both change over time and the changes are related. As an institution, property—and any particular system of property—is a man-made device which establishes certain relations between people. Like all such devices, its maintenance requires at least the acquiescence of the bulk of the people, and the positive support of any leading classes. Such support requires a belief that the institution serves some purpose or fills some need. That belief requires, in turn, that there be a theory which both explains and justifies the institution in terms of the purpose served or the need filled. As needs change new theories are developed, and the institution itself is changed by political action. Changes in the theory and in the institution may come in either order; or they may come bit by bit, each reinforcing the other by such small stages that one cannot assign priority to either. But the general pattern seems to be, first, a change in perceived needs or wants which the institution could serve, then a change in the concept and theory of what the institution is and could be, then political action (ranging from legislation and judicial and administrative action to revolution) to change the institution. Some support for this generalization is offered in the following sections of this essay.

When the theory of property is examined, historically and logically, it turns out to be more flexible than the classical liberals or their twentieth-century followers have allowed for. The concept of property has changed more than once, and in more than one way, in the past few centuries. It changed in discernible ways with the rise of modern capitalism, and it is changing again now with the matura-

---

[1] It might be argued that in an ultimately ideal non-extractive society, from which the possessive ethos had disappeared, no institution of property would be needed. But short of that, and certainly in a transition period of indefinite duration, some institution of property would be needed.

tion of capitalism. The more fully we can understand these changes and the reasons for them, the more able we shall be to see the necessary and the possible directions of future change.

It may even be that the breakthrough of consciousness . . . which would release us from the false image of man as infinite consumer and infinite appropriator, will come through a further transformation of the notion of property, induced by changes now already visible in the institution of property itself and in the needs which it serves.

I want now to argue

(1) that the concept of property which now prevails in Western societies is largely an invention of the seventeenth and eighteenth centuries, and is fully appropriate only to an autonomous capitalist market society: this is the concept of property as (a) identical with private property—an individual (or corporate) right to exclude others from the use or benefit of something; (b) a right in or to material things rather than a right to a revenue (and even, in common usage, as the things themselves rather than the rights); and (c) having as its main function to provide an incentive to labour, as well as (or rather than) being an instrument for the exercise of human capacities;

(2) that this concept of property has already begun to change, noticeably first in respect of (b): property is increasingly being seen again as a right to a revenue; and that for most people this must now be a right to *earn* an income, which is a right of access to the means of labour;

(3) that any society which claims to be democratic (i.e. to enable individuals equally to use and develop their human capacities) will have to acknowledge that individual property must increasingly consist in the individual right not to be excluded from access to the means of labour, now mainly corporately or socially owned: so that a democratic society must broaden the concept again from property as an individual right to exclude others, by adding property as an individual right not to be excluded by others; and

(4) that the concept of property as a right of access to the means of labour (in the narrow sense of labour devoted to material production) will in turn become obsolete, as and to the extent that technological change makes current labour less necessary; that, if the concept (and the institution) of property is to be compatible with any real democracy (including any real liberal democracy), it will have to change *from* access to the means of labour *to* access to the means of a fully human life, and will therefore have to become (a) a right to a share in political power to control the uses of the amassed capital and the natural resources of the society, and (b), beyond that, a right to a kind of society, a set of power relations throughout the society, essential to a fully human life. . . .

Mid-Twentieth-Century Changes in the Concept of Property

The concept of property . . . which became dominant with the full development of capitalism in the nineteenth and twentieth centuries . . . is already undergoing changes. The most general change is that property is again being seen as a right to a revenue or an income, rather than as rights in specific material things. The change is evident in all sectors of advanced capitalist societies: the changed view is common to investors, beneficiaries of the welfare state, independent enterprisers, and wage and salary earners.

Investors, to the extent that they are pure *rentiers*, have of course always seen their property as a right to a revenue. But with the rise of the modern corporation, and the predominance of corporate property, more individual investors of all sorts become *rentiers* and become aware that that is what they are. Their property consists less of their ownership of some part of the corporation's physical plant and stock of materials and products than of their right to a revenue from the ability of the corporation to manoeuvre profitably in a very imperfect market. True, an investor may see his property as a right to expected capital gains rather than to expected dividends, but this is still a right to a revenue (a more sophisticated one, less subject perhaps to reduction by the income tax). Moreover, with the spread of affluence and of security-consciousness, increasing numbers of people have some property in the form of rights in pension funds or annuities, if not of rights to a revenue from stocks or bonds. This of course has not turned the whole population into *rentiers*, but it is making members of all classes more revenue-conscious than many of them were before.

The rise of the welfare state has created new forms of property and distributed them widely—all of them being rights to a revenue. The old-age pensioner, the unemployed, and the unemployable, may have as his sole property the right to such a revenue as his condition entitles him to receive from the state. Where in addition the state provides such things as family allowances and various free or subsidized services, almost everyone has some property in such rights to a revenue.

But while almost everyone may get some of his income from the welfare state, and increasing numbers get some of theirs (at least indirectly) as investors, most people still have to work for most of their income. Their main property is their right to *earn* an income, whether as self-employed persons or as wage or salary earners.Whichever way they earn their income, they are coming to see their main property as the right to do so, and to see that this depends on factors outside their control.

Those who may still be counted as independent enterprisers—the self-employed, from taxi operators to doctors—find that their property in their enterprises increasingly depends on governmental licences to ply their trade or exercise their profession: their property is an expectation of a revenue dependent on their conformity to increasingly stringent regulations laid down by the state or its agents "in the public interest."[2]

[2]The proliferation of the regulatory powers of the state, and the extent to which this has replaced the older forms of property by a "new property" in government licences (and government largess), is strikingly documented by Professor Charles Reich: "The New Property," *Yale Law Journal*, Vol. 73 (April 1964). A shorter version of his paper, with the same title, is printed in *The Public Interest*, no. 3 (Spring 1966). . . .

However, the bulk of those whose main income is from their work is now made up of wage and salary earners. And they are increasingly coming to see their property as the right to a job, the right to be employed. Since they are by definition employed by others, that right amounts to a right of access to the means of labour which they do not own. What is new is not the fact, but the increasing perception of it.

That an individual's access to the means of labour is his most important property has been true for most men in most societies. For wherever a society's flow of income requires the current labour of most of its members, and wherever most individuals' incomes depend on their contributing their labour, most men's property in the means of life depends on their access to the means of labour. In a simple society most might have access by communal or tribal rights, or, where there was private property in land but still plenty of land, most might have access by owning, that is, having some exclusive right in, the land or materials which were their necessary means of labour. In a capitalist society, where most do not own their own means of labour, their right to the means of life is reduced to their right of access to means of labour owned by others.

It was all very well for Locke and subsequent liberal theorists to suggest that a man's labour was his most important property: the fact was that the value of a man's labour was zero if he had no access to land or capital. The value of the property in one's labour depended on one's access to the means of labour owned by others. It has been so ever since the predominance of the capitalist market system. It still is so. One's main property is still, for most men, one's right of access to the means of labour. This, as I have said, is not new.

What is new in mid-twentieth century is that this fact is being more widely recognized. It was seen in the nineteenth century only by a handful of radicals and socialists: it is now seen by a large part of the non-socialist organized labour movement, which thinks of the worker's main property as his right to the job. This is a considerable transformation of the concept of property. And it can have explosive consequences. For to see as one's property a right to earn an income through employment is to see (or to come close to seeing) as one's property a right of access to some of the existent means of labour, that is, to some of the accumulated productive resources of the whole society (natural resources plus the productive resources created by past labour), no matter by whom they are owned.

An Impending Change in the
Concept of Property

It can now be forecast that the concept of property as solely private property, the right to exclude others from some use or benefit of something, which is already a concept of an individual right to a revenue, will have to be broadened to include property as an individual right not to be excluded from the use or benefit of the accumulated productive resources of the whole society.

The forecast is made on two grounds: (a) that property as an exclusive alienable "absolute" right is no longer as much needed in the quasi-market society of the late twentieth century as it was in the earlier, relatively uncontrolled, full market society; and (b) that democratic pressures on those governments which uphold capitalist property rights are becoming strong enough that any such government which claims also to be furthering a democratic society (i.e. to be enabling individuals equally to use and develop their human capacities), will have to acknowledge that property as a right of access must be increasingly an individual right not to be excluded from access.

(a) The Change from Market to Quasi-Market Society

We noticed above that property as exclusive, alienable, "absolute," individual, or corporate rights in things was required by the full market society because and in so far as the market was expected to do the whole work of allocation of natural resources and capital and labour among possible uses. In such an autonomous market society there is very little room for common property, since common property by definition withholds from the play of the market those resources in which there is common property and so interferes with total market allocation of resources (and of labour, since the more common property there is, the less dependent on employment, i.e. the less compelled to enter his labour in the market, is each individual who lacks material productive resources of his own).

There is of course still a place in capitalist market society for some state property, such as transportation and communications facilities that are necessary for, but not profitable to, private enterprise. But such state property is sharply distinct from common property, as we have seen above. State property may assist, but common property hinders, market allocation.

As long as the market was expected to do the whole job of allocation, then, the concept of property that was needed was the concept of private, exclusive, alienable right. But now, even in the most capitalist countries, the market is no longer expected to do the whole work of allocation. We have moved from market society to quasi-market society. In all capitalist countries, the society as a whole, or the most influential sections of it, operating through the instrumentality of the welfare state and the warfare state—in any case, the regulatory state—is doing more and more of the work of allocation. Property as exclusive, alienable, "absolute," individual, or corporate rights in things therefore becomes less necessary.

This does not mean that this kind of property is any less desired by the corporations and individuals who still have it in any quantity. But it does mean that as this kind of property becomes less demonstrably necessary to the work of allocation, it becomes harder to defend this kind as the very essence of property. Again, no one would suggest that the removal or reduction of the necessity of this kind of property would by itself result in the disappearance or weakening of this as the very image of property: positive social pressures would also be required.

(b) Democratic Pressures on Governments

Democratic pressures for more equitable and more secure access to the means of labour and the means of life are clearly increasing. They are, I think, now reaching such a strength that governments which still uphold the exclusive property rights of a capitalist society, and which claim also, as they all do, that they are promoting a fully democratic society—one in which all individuals are enabled equally to use and develop their human capacities—will have to acknowledge that property can no longer be considered to consist solely of private property—an individual right to exclude others from some use or benefit of something—but must be stretched to cover the opposite kind of individual property—an individual right not to be excluded from the use or benefit of something. This means the creation, by law, either of more common property or of more guaranteed access to the means of labour and the means of life which remain privately owned, i.e. a diminution of the extent to which private property, especially in productive resources, is a right to exclude.

The pressure comes from several directions. There is the already mentioned insistence by many sectors of organized labour on "the right to the job," an insistence which the modern state and its agencies have found themselves in a weak position to resist. There is the markedly increasing public awareness of the menaces of air and water and earth pollution, which are seen as a denial of a human right to a decent environment, a denial directly attributable to the hitherto accepted idea of the sanctity of private (including corporate) property. Air and water, which hitherto had scarcely been regarded as property at all, are now being thought of as common property—a right to clean air and water is coming to be regarded as a property from which nobody should be excluded.

So the identification of property with exclusive private property, which we have seen has no standing in logic, is coming to have less standing in fact. It is no longer as much needed, and no longer as welcomed, as it was in the earlier days of the capitalist market society.

The pressures against it can only be strengthened by the logic of the situation. Private property as an institution has always needed a moral justification. The justification of private property (which became the justification of all property, as capitalism took hold and reduced common property to insignificance) has always ultimately gone back either to the individual right to life at a more than animal level (and hence a right to the means of such a life), or to the right to one's own body, hence to one's own labour, hence to the fruits of one's own labour, and hence also to the means of one's labour.

Sometimes the case is made on a ground that appears to be different from either of these, namely, that individual exclusive property is essential to individual freedom both economic and political—freedom from coerced labour and from arbitrary government. This is the case that Jefferson made much of. He argued convincingly that property in the means of one's own labour was not only rightful in itself but was also an indispensable safeguard of individual liberty. With one's own small property one could not be made subservient. And small property was the great guarantee against government tyranny as well as against economic oppression. It was to secure individual liberty, and all the virtues that can flourish only with sturdy independence, that Jefferson wanted America to remain a country of small proprietors.

This justification of property rests, in the last analysis, on the right to life at a more than animal level: freedom from coerced labour and from arbitrary government are held to be part of what is meant by a fully human life. At the same time this justification is an assertion of the right to the means of labour: the whole point is that by working on his own land or other productive resources a man can be independent and uncoerced. However, while the Jeffersonian argument is a branch of the case resting on the right of life, it is important enough to be treated separately: its emphasis on property as a prerequisite of freedom adds something important to the narrow Utilitarian case for property as a prerequisite of a flow of the consumable material means of life. So we have three principles on which individual property is based: the right to the material means of life, the right to a free life, and the right to the (current and accumulated) fruits of one's labour.

It can easily be seen that, in the circumstances of mature capitalism, all three principles require that the concept of property be broadened—that it no longer be confined to the individual right to exclude others, but be extended to include each individual's right not to be excluded from the use or benefit of things, and productive powers, that can be said to have been created by the joint efforts of the whole society. (i) A right to the means of life must either be a direct right, irrespective of work, to a share in the society's current output of goods and services, which is a right not to be excluded from its flow of benefits; or a right to earn an income, which requires that one should not be excluded from the use of the accumulated means of labour. (ii) A right to the fruits of one's labour requires that one should be able to labour, that is, requires access to the means of labour, or non-exclusion from the accumulated means of labour. (iii) A right to a free life can no longer be secured, as it could in Jefferson's day, by each man having his own small property in his means of labour: it can only be secured by guarantees of access on equal terms to the means of labour that are now mainly corporately or socially owned.

Thus the rationale of property, in any of its three justifications, requires the recognition of property as the right not to be excluded—either the right not to be excluded from a share in the society's whole material output, or the right not to be excluded from access to the accumulated means of labour. Of these, the latter has been up to now much the most important. But this is likely to change.

Beyond Property as Access to the Means of Labour

We can now forecast that the concept of property as essentially access to the means of labour will in turn become inadequate, as and to the extent that technological advances make current human labour less necessary; and that, if property is to be consistent with any real democracy, the concept of property will have to be broadened again to include the right to a share in political power, and, even beyond that, a right to a kind of society or set of power relations which will enable the individual to live a fully human life. This is to take to a higher level the concept of property as the prerequisite of a free life.

(a) Property as Political Power

The importance to each individual of access to the means of labour will clearly diminish if and in so far as the amount of current human labour required to produce an acceptable flow of the means of life for all diminishes. For as less labour is needed, the requirement to work is less needed. The right to *earn* an income becomes less a prerequisite or co-requisite of the right *to* an income.

Already, for technical economic reasons as well as from social and political pressures, the most advanced capitalist countries are beginning to move in the direction of providing a "guaranteed annual income" or setting up a "negative income tax." The effect of such measures is to give everyone an income (though it may at first be a small one) unrelated to work. It the amount of such income should become substantial, the right to *earn* an income would clearly decline in importance as a form of property. It is too early to say for certain whether, or when, future increases in the productivity of modern societies will so diminish the amount of socially required human labour that income can be detached entirely from labour expended. But we can say that, to the extent that this happens, property as a valuable individual right will again change its nature.

The change in that case will be more striking than any of the changes we have seen so far. It will be a change from property as a right of access to the means of labour, to property as a right to the means of a fully human life. This seems to move us back through the centuries, to bring us back again to the idea that property in the means of life (a "good" life) is the main form of property, as it was for the earliest theorists, e.g. Aristotle, before emphasis shifted to property in land and capital (the means of producing the means of life).

So it does, but the outcome is not the same. For, in the assumed circumstances of greatly increased productivity, the crucial question will no longer be how to provide a sufficient flow of the material means of life: it will be a question of getting the quality and kinds of things wanted for a full life, and, beyond that, of the quality of life itself. And both of these matters will require a property in the control of the mass of productive resources. If one envisages the extreme of an automated society in which nobody has to labour in order to produce the material means of life, the property in the massed productive resources of the whole society becomes of utmost importance. The property that would then be most important to the individual would no longer be the right of access to the means of labour; it would be instead, the right to a share in the control of the massed productive resources. That right would presumably have to be exercised politically. Political power then becomes the most important kind of property. Property, as an individual right, becomes essentially the individual's share in political power.

This becomes *the* important form of property, not only because it is the individual's guarantee of sharing equitably in the flow of consumables, in some part of which he will of course still need a property in the sense of an exclusive right. It becomes important also because only by sharing the control can he be assured of the means of the good or commodious or free life, which would then be seen to consist of more than a flow of consumables.

Property has always been seen as instrumental to life, and justified as instrumental to a fully human life. In the circumstances of material plenty which we now envisage, the relative importance, for a fully human life, of a merely sufficient flow of consumables will diminish, and the importance of all the means of a life of action and enjoyment of one's human capacities will increase.

(b) Property as a Right to a Kind of Society

If property is to remain justified as instrumental to a full life, it will have to become the right not to be excluded from the means of such a life. Property will, in such circumstances, increasingly have to become a right to a set of social relations, a right to a kind of society. It will have to include not only a right to a share in political power as instrumental in determining the kind of society, but a right to that kind of society which is instrumental to a full and free life.

The idea that individual property extends to, and that a crucially important part of it is, a right to a set of power relations that permits a full life of enjoyment and development of one's human capacities, may seem fanciful. How can such a right be reduced to a set of enforceable claims of the individual (failing which, it would not meet an essential criterion of the idea of property)? It could not easily so be reduced merely by amendments to the existing laws of property. The claims that will have to be made enforceable are much broader than those which "property" has comprised in the liberal society up to now.

There is, in principle, no reason why such broader claims could not be made enforceable, as certain rights to life and liberty are now. But I am suggesting that the broader claims will not be firmly anchored unless they are seen as property. For, in the liberal ethos which prevails in our liberal-democratic societies, property has more prestige than has almost anything else. And if the new claims are not brought under the head of property, the narrow idea of property will be used, with all the prestige of property, to combat them. In short, the now foreseeable and justifiable demands of the members of at least the most technically advanced societies cannot now be met without a new concept of property.

What makes this urgent is the fact that the conquest of scarcity is now not only foreseeable but actually foreseen. In the conditions of material scarcity that have always prevailed up to now,[3] property has been a matter of a right to a *material*

[3]To say that scarcity has always prevailed up to now and that its conquest is now foreseeable is not to say that it has all been the result of hitherto inadequate technology, or that its conquest will be automatically accomplished by technological advances. Much of the scarcity in capitalist societies is created by the very requirements of the system of capitalist production, which (i) generates ever-increasing consumer demands, in relation to which there is scarcity by definition, . . . and which (ii) distributes the whole social output in such a way that the poor are subject to real scarcity. But whether the scarcity is real or artificial, it is scarcity.

revenue. With the conquest of scarcity that is now foreseen, property must become rather a right to an *immaterial* revenue, a revenue of enjoyment of the quality of life. Such a revenue cannot be reckoned in material quantities. The right to such a revenue can only be reckoned as a right to participation in a satisfying set of social relations.

If we achieve this concept of property we shall have reached again, but now on a more effective level, and for more people, that broader idea of property that prevailed in the period just before the individual was at once released and submerged by the capitalist market—the idea that a man has a property not just in the material means of life, but in his life itself, in the realization of all his active potentialities. It is worth emphasizing here that in the seventeenth century the word "property" was used in a far wider sense than it has had ever since then. Political writers in the seventeenth century spoke of a man's property as including not only his rights in material things and revenues, but also in his life, his person, his faculties, his liberty, his conjugal affection, his honour, etc.; and material property might be ranked lower than some of the others, as it was specifically by Hobbes. [4]

The fact that property once had such a wider meaning opens up the possibility, which our narrower concept has not allowed, that property may once again be seen as more than rights in material things and revenues. The seventeenth-century broad concept of property may strike us as very odd, even quaint and unrealistic. But it seems odd only because we have become accustomed to a narrow concept which was all that was needed by and suited to a market society in which maximization of material wealth became the overriding value. Now that we have the possibility, and as I have argued the democratic need, to downgrade material maximization, the broader concept of property becomes the more realistic.

Property can and should become again a right to life and liberty; and it can now, in the measure that we conquer scarcity, become a right to a fuller and freer life, for more people, than was attainable (though it was dreamed of) in the seventeenth century. And the right to live fully cannot be less than the right to share in the determination of the power relations that prevail in the society. Property then, we may say, needs to become a right to participate in a system of power relations which will enable the individual to live a fully human life.

It may *need* become so, but *can* it become so? My argument has been that both the concept and the actual institution of property need to be broadened in this way if they are to be consistent with the needs and the possibility of a society fully democratic and fully free. I have indicated ways in which the concept, and even the institution, are beginning to change in that direction. Whether or how far those

---

[4] Of things held in propriety, those that are dearest to a man are his own life, & limbs; and in the next degree, (in most men,) those that concern conjugall affection; and after them riches and means of living" (*Leviathan*, Chapter 30, pp. 382–3, Pelican edition). Locke, when he defined property in the broad sense, also put life and liberty ahead of "estate," and "person" ahead of "goods" (*Second Treatise of Government*, sections 87, 123, 173). On seventeenth-century usage generally, see my *Political Theory of Possessive Individualism*, index entry "Property."

changes will proceed depends on both the degree of democratic pressure on governments and the extent of consciousness of what the issues are, and each of these depends partly on the other. The seriousness of the obstacles should not be underestimated. But nor should the possibility of their being overcome: not by goodwill, nor by any improbable conversion of ruling élites to a new morality; nor necessarily by traumatic revolutionary action; but by a conjuncture . . . of partial breakdowns of the political order and partial breakthroughs of public consciousness.

The former, it may now be seen, may well come through failures of the system to respond adequately to growing demands for access to the means of labour, that is, by failure to put such new limitations on exclusive property rights as are needed to meet those demands. The latter might come naturally enough as a growing, even a fairly sudden, realization that a new property in the quality of life and liberty is now within reach. And each of these changes would reinforce the other.

Rights and Dollars
●
Arthur M. Okun

American society proclaims the worth of every human being. All citizens are guaranteed equal justice and equal political rights. Everyone has a pledge of speedy response from the fire department and access to national monuments. As American citizens, we are all members of the same club.

Yet at the same time, our institutions say "find a job or go hungry," "succeed or suffer." They prod us to get ahead of our neighbors economically after telling us to stay in line socially. They award prizes that allow the big winners to feed their pets better than the losers can feed their children.

Such is the double standard of a capitalist democracy, professing and pursuing an egalitarian political and social system and simultaneously generating gaping disparities in economic well-being. This mixture of equality and inequality sometimes smacks of inconsistency and even insincerity. Yet I believe that, in many cases, the institutional arrangements represent uneasy compromises rather than fundamental inconsistencies. The contrasts among American families in living standards and in material wealth reflect a system of rewards and penalties that is intended to encourage effort and channel it into socially productive activity. To the extent that the system succeeds, it generates an efficient economy. But that pursuit of efficiency necessarily creates inequalities. And hence society faces a tradeoff between equality and efficiency.

Tradeoffs are the central study of the economist. "You can't have your cake and eat it too" is a good candidate for the fundamental theorem of economic analysis. Producing more of one thing means using labor and capital that could be devoted to more output of something else. Consuming more now means saving less for the future. Working longer impinges on leisure. The crusade against infla-

From Arthur M. Okun, *Equality and Efficiency: The Big Tradeoff* (Washington, D.C.: The Brookings Institution, 1975), pp. 1–10, 15–22. Copyright © 1975 by The Brookings Institution. Reprinted by permission.

Arthur Okun is a senior fellow at The Brookings Institution and a former chairman of the Council of Economic Advisers.

tion demands the sacrifice of output and employment—posing the tradeoff that now concerns the nation most seriously. . . .

To the economist, as to the engineer, efficiency means getting the most out of a given input. The inputs applied in production are human effort, the services of physical capital such as machines and buildings, and the endowments of nature like land and mineral resources. The outputs are thousands of different types of goods and services. If society finds a way, with the same inputs, to turn out more of some products (and no less of the others), it has scored an increase in efficiency.

This concept of efficiency implies that more is better, insofar as the "more" consists of items that people want to buy. In relying on the verdicts of consumers as indications of what they want, I, like other economists, accept people's choices as reasonably rational expressions of what makes them better off. To be sure, by a different set of criteria, it is appropriate to ask skeptically whether people are made better off (and thus whether society really becomes more efficient) through the production of more whiskey, more cigarettes, and more big cars. That inquiry raises several intriguing further questions. Why do people want the things they buy? How are their choices influenced by education, advertising, and the like? Are there criteria by which welfare can be appraised that are superior to the observation of the choices people make? Without defense and without apology, let me simply state that I will not explore those issues despite their importance. That merely reflects my choices, and I hope they are accepted as reasonably rational.

I have greater conviction in essentially ignoring a second type of criticism of the "more is better" concept of efficiency. Some warn that the economic growth that generates more output today may plunder the earth of its resources and make for lower standards of living in the future. Other economists have recently accepted the challenge of the "doomsday" school and, in my judgment, have effectively refuted its dire predictions.[1]

The concept of economic equality also poses its problems. . . . Impressionistically, I shall speak of more or less equality as implying smaller or greater disparities among families in their maintainable standards of living, which in turn implies lesser or greater disparities in the distribution of income and wealth, relative to the needs of families of different sizes. Equal standards of living would not mean that people would choose to spend their incomes and allocate their wealth identically. Economic equality would not mean sameness or drabness or uniformity, because people have vastly different tastes and preferences. Within any income stratum today, some families spend far more on housing and far less on education than do others. Economic equality is obviously different from equality of opportunity, as I shall use the terms. . . .

The presence of a tradeoff between efficiency and equality does not mean that everything that is good for one is necessarily bad for the other. Measures that might soak the rich so much as to destroy investment and hence impair the quality

---

[1] See William D. Nordhaus, "World Dynamics: Measurement without Data," *Economic Journal*, Vol. 83 (December 1973), pp. 1156–83; and Robert M. Solow, "Is the End of the World at Hand?" in Andrew Weintraub, Eli Schwartz, and J. Richard Aronson (eds.), *The Economic Growth Controversy* (International Arts and Sciences Press, 1973), pp. 39–61.

and quantity of jobs for the poor could worsen both efficiency and equality. On the other hand, techniques that improve the productivity and earnings potential of unskilled workers might benefit society with greater efficiency *and* greater equality. Nonetheless, there are places where the two goals conflict, and those pose the problems. . . .

In this chapter, I will examine the ways in which American society promotes equality (and pays some costs in terms of efficiency) by establishing social and political rights that are distributed equally and universally and that are intended to be kept out of the marketplace. Those rights affect the functioning of the economy and, at the same time, their operation is affected by the market. They lie basically in the territory of the political scientist, which is rarely invaded by the economist. But at times the economist cannot afford to ignore them. The interrelationships between market institutions and inequality are clarified when set against the background of the entire social structure, including the areas where equality is given high priority.

A society that is both democratic and capitalistic has a split-level institutional structure, and both levels need to be surveyed. When only the capitalistic level is inspected, issues concerning the distribution of material welfare are out of focus. In an economy that is based primarily on private enterprise, public efforts to promote equality represent a deliberate interference with the results generated by the marketplace, and they are rarely costless. When the question is posed as: "Should the government tamper with the market?" the self-evident answer is a resounding "No." Not surprisingly, this is a common approach among anti-egalitarian writers. Forget that the Declaration of Independence proclaims the equality of human beings, ignore the Bill of Rights, and one can write that only intellectuals—as distinguished sharply from people—care much about equality.[2] With these blinders firmly in place, egalitarianism in economics can be investigated as though it were an idiosyncrasy, perhaps even a type of neurosis.[3]

It is just as one-sided to view enormous wealth or huge incomes as symptoms of vicious or evil behavior by their owners, or as an oversight of an egalitarian society. The institutions of a market economy promote such inequality, and they are as much a part of our social framework as the civil and political institutions that pursue egalitarian goals. To some, "profits" and "rich" may be dirty words, but their views have not prevailed in the rules of the economic game.

To get a proper perspective, even an economist with no training in other social sciences had better tread—or at least tiptoe—into social and political territory. And that is where I shall begin. I shall travel through the places where society deliberately opts for equality, noting the ways these choices compromise efficiency and curb the role of the market, and examining the reasons why society may choose

[2] Irving Kristol, "About Equality," *Commentary*, Vol. 54 (November 1972), pp. 41–47.

[3] Harry G. Johnson, "Some Micro-Economic Reflections on Income and Wealth Inequalities," *Annals of the American Academy of Political and Social Science*, Vol. 409 (September 1973), p. 54. Johnson attributes the concern with inequality, in part, to "a naïve and basically infantile anthropomorphism."

to distribute some of its entitlements equally. I shall focus particularly on some of the difficulties in establishing and implementing the principle that the equally distributed rights ought not to be bought and sold for money.

The Domain of Rights

A vast number of entitlements and privileges are distributed universally and equally and free of charge to all adult citizens of the United States. Our laws bestow upon us the right to obtain equal justice, to exercise freedom of speech and religion, to vote, to take a spouse and procreate, to be free in our persons in the sense of immunity from enslavement, to disassociate ourselves from American society by emigration, as well as various claims on public services such as police protection and public education. For convenience, I shall call all of these universal entitlements "rights," recognizing that this is a broader use of the term than most political theorists employ and that it lumps together freedom of speech and free access to visit the Capitol.

Rights have their negative side as well, in the form of certain duties that are imposed on all citizens. For example, everyone has a responsibility to obey the law—anyone who would merely balance the cost of risking a prison sentence against the benefits obtainable from stealing a wallet is violating that duty. Military conscription and jury service are examples of duties assigned—in principle, if not always in practice—by random selection and not according to the preferences or status of individuals.

An obvious feature of rights—in sharp contrast with economic assets—is that they are acquired and exercised without any monetary charge. Because citizens do not normally have to pay a price for using their rights,[4] they lack the usual incentive to economize on exercising them. If the fire department charged for its services, people would be at least a little more reluctant to turn in an alarm and perhaps a bit more systematic about fire prevention. If speaking out on public issues had a price tag, citizens might be more thoughtful before they sounded off—and perhaps that would improve the quality of debate. But society does not try to ration the exercise of rights.

Second, because rights are universally distributed, they do not invoke the economist's principle of comparative advantage that tells people to specialize in the things they do particularly well. Everybody can get into the act, including some who are not talented actors. Some people with great skill in their civilian pursuits make hopelessly inept soldiers; thus, the draft cannot provide the most efficient army, yet it is the way we raise wartime military forces. Surely, voters do not have equal ability, equal information or education, or an equal stake in political decisions. Since those decisions are concentrated on taxing and spending, property owners and taxpayers may have a greater stake in them; that relative difference is ignored in the acceptance of universal suffrage. We have dismissed Edmund Burke's con-

[4]Money may be relevant indirectly. Visiting the Capitol involves the cost of transportation. More seriously, the cost of obtaining equal justice before the law creates problems. . . .

tention that a limitation of suffrage to property owners might help to ensure a thoughtful approach to social policy.[5] Similarly, although children are excluded from voting rights, we forgo the use of even a minimum test of competence like literacy as a qualification.

We have rejected John Stuart Mill's proposal that differential voting powers should be based on achievement and intelligence, despite his insistence that such a system was "not . . . necessarily invidious. . . ."[6] Recently, a writer on the op-ed page of the *New York Times* reinvented Mill's wheel, proposing a "system of proportional representation that would weight each man's vote in proportion to his demonstrated capability to make intelligent choices."[7] Such proposals imply that the division of labor is relevant to the distribution of voting rights, and given that fundamental premise, they might make sense. But rejecting the premise, many of us find them preposterous.

A third characteristic of rights is that they are not distributed as incentives, or as rewards and penalties. Unlike the dollar prizes of the marketplace or the nonpecuniary honors and awards elsewhere, extra rights and duties are not used to channel behavior into socially constructive pursuits. In principle, people could be offered extra votes or exemptions from the draft in recognition of outstanding performance, and those rewards might serve as added incentives to productive achievement. But only in a few limited and extreme cases, like the loss of the right to vote by convicted felons, does society establish a quid pro quo in the domain of rights.

A century ago, that advocate of thoroughgoing laissez-faire, Herbert Spencer, opposed a host of universally distributed public services, resting his criticisms on several grounds, including disincentive effects. Even public libraries drew his scorn.[8] After all, they offer people real income without requiring any effort in return. Indeed, free books may be doubly damned because they are a form of real income that increases the value of leisure. Spencer certainly was revealing some bizarre social attitudes, but he had a point in recognizing the inefficiency of rights.[9]

Fourth, the distribution of rights stresses equality even at the expense of equity and freedom. When people differ in capabilities, interests, and preferences, identical treatment is not equitable treatment, at least by some standards. It would be hard to defend the provision of public education out of tax revenue as equitable to the childless or the patrons of private schools, however compelling its other merits. People are not forced to exercise their rights—freedom of speech includes the right to be silent, and universal suffrage does not impose a requirement to go to the polls. But duties clearly encroach on freedom. Moreover, people are forcibly prevented from buying and selling rights; and that deprives them of freedom.

[5] Edmund Burke, *Reflections on the Revolution in France* (1st ed., 1790; Penguin Books, 1969), pp. 140–41.

[6] John Stuart Mill, *Considerations on Representative Government* (1st ed., 1875; Bobbs-Merrill, 1958), p. 136.

[7] Joseph Farkas, "One Man, ¼ Vote," *New York Times*, March 29, 1974.

[8] Herbert Spencer, *The Man versus the State* (Appleton, 1884), p. 33.

[9] To be sure, the efficiency argument is not clear-cut for public libraries, since access to books may build human capital.

That important principle—that rights cannot be bought and sold*—is the final characteristic on my list. The owner may not trade a right away to another individual either for extra helpings of other rights or for money or goods. Such bans fly in the face of the economist's traditional approach to the maximization of welfare. As James Tobin of Yale University put it, "Any good second year graduate student in economics could write a short examination paper proving that voluntary transactions in votes would increase the welfare of the sellers as well as the buyers."[10]

It takes only a little imagination to envision many new markets in rights that might arise if trades were permitted. The ban on indentured service is an obviously coercive limitation on free trade; it discourages investments by businessmen in the training and skills of their employees, and prevents bargains that might be beneficial to both the seller of his person and the buyer. The one-person, one-spouse rule could be altered to permit voluntary exchange by giving each person a marketable ticket to a spouse rather than a nontransferable right to marry one (and no more than one) person at a time. Since jury trials are expensive, society might offer any defendant who waived that right some portion of the savings. Trade in military draft obligations is easy to conceive and, in fact, has occurred in the past. Even the obligation to obey the law might be made marketable, as it was, in a figurative sense, when the Church sold indulgences during the Middle Ages.[11]

In short, the domain of rights is full of infringements on the calculus of economic efficiency. Our rights can be viewed as inefficient, because they preclude prices that would promote economizing, choices that would invoke comparative advantage, incentives that would augment socially productive effort, and trades that potentially would benefit buyer and seller alike. . . .

How and where does society draw the boundary lines between the domain of rights and that of the marketplace? It is tempting to say that rights deal with noneconomic assets while the market handles economic assets. But that is circular. Since rights may not be bought and sold for dollars, and since they are distributed freely to citizens, they automatically lack the price-tag hallmark of economic "things." In that sense, rights define and delimit the range of economic assets. The Emancipation Proclamation took human beings off the list of commodities for which the market could set price tags. Less dramatically, if fire departments operated as public utilities and thus charged for their services, they would be viewed in economic terms. Because these services are provided as a right, they are pulled outside the framework of the market. But they nonetheless involve the use of labor

---

*Editor's note: Except for those rights to possess and control things specifically provided by property rights.

[10]James Tobin, "On Limiting the Domain of Inequality," *Journal of Law and Economics*, Vol. 13 (October 1970), p. 269.

[11]According to the *Encyclopaedia Britannica*, it is a "popular misconception" that an indulgence granted "permission to commit sin." It is suggested instead that "an indulgence can perhaps be best compared to a pardoning of part of the sentence of a prisoner who has performed some good work not directly connected with either his crime or his sentence." By any interpretation, the purchaser of the indulgence was buying some amelioration of the usual workings of holy law.

and capital; they are paid for collectively through taxation; and their resource costs make them "economic."

To be sure, resource costs influence the boundary line. Any entitlement is more likely to be established as a right when it has relatively low resource costs, when economizing and comparative advantage and the other verities of the marketplace are relatively unimportant compared with the significance of broad sharing and common access.[12] It is much less expensive, in every sense, to fulfill the right to free speech than a "right" to free food. But society does provide some costly or resource-using rights, like public education. And one way proponents of equality seek to narrow the differences in standards of living among Americans is to lengthen the list of resource-using rights. A government obligation to provide suitable housing or adequate diets for every citizen would, in effect, set a higher basic minimum of real income for all families. The advocacy of new rights can be carried to extremes. I once got into a heated debate with an audience of medical administrators when, taking what I viewed as an outlandish example, I suggested that any national health program should not grant me at public expense all the pairs of eyeglasses I might like. I learned to my surprise that they favored an unlimited right to eyeglasses.

Economists run into such surprises frequently. Nearly all members of my profession would favor some reliance on "effluent fees"—prices imposed on pollutants—rather than total commitment to complex, detailed regulations, as a means of allocating the safe and tolerable amount of discharge into air and water. But most legislators denounce such proposals as selling licenses to pollute to the rich. Suggestions that stiffer tolls might unclog our highways and bridges get a hostile reception. Arguments that interest rates should be flexible enough to clear financial markets that have ample competition are greeted with derision. Apparently, many public officials and their constituents want these items to be treated as rights and kept out of the marketplace. On a first reaction, I am baffled: When money buys bread and baby's shoes, why should it not buy these things? On second thought, a glimmer of understanding shines through. I think some of the critics are most concerned about extending the list of marketable assets, in general, rather than about including these particular items. They believe the scope of the marketplace is already too great, and they oppose any changes that would add new dimensions of economic inequality.

The Fuzzy Right to Survival

While I am not persuaded by the arguments for many proposed new rights, the case for a right to survival is compelling. The assurance of dignity for every member of the society requires a right to a decent existence—to some minimum standard of nutrition, health care, and other essentials of life. Starvation and dignity do not mix well. The principle that the market should not legislate life

---

[12]Even the dividing line between the trivial "right" of free parking spaces and the economic good of metered parking fits this description. For the former, economizing through a price tag isn't worthwhile.

and death is a cliché. I do not know anyone today who would disagree, in principle, that every person, regardless of merit or ability to pay, should receive medical care and food in the face of serious illness or malnutrition. Attitudes about this issue have changed dramatically during the past century. At least some devotees of laissez-faire capitalism in the nineteenth century opposed in principle any *right* to survival, beyond the right to beg from private philanthropists. [13] To them, economic efficiency required the forceful implementation of the rule that those who do not work shall not eat.

Although the right to survival now seems to be generally accepted, it has not been explicitly written into our statute books. It has been kept fuzzy, because its fulfillment could be very expensive. A formal and clear commitment that individuals could count on would increase the number who call for help. Uncertainty holds down the resource cost. To the needy, help is where they find it. Sometimes, it is found more easily from philanthropic organizations than from public emergency facilities. Sometimes, it is available only through some demeaning proof of dire need—thus imposing a toll of shame in lieu of cash, or a sacrifice of pride for a dinner.

Ever since the days of the New Deal, however, the federal government has increasingly assumed some of these obligations and formalized some commitments. In particular, the right to some minimum standard of consumption has been established for the elderly. The evolution of old-age retirement benefits into a right is instructive. The basic philosophy of social security has been and remains contributory, stressing the obligation of people to provide for themselves. Initially, those who had not been covered by the contributory system during their working careers were not entitled to benefits upon their retirement. For the first time, legislation enacted in 1966 bestowed some minimum benefits on all Americans over the age of 72, regardless of whether they had ever contributed to the system. Since then, the level of minimal entitlements has been increased and the age requirement reduced to 65 through additional programs that supplement the standard system of old-age benefits. Currently, the principle of contribution serves mainly to preserve pride while fulfilling the right to survival. [14]

[13] Herbert Spencer, for example, wrote in *Social Statics and Man versus the State*, published in 1884: "The command 'if any would not work neither should he eat,' is simply a Christian enunciation of that universal law of Nature under which life has reached its present height—the law that a creature not energetic enough to maintain itself must die. . . ." Spencer was even skeptical of private philanthropy, arguing against the "injudicious charity" that permits "the recipients to elude the necessities of our social existence." These passages are cited in *Introduction to Contemporary Civilization in the West*, A Source Book Prepared by the Contemporary Civilization Staff of Columbia University, Vol. 2 (Columbia University Press, 1946), pp. 553, 555. Polanyi offers other examples of eighteenth and nineteenth century extremism in *The Great Transformation* (Farrar, 1944; Beacon, 1957), pp. 86–118, passim. Rereading the old-time libertarians made me realize how moderate most of the contemporary brand is by comparison.

[14] The establishment of old-age payroll-tax "contributions" as mandatory is also interesting. Once society decides it will not let old people starve (regardless of any previous profligacy or imprudence on their part), it cannot realistically permit workers to opt out of the social security system.

Issues surrounding the extension and implementation of a formal right to a decent existence are the heart of today's controversies about health insurance, the negative income tax, and welfare reform. Fulfilling that right is an urgent and feasible step toward economic equality in America. . . .

Rights of survival set floors under the consumption of the various items identified as essential. They thus preserve some incentives for economizing, and leave considerable scope for the marketplace in determining the production and distribution of food, health care, housing, and the like, for the majority of citizens who wish to, and are able to, spend more than the basic minimum that is guaranteed to all. In this respect they differ from free fire-fighting services, which are essentially unlimited and adequate to serve the needs of virtually all citizens. They also contrast with those political and civil rights that money is not allowed to buy.

Bans on Exchange

Once political and civil rights are seen as integral to human dignity, it becomes clear why they shouldn't be bought or sold for money. If someone can buy your vote, or your favorable draft number, or a contract for your indentured service, he can buy part of your dignity; he can buy power over you. By prohibiting your sale of rights, society is encroaching on your freedom, but it is also protecting you from others who might want to take your rights away. Your creditors cannot make you part with your dignity. They cannot force you into trades that are made as a last resort, which could not be fair trades and which would be distorted by vast differences in the bargaining power of the participants and by the desperation that spawns them. Any rational person who would sign a contract for indentured service must be in desperate straits. Similarly, anyone taking out a loan to cover basic consumption needs must be operating under extreme pressure; hence the religious bans on usury during the Middle Ages.[15]

Whenever the law bans trades of last resort, it shuts some potential escape valve for the person in desperate straits. In shutting the valve, society implies that there must be better ways of preventing or alleviating that desperation. When, for example, child labor was restricted, widowed mothers and disabled fathers were deprived of the opportunity to make ends meet out of the earnings of their young children. When the battle over child labor was fought in Great Britain, the proponents of the ban viewed it as part of a larger program in which society would provide the disadvantaged with aid in another and better form.[16]

Minimum-wage laws and work-safety legislation can be viewed most fruitfully as further examples of prohibitions on exchanges born of desperation, extending the logic of the ban on indentured service. Some economists strain to

[15] See Henri Pirenne, *Economic and Social History of Medieval Europe* (Harcourt, Brace, 1937), pp. 137–38.
[16] See Pigou, *Economics of Welfare*, pp. 788–90.

understand the sources of minimum-wage laws.[17] Are they justified as an offset to monopoly power in hiring labor? Do they emerge out of a conspiracy by skilled workers to reduce the job opportunities of the unskilled? Or are they urged by the skilled on the premise that wages will be raised all along the line as customary differentials are preserved? Are they well-intentioned but misguided efforts to help the poor? Similarly, some economists wonder whether work-safety legislation is warranted by lack of information about on-the-job dangers.

As I read the laws, they declare that anyone who takes an absurdly underpaid or extremely risky job must be acting out of desperation. That desperation may result from ignorance, immobility, or genuine lack of alternatives, but it should be kept out of the marketplace. Recognizing that objective still leaves plenty of room for debate about the proper scope of these laws. With these bans, society assumes a commitment to provide jobs that are not excessively risky or woefully underpaid. That commitment is often regrettably unfulfilled, and perhaps, if it were fulfilled, the bans would be unnecessary. Still, closing a bad escape valve may be an efficient way of promoting the development of better ones through the political process.

Prohibitions on exchange thus protect a variety of rights and institutions from contamination by the market. But they can also be manipulated to insulate unequal, oppressive, and hierarchical institutions from ventilation by the market. Historically, caste positions, feudal obligations, entailed land, and guild memberships have been maintained among the things that money should not buy and sell. Those bans served to promote inequality as well as economic inefficiency. Indeed, across the spectrum of primitive, ancient, medieval, and modern societies, the market has been restricted more often to preserve unequal power and distinction for the few than to guarantee equal rights for the many.[18] Tyrants, warriors, religious zealots, and dictators rarely tolerated the rivalry of the marketplace in their ordered societies. The social consequences of keeping the market in its place can be good or bad, depending on what is put in the other places. The determination to fill many of them with equal rights is a unique characteristic of a democracy. . . .

[17]A summary of the diverse justifications of economists and others for minimum-wage laws is contained in David E. Kaun, "The Fair Labour Standards Act," *South African Journal of Economics*, Vol. 33 (June 1965), pp. 131–39. For a discussion of the efficacy of minimum-wage laws in alleviating poverty and in offsetting employer control in the labor market, see George J. Stigler, "The Economics of Minimum Wage Legislation," *American Economic Review*, Vol. 36 (June 1946), pp. 358–65.

[18]Polanyi's discussions of past social arrangements illustrate this point again and again. But I doubt that he would agree with my generalization. Money arrangements generally get the lowest grades in his evaluation. Charles Kindleberger, a fellow admirer of Polanyi, also notes critically his eagerness to conclude that ". . . interferences in the market economy are justified by the need to preserve the pattern of society and the status of its members." See Charles P. Kindleberger, "The Great Transformation," *Daedalus*, Vol. 103 (Winter 1974), p. 50.

Appendix

Universal Declaration of Human Rights

•

**General Assembly
of the
United Nations**

Preamble

Whereas recognition of the inherent dignity and of the equal and inalienable rights of all members of the human family is the foundation of freedom, justice and peace in the world.

Whereas disregard and contempt for human rights have resulted in barbarous acts which have outraged the conscience of mankind, and the advent of a world in which human beings shall enjoy freedom of speech and belief and freedom from fear and want has been proclaimed as the highest aspiration of the common people,

Whereas it is essential, if man is not to be compelled to have recourse, as a last resort, to rebellion against tyranny and oppression, that human rights should be protected by the rule of law,

Whereas it is essential to promote the development of friendly relations between nations,

Whereas the peoples of the United Nations have in the Charter reaffirmed their faith in fundamental human rights, in the dignity and worth of the human person and in the equal rights of men and women and have determined to promote social progress and better standards of life in larger freedom,

Whereas Member States have pledged themselves to achieve, in co-operation with the United Nations, the promotion of universal respect for and observance of human rights and fundamental freedoms,

Whereas a common understanding of these rights and freedoms is of the greatest importance for the full realisation of this pledge,

Adopted by the General Assembly of the United Nations on 10 December 1948, at the Palais de Chaillot, Paris.

Now therefore

THE GENERAL ASSEMBLY proclaims

This Universal Declaration of Human Rights as a common standard of achievement for all peoples and all nations, to the end that every individual and every organ of society, keeping this Declaration constantly in mind, shall strive by teaching and education to promote respect for these rights and freedoms and by progressive measures, national and international, to secure their universal and effective recognition and observance, both among the peoples of Member States themselves and among the peoples of territories under their jurisdiction.

Article 1. All human beings are born free and equal in dignity and rights. They are endowed with reason and conscience and should act towards one another in a spirit of brotherhood.

Article 2. Everyone is entitled to all the rights and freedoms set forth in this Declaration, without distinction of any kind, such as race, colour, sex, language, religion, political or other opinion, national or social origin, property, birth or other status. Furthermore, no distinction shall be made on the basis of the political, jurisdictional or international status of the country or territory to which a person belongs, whether it be independent, trust, non-self-governing or under any other limitation of sovereignty.

Article 3. Everyone has the right to life, liberty and security of person.

Article 4. No one shall be held in slavery or servitude; slavery and the slave trade shall be prohibited in all their forms.

Article 5. No one shall be subjected to torture or to cruel, inhuman or degrading treatment or punishment.

Article 6. Everyone has the right to recognition everywhere as a person before the law.

Article 7. All are equal before the law and are entitled without any discrimination to equal protection of the law. All are entitled to equal protection against any discrimination in violation of this Declaration and against any incitement to such discrimination.

Article 8. Everyone has the right to an effective remedy by the competent national tribunals for acts violating the fundamental rights granted him by the constitution or by law.

Article 9. No one shall be subjected to arbitrary arrest, detention or exile.

Article 10. Everyone is entitled in full equality to a fair and public hearing by an independent and impartial tribunal, in the determination of his rights and obligations and of any criminal charge against him.

Article 11. (1) Everyone charged with a penal offence has the right to be presumed innocent until proved guilty according to law in a public trial at which he has had all the guarantees necessary for his defence.

(2) No one shall be held guilty of any penal offence on account of any act or omission which did not constitute a penal offence, under national or international

law, at the time when it was committed. Nor shall a heavier penalty be imposed than the one that was applicable at the time the penal offence was committed.

Article 12. No one shall be subjected to arbitrary interference with his privacy, family, home or correspondence, nor to attacks upon his honour and reputation. Everyone has the right to the protection of the law against such interference or attacks.

Article 13. (1) Everyone has the right to freedom of movement and residence within the borders of each state.

(2) Everyone has the right to leave any country, including his own, and to return to his country.

Article 14. (1) Everyone has the right to seek and to enjoy in other countries asylum from persecution.

(2) This right may not be invoked in the case of prosecutions genuinely arising from non-political crimes or from acts contrary to the purposes and principles of the United Nations.

Article 15. (1) Everyone has the right to a nationality.

(2) No one shall be arbitrarily deprived of his nationality nor denied the right to change his nationality.

Article 16. (1) Men and women of full age, without any limitation due to race, nationality or religion, have the right to marry and to found a family. They are entitled to equal rights as to marriage, during marriage and at its dissolution.

(2) Marriage shall be entered into only with the free and full consent of the intending spouses.

(3) The family is the natural and fundamental group unit of society and is entitled to protection by society and the State.

Article 17. (1) Everyone has the right to own property alone as well as in association with others.

(2) No one shall be arbitrarily deprived of his property.

Article 18. Everyone has the right to freedom of thought, conscience and religion; this right includes freedom to change his religion or belief, and freedom, either alone or in community with others and in public or private, to manifest his religion or belief in teaching, practice, worship and observance.

Article 19. Everyone has the right to freedom of opinion and expression; this right includes freedom to hold opinions without interference and to seek, receive and impart information and ideas through any media and regardless of frontiers.

Article 20. (1) Everyone has the right of freedom of peaceful assembly and association.

(2) No one may be compelled to belong to an association.

Article 21. (1) Everyone has the right to take part in the government of his country, directly or through freely chosen representatives.

(2) Everyone has the right of equal access to public service in his country.

(3) The will of the people shall be the basis of the authority of government; this will shall be expressed in periodic and genuine elections which shall be by

universal and equal suffrage and shall be held by secret vote or by equivalent free voting procedures.

Article 22. Everyone, as a member of society, has the right to social security and is entitled to realisation, through national effort and international co-operation and in accordance with the organisation and resources of each State, of the economic, social and cultural rights indispensable for his dignity and the free development of his personality.

Article 23. (1) Everyone has the right to work, to free choice of employment, to just and favourable conditions of work and to protection against unemployment.

(2) Everyone, without any discrimination, has the right to equal pay for equal work.

(3) Everyone who works has the right to just and favourable remuneration insuring for himself and his family an existence worthy of human dignity, and supplemented, if necessary, by other means of social protection.

(4) Everyone has the right to form and to join trade unions for the protection of his interests.

Article 24. Everyone has the right to rest and leisure, including reasonable limitation of working hours and periodic holidays with pay.

Article 25. (1) Everyone has the right to a standard of living adequate for the health and well-being of himself and of his family, including food, clothing, housing and medical care and necessary social services, and the right to security in the event of unemployment, sickness, disability, widowhood, old age or other lack of livelihood in circumstances beyond his control.

(2) Motherhood and childhood are entitled to special care and assistance. All children, whether born in or out of wedlock, shall enjoy the same social protection.

Article 26. (1) Everyone has the right to education. Education shall be free, at least in the elementary and fundamental stages. Elementary education shall be compulsory. Technical and professional education shall be made generally available and higher education shall be equally accessible to all on the basis of merit.

(2) Education shall be directed to the full development of the human personality and to the strengthening of respect for human rights and fundamental freedoms. It shall promote understanding, tolerance and friendship among all nations, racial or religious groups, and shall further the activities of the United Nations for the maintenance of peace.

(3) Parents have a prior right to choose the kind of education that shall be given to their children.

Article 27. (1) Everyone has the right freely to participate in the cultural life of the community, to enjoy the arts and to share in scientific advancement and its benefits.

(2) Everyone has the right to the protection of the moral and material interests resulting from any scientific, literary or artistic production of which he is the author.

Article 28. Everyone is entitled to a social and international order in which the rights and freedoms set forth in this Declaration can be fully realised.

Article 29. (1) Everyone has duties to the community in which alone the free and full development of his personality is possible.

(2) In the exercise of his rights and freedoms, everyone shall be subject only to such limitations as are determined by law solely for the purpose of securing due recognition and respect for the rights and freedoms of others and of meeting the just requirements of morality, public order and the general welfare in a democratic society.

(3) These rights and freedoms may in no case be exercised contrary to the purposes and principles of the United Nations.

Article 30. Nothing in this Declaration may be interpreted as implying for any State, group or person any right to engage in any activity or to perform any act aimed at the destruction of any of the rights and freedoms set forth herein.

Wyman,
*Commissioner of New York
Department of Social Services,
et al.* v. *James*
•

Supreme Court of the United States

Mr. Justice Blackmun delivered the opinion of the Court.

This appeal presents the issue whether a beneficiary of the program for Aid to Families with Dependent Children (AFDC) may refuse a home visit by the caseworker without risking the termination of benefits.

The New York State and City social services commissioners appeal from a judgment and decree of a divided three-judge District Court. . . .

The District Court majority held that a mother receiving AFDC relief may refuse, without forfeiting her right to that relief, the periodic home visit which the cited New York statutes and regulations prescribe as a condition for the continuance of assistance under the program. The beneficiary's thesis, and that of the District Court majority, is that home visitation is a search and, when not consented to or when not supported by a warrant based on probable cause, violates the beneficiary's Fourth and Fourteenth Amendment rights. . . .

Plaintiff Barbara James is the mother of a son, Maurice, who was born in May 1967. They reside in New York City. Mrs. James first applied for AFDC assistance shortly before Maurice's birth. A caseworker made a visit to her apartment at that time without objection. The assistance was authorized.

Two years later, on May 8, 1969, a caseworker wrote Mrs. James that she would visit her home on May 14. Upon receipt of this advice, Mrs. James telephoned the worker that, although she was willing to supply information "reasonable and relevant" to her need for public assistance, any discussion was not to take place at her home. The worker told Mrs. James that she was required by law to visit in her home and that refusal to permit the visit would result in the termination of assistance. Permission was still denied. . . .

400 U.S. 309 (1971). Decided January 12, 1971.

A notice of termination issued on June 2.

Thereupon, without seeking a hearing at the state level, Mrs. James, individually and on behalf of Maurice, and purporting to act on behalf of all other persons similarly situated, instituted the present civil rights suit. . . .

When a case involves a home and some type of official intrusion into that home, as this case appears to do, an immediate and natural reaction is one of concern about Fourth Amendment rights and the protection which that Amendment is intended to afford. Its emphasis indeed is upon one of the most precious aspects of personal security in the home: "The right of the people to be secure in their persons, houses, papers, and effects. . . ." This Court has characterized that right as "basic to a free society. . . ." And over the years the Court consistently has been most protective of the privacy of the dwelling. . . .

This natural and quite proper protective attitude, however, is not a factor in this case, for the seemingly obvious and simple reason that we are not concerned here with any search by the New York social service agency in the Fourth Amendment meaning of that term. It is true that the governing statute and regulations appear to make mandatory the initial home visit and the subsequent periodic "contacts" (which may include home visits) for the inception and continuance of aid. It is also true that the caseworker's posture in the home visit is perhaps, in a sense, both rehabilitative and investigative. But this latter aspect, we think, is given too broad a character and far more emphasis than it deserves if it is equated with a search in the traditional criminal law context. We note, too, that the visitation in itself is not forced or compelled, and that the beneficiary's denial of permission is not a criminal act. If consent to the visitation is withheld, no visitation takes place. The aid then never begins or merely ceases, as the case may be. There is no entry of the home and there is no search. . . .

. . . It is unreasonableness which is the Fourth Amendment's standard. . . .

There are a number of factors that compel us to conclude that the home visit proposed for Mrs. James is not unreasonable.

The public's interest in this particular segment of the area of assistance to the unfortunate is protection and aid for the dependent child whose family requires such aid for that child. . . . The dependent child's needs are paramount, and only with hesitancy would we relegate those needs, in the scale of comparative values, to a position secondary to what the mother claims as her rights.

The agency, with tax funds provided from federal as well as from state sources, is fulfilling a public trust. The State, working through its qualified welfare agency, has appropriate and paramount interest and concern in seeing and assuring that the intended and proper objects of that tax-produced assistance are the ones who benefit from the aid it dispenses. . . .

One who dispenses purely private charity naturally has an interest in and expects to know how his charitable funds are utilized and put to work. The public, when it is the provider, rightly expects the same. It might well expect more, because of the trust aspect of public funds, and the recipient, as well as the caseworker, has not only an interest but an obligation. . . .

We therefore conclude that the home visitation as structured by the New York statutes and regulations is a reasonable administrative tool; that it serves a valid and proper administrative purpose for the dispensation of the AFDC program; that it is not an unwarranted invasion of personal privacy; and that it violates no right guaranteed by the Fourth Admendment.

Reversed and remanded with directions to enter a judgment of dismissal.

It is so ordered. . . .

MR. JUSTICE DOUGLAS, dissenting. . . .

In 1969 roughly 127 billion dollars were spent by the federal, state, and local governments on "social welfare." To farmers alone almost four billion dollars were paid, in part for not growing certain crops. . . .

Yet almost every beneficiary whether rich or poor, rural or urban, has a "house"—one of the places protected by the Fourth Amendment against "unreasonable searches and seizures." The question in this case is whether receipt of largesse from the government makes the *home* of the beneficiary subject to access by an inspector of the agency of oversight, even though the beneficiary objects to the intrusion and even though the Fourth Amendment's procedure for access to one's *house* or *home* is not followed. The penalty here is not, of course, invasion of the privacy of Barbara James, only her loss of federal or state largesse. That, however, is merely rephrasing the problem. Whatever the semantics, the central question is whether the government by force of its largesse has the power to "buy up" rights guaranteed by the Constitution. But for the assertion of her constitutional right, Barbara James in this case would have received the welfare benefit. . . .

. . . In *See* we [decided] that the "businessman, like the occupant of a residence, has a constitutional right to go about his business free from unreasonable official entries upon his private commercial property." *Id.,* at 543. There is not the slightest hint in *See* that the Government could condition a business license on the "consent" of the licensee to the administrative searches we held violated the Fourth Amendment. It is a strange jurisprudence indeed which safeguards the businessman at his place of work from warrantless searches but will not do the same for a mother in her *home*.

Is a search of her home without a warrant made "reasonable" merely because she is dependent on government largesse?

Judge Skelly Wright has stated the problem succinctly:

> *"Welfare has long been considered the equivalent of charity and its recipients have been subjected to all kinds of dehumanizing experiences in the government's effort to police its welfare payments. In fact, over half a billion dollars are expended annually for administration and policing in connection with the Aid to Families with Dependent Children program. Why such large sums are necessary for administration and policing has never been adequately explained. No such sums are spent policing the government subsidies granted to farmers, airlines, steamship companies, and junk mail dealers, to name but a few. The truth is that in this subsidy area society has simply adopted a double standard, one for aid to business*

and the farmer and a different one for welfare." Poverty, Minorities, and Respect For Law, 1970 Duke L. J. 425, 437–438.

I would sustain the judgment of the three-judge court in the present case.

MR. JUSTICE MARSHALL, whom MR. JUSTICE BRENNAN joins, dissenting.

. . . The record plainly shows . . . that Mrs. James offered to furnish any information that the appellants desired and to be interviewed at any place other than her home. Appellants rejected her offers and terminated her benefits solely on the ground that she refused to permit a home visit. In addition, appellants make no contention that any sort of probable cause exists to suspect appellee of welfare fraud or child abuse.

Simply stated, the issue in this case is whether a state welfare agency can require all recipients of AFDC benefits to submit to warrantless "visitations" of their homes. In answering that question, the majority dodges between constitutional issues to reach a result clearly inconsistent with the decisions of this Court. We are told that there is no search involved in this case; that even if there were a search, it would not be unreasonable; and that even if this were an unreasonable search, a welfare recipient waives her right to object by accepting benefits. I emphatically disagree with all three conclusions. . . .

. . . In an era of rapidly burgeoning governmental activities and their concomitant inspectors, caseworkers, and researchers, a restriction of the Fourth Amendment to "the traditional criminal law context" tramples the ancient concept that a man's home is his castle. Only last Term, we reaffirmed that this concept has lost none of its vitality. . . .

. . . [I]t is argued that the home visit is justified to protect dependent children from "abuse" and "exploitation." These are heinous crimes, but they are not confined to indigent households. Would the majority sanction, in the absence of probable cause, compulsory visits to all American homes for the purpose of discovering child abuse? Or is this Court prepared to hold as a matter of constitutional law that a mother, merely because she is poor, is substantially more likely to injure or exploit her children? Such a categorical approach to an entire class of citizens would be dangerously at odds with the tenets of our democracy. . . .

Although the Court does not agree with my conclusion that the home visit is an unreasonable search, its opinion suggests that even if the visit were unreasonable, appellee has somehow waived her right to object. Surely the majority cannot believe that valid Fourth Amendment consent can be given under the threat of the loss of one's sole means of support. . . .

In deciding that the homes of AFDC recipients are not entitled to protection from warrantless searches by welfare caseworkers, the Court declines to follow prior case law and employs a rationale that, if applied to the claims of all citizens, would threaten the vitality of the Fourth Amendment. . . . Perhaps the majority has explained why a commercial warehouse deserves more protection than does this poor woman's home. I am not convinced; and, therefore, I must respectfully dissent.

San Antonio Independent School District et al. v. Rodriguez et al.

•

Supreme Court of the United States

MR. JUSTICE POWELL delivered the opinion of the Court.

This suit attacking the Texas system of financing public education was initiated by Mexican-American parents whose children attend the elementary and secondary schools in the Edgewood Independent School District, an urban school district in San Antonio, Texas. They brought a class action on behalf of schoolchildren throughout the State who are members of minority groups or who are poor and reside in school districts having a low property tax base. Named as defendants were the State Board of Education, the Commissioner of Education, the State Attorney General, and the Bexar County (San Antonio) Board of Trustees. The complaint was filed in the summer of 1968 and a three-judge court was impaneled in January 1969. In December 1971 the panel rendered its judgment in a *per curiam* opinion holding the Texas school finance system unconstitutional under the Equal Protection Clause of the Fourteenth Amendment. The State appealed, and we noted probable jurisdiction to consider the far-reaching constitutional questions presented. . . . For the reasons stated in this opinion, we reverse the decision of the District Court. . . .

The school district in which appellees reside, the Edgewood Independent School District, has been compared throughout this litigation with the Alamo Heights Independent School District. This comparison between the least and most affluent districts in the San Antonio area serves to illustrate the manner in which the dual system of finance operates and to indicate the extent to which substantial disparities exist despite the State's impressive progress in recent years. Edgewood is one of seven public school districts in the metropolitan area. Approximately 22,000 students are enrolled in its 25 elementary and secondary schools. The district is situated in the core-city sector of San Antonio in a residential neighborhood that has little commercial or industrial property. The residents are predominantly of

411 U.S. 1 (1973). Decided March 21, 1973.

Mexican-American descent: approximately 90% of the student population is Mexican-American and over 6% is Negro. The average assessed property value per pupil is $5,960—the lowest in the metropolitan area—and the median family income ($4,686) is also the lowest. At an equalized tax rate of $1.05 per $100 of assessed property—the highest in the metropolitan area—the district contributed $26 to the education of each child for the 1967–1968 school year above its Local Fund Assignment for the Minimum Foundation Program. The Foundation Program contributed $222 per pupil for a state-local total of $248. Federal funds added another $108 for a total of $356 per pupil.

Alamo Heights is the most affluent school district in San Antonio. Its six schools, housing approximately 5,000 students, are situated in a residential community quite unlike the Edgewood District. The school population is predominantly "Anglo," having only 18% Mexican-Americans and less than 1% Negroes. The assessed property value per pupil exceeds $49,000, and the median family income is $8,001. In 1967–1968 the local tax rate of $.85 per $100 of valuation yielded $333 per pupil over and above its contribution to the Foundation Program. Coupled with the $225 provided from that Program, the district was able to supply $558 per student. Supplemented by a $36 per-pupil grant from federal sources, Alamo Heights spent $594 per pupil. . . .

. . . [T]hese disparities, largely attributable to differences in the amounts of money collected through local property taxation . . . led the District Court to conclude that Texas' dual system of public school financing violated the Equal Protection Clause. The District Court held that the Texas system discriminates on the basis of wealth in the manner in which education is provided for its people. . . . Finding that *wealth* is a *"suspect"* classification and that *education* is a *"fundamental"* interest, the District Court held that the Texas system could be sustained only if the State could show that it was premised upon some compelling state interest. *Id.*, at 282–284. On this issue the court concluded that "[n]ot only are defendants unable to demonstrate compelling state interests . . . they fail even to establish a reasonable basis for these classifications." . . .

Texas virtually concedes that its historically rooted dual system of financing education could not withstand the strict judicial scrutiny that this Court has found appropriate in reviewing legislative judgments that interfere with fundamental constitutional rights or that involve suspect classifications. If, as previous decisions have indicated, strict scrutiny means that the State's system is not entitled to the usual presumption of validity, that the State rather than the complainants must carry a "heavy burden of justification," that the State must demonstrate that its educational system has been structured with "precision," and is "tailored" narrowly to serve legitimate objectives and that it has selected the "less drastic means" for effectuating its objectives, the Texas financing system and its counterpart in virtually every other State will not pass muster. . . . [T]he State defends the system's rationality with vigor and disputes the District Court's finding that it lacks a "reasonable basis."

This, then, establishes the framework for our analysis. We must decide, first, whether the Texas system of financing public education operates to the disadvantage of some suspect class or impinges upon a fundamental right explicitly or implicitly protected by the Constitution, thereby requiring strict judicial scrutiny. If so, the judgment of the District Court should be affirmed. If not, the Texas scheme must still be examined to determine whether it rationally furthers some legitimate, articulated state purpose and therefore does not constitute an invidious discrimination in violation of the Equal Protection Clause of the Fourteenth Amendment.

The District Court's opinion does not reflect the novelty and complexity of the constitutional questions posed by appellees' challenge to Texas' system of school financing. In concluding that strict judicial scrutiny was required, that court relied on decisions dealing with the rights of indigents to equal treatment in the criminal trial and appellate processes, and on cases disapproving wealth restrictions on the right to vote. Those cases, the District Court concluded, established wealth as a suspect classification. Finding that the local property tax system discriminated on the basis of wealth, it regarded those precedents as controlling. It then reasoned, based on decisions of this Court affirming the undeniable importance of education, that there is a fundamental right to education and that, absent some compelling state justification, the Texas system could not stand.

We are unable to agree that this case, which in significant aspects is *sui generis,* may be so neatly fitted into the conventional mosaic of constitutional analysis under the Equal Protection Clause. Indeed, for the several reasons that follow, we find neither the suspect-classification nor the fundamental-interest analysis persuasive.

The wealth discrimination discovered by the District Court in this case, and by several other courts that have recently struck down school-financing laws in other States,* is quite unlike any of the forms of wealth discrimination heretofore reviewed by this Court. Rather than focusing on the unique features of the alleged discrimination, the courts in these cases have virtually assumed their findings of a suspect classification through a simplistic process of analysis: since, under the traditional systems of financing public schools, some poorer people receive less expensive educations than other more affluent people, these systems discriminate on the basis of wealth. This approach largely ignores the hard threshold questions, including whether it makes a difference for purposes of consideration under the Constitution that the class of disadvantaged "poor" cannot be identified or defined in customary equal protection terms, and whether the relative—rather than absolute—nature of the asserted deprivation is of significant consequence. Before a State's laws and the justifications for the classifications they create are subjected to strict judicial scrutiny, we think these threshold considerations must be analyzed more closely than they were in the court below. . . .

. . . The individuals, or groups of individuals, who constituted the class discriminated against in our prior cases shared two distinguishing characteristics:

Serrano v. *Priest,* 5 Cal. 3d 584, 487 P. 2d 1241 (1971); *Van Dusartz* v. *Hatfield,* 334 F. Supp. 870 (Minn. 1971); *Robinson* v. *Cahill,* 118 N. J. Super. 223, 287 A. 2d 187 (1972); *Milliken* v. *Green,* 389 Mich. 1, 203 N. W. 2d 457 (1972), rehearing granted, Jan. 1973.

because of their impecunity they were completely unable to pay for some desired benefit, and as a consequence, they sustained an absolute deprivation of a meaningful opportunity to enjoy that benefit. . . .

. . . [N]either appellees nor the District Court addressed the fact that, unlike the foregoing cases, lack of personal resources has not occasioned an absolute deprivation of the desired benefit. The argument here is not that the children in districts having relatively low assessable property values are receiving no public education; rather, it is that they are receiving a poorer quality education than that available to children in districts having more assessable wealth. Apart from the unsettled and disputed question whether the quality of education may be determined by the amount of money expended for it, a sufficient answer to appellees' argument is that, at least where wealth is involved, the Equal Protection Clause does not require absolute equality or precisely equal advantages. . . .

. . . [I]n recognition of the fact that this Court has never heretofore held that wealth discrimination alone provides an adequate basis for invoking strict scrutiny, appellees have not relied solely on this contention. They also assert that the State's system impermissibly interferes with the exercise of a "fundamental" right and that accordingly the prior decisions of this Court require the application of the strict standard of judicial review. . . . It is this question—whether education is a fundamental right, in the sense that it is among the rights and liberties protected by the Constitution—which has so consumed the attention of courts and commentators in recent years.

In *Brown* v. *Board of Education,* . . . a unanimous Court recognized that "education is perhaps the most important function of state and local governments." *Id.,* at 493. What was said there in the context of racial discrimination has lost none of its vitality with the passage of time. . . .

> *". . . In these days, it is doubtful that any child may reasonably be expected to succeed in life if he is denied the opportunity of an education. Such an opportunity, where the state has undertaken to provide it, is a right which must be made available to all on equal terms."* . . .

. . . But the importance of a service performed by the State does not determine whether it must be regarded as fundamental for purposes of examination under the Equal Protection Clause. . . .

. . . It is not the province of this Court to create substantive constitutional rights in the name of guaranteeing equal protection of the laws. Thus, the key to discovering whether education is "fundamental" is not to be found in comparisons of the relative societal significance of education as opposed to subsistence or housing. Nor is it to be found by weighing whether education is as important as the right to travel. Rather, the answer lies in assessing whether there is a right to education explicitly or implicitly guaranteed by the Constitution. . . .

Education, of course, is not among the rights afforded explicit protection under our Federal Constitution. Nor do we find any basis for saying it is implicitly so protected. . . . It is appellees' contention, however, that education is distinguishable from other services and benefits provided by the State because it bears a peculiarly close relationship to other rights and liberties accorded protection under the Constitution. Specifically, they insist that education is itself a fundamental personal right because it is essential to the effective exercise of First Amendment freedoms and to intelligent utilization of the right to vote. In asserting a nexus between speech and education, appellees urge that the right to speak is meaningless unless the speaker is capable of articulating his thoughts intelligently and persuasively. The "marketplace of ideas" is an empty forum for those lacking basic communicative tools. Likewise, they argue that the corollary right to receive information becomes little more than a hollow privilege when the recipient has not been taught to read, assimilate, and utilize available knowledge.

A similar line of reasoning is pursued with respect to the right to vote. Exercise of the franchise, it is contended, cannot be divorced from the educational foundation of the voter. The electoral process, if reality is to conform to the democratic ideal, depends on an informed electorate: a voter cannot cast his ballot intelligently unless his reading skills and thought processes have been adequately developed. . . .

. . . Whatever merit appellees' argument might have if a State's financing system occasioned an absolute denial of educational opportunities to any of its children, that argument provides no basis for finding an interference with fundamental rights where only relative differences in spending levels are involved. . . .

. . . [T]he logical limitations on appellees' nexus theory are difficult to perceive. How, for instance, is education to be distinguished from the significant personal interests in the basics of decent food and shelter? Empirical examination might well buttress an assumption that the ill-fed, ill-clothed, and ill-housed are among the most ineffective participants in the political process, and that they derive the least enjoyment from the benefits of the First Amendment. . . .

We have carefully considered each of the arguments supportive of the District Court's finding that education is a fundamental right or liberty and have found those arguments unpersuasive. . . .

MR. JUSTICE MARSHALL, with whom MR. JUSTICE DOUGLAS concurs, dissenting.

The Court today decides, in effect, that a State may constitutionally vary the quality of education which it offers its children in accordance with the amount of taxable wealth located in the school districts within which they reside. The majority's decision represents an abrupt departure from the mainstream of recent state and federal court decisions concerning the unconstitutionality of state educational financing schemes dependent upon taxable local wealth. More unfortunately, though, the majority's holding can only be seen as a retreat from our historic commitment to equality of educational opportunity and as unsupportable acquiescence in a system which deprives children in their earliest years of the chance to reach their full potential as citizens. The Court does this despite the absence of any substantial justification for a scheme which arbitrarily channels educational resources in accordance with the fortuity of the amount of taxable wealth within each district.

In my judgment, the right of every American to an equal start in life, so far as the provision of a state service as important as education is concerned, is far too vital to permit state discrimination on grounds as tenuous as those presented by this record. Nor can I accept the notion that it is sufficient to remit these appellees to the vagaries of the political process which, contrary to the majority's suggestion, has proved singularly unsuited to the task of providing a remedy for this discrimination. I, for one, am unsatisfied with the hope of an ultimate "political" solution sometime in the indefinite future while, in the meantime, countless children unjustifiably receive inferior educations that "may affect their hearts and minds in a way unlikely ever to be undone." *Brown* v. *Board of Education*, 347 U.S. 483, 494 (1954). I must therefore respectfully dissent. . . .

. . . [T]his Court has never suggested that because some "adequate" level of benefits is provided to all, discrimination in the provision of services is therefore constitutionally excusable. The Equal Protection Clause is not addressed to the minimal sufficiency but rather to the unjustifiable inequalities of state action. It mandates nothing less than that "all persons similarly circumstanced shall be treated alike." . . .

Even if the Equal Protection Clause encompassed some theory of constitutional adequacy, discrimination in the provision of educational opportunity would certainly seem to be a poor candidate for its application. Neither the majority nor appellants inform us how judicially manageable standards are to be derived for determining how much education is "enough" to excuse constitutional discrimination. One would think that the majority would heed its own fervent affirmation of judicial self-restraint before undertaking the complex task of determining at large what level of education is constitutionally sufficient. . . .

In my view, then, it is inequality—not some notion of gross inadequacy—of educational opportunity that raises a question of denial of equal protection of the laws.

. . . A principled reading of what this Court has done reveals that it has applied a spectrum of standards in reviewing discrimination allegedly violative of the Equal Protection Clause. This spectrum clearly comprehends variations in the degree of care with which the Court will scrutinize particular classifications, depending, I believe, on the constitutional and societal importance of the interest adversely affected and the recognized invidiousness of the basis upon which the particular classification is drawn. . . .

I therefore cannot accept the majority's labored efforts to demonstrate that fundamental interests, which call for strict scrutiny of the challenged classification, encompass only established rights which we are somehow bound to recognize from the text of the Constitution itself. To be sure, some interests which the Court has deemed to be fundamental for purposes of equal protection analysis are themselves constitutionally protected rights. Thus, discrimination against the guaranteed right of freedom of speech has called for strict judicial scrutiny. . . . But it will not do to suggest that the "answer" to whether an interest is fundamental for purposes of equal protection analysis is *always* determined by whether that interest "is a right . . . explicitly or implicitly guaranteed by the Constitution." . . .

I would like to know where the Constitution guarantees the right to procreate . . . or the right to vote in state elections, . . . or the right to an appeal from a criminal conviction. . . . These are instances in which, due to the importance of the interests at stake, the Court has displayed a strong concern with the existence of discriminatory state treatment. But the Court has never said or indicated that these are interests which independently enjoy full-blown constitutional protection. . . .

. . . This Court has frequently recognized that discrimination on the basis of wealth may create a classification of a suspect character and thereby call for exacting judicial scrutiny. See, *e.g., Griffin* v. *Illinois,* 351 U.S. 12 (1956); *Douglas* v. *California,* 372 U.S. 353 (1963); *McDonald* v. *Board of Election Comm'rs of Chicago,* 394 U.S. 802, 807 (1969). The majority, however, considers any wealth classification in this case to lack certain essential characteristics which it contends are common to the instances of wealth discrimination that this Court has heretofore recognized. We are told that in every prior case involving a wealth classification, the members of the disadvantaged class have "shared two distinguishing characteristics: because of their impecunity they were completely unable to pay for some desired benefit, and as a consequence, they sustained an absolute deprivation of a meaningful opportunity to enjoy that benefit." . . . I cannot agree. The Court's distinctions . . . are not in fact consistent with the decisions in *Harper* v. *Virginia Bd. of Elections,* . . . or *Griffin* v. *Illinois,* . . . or *Douglas* v. *California.* . . .

In *Harper,* the Court struck down as violative of the Equal Protection Clause an annual Virginia poll tax of $1.50, payment of which by persons over the age of 21 was a prerequisite to voting in Virginia elections. . . . [T]he Court struck down the poll tax *in toto;* it did not order merely that those too poor to pay the tax be exempted; complete impecunity clearly was not determinative of the limits of the disadvantaged class, nor was it essential to make an equal protection claim.

Similarly, *Griffin* and *Douglas* refute the majority's contention that we have in the past required an absolute deprivation before subjecting wealth classifications to strict scrutiny. The Court characterizes *Griffin* as a case concerned simply with the denial of a transcript or an adequate substitute therefor, and *Douglas* as involving the denial of counsel. But in both cases the question was in fact whether "a State that [grants] *appellate review* can do so in a way that discriminates against some convicted defendants on account of their poverty." *Griffin* v. *Illinois, supra,* at 18 (emphasis added). In that regard, the Court concluded that inability to purchase a transcript denies "the poor an adequate *appellate review* accorded to all who have money enough to pay the costs in advance," *ibid.* (emphasis added), and that "the type of an *appeal* a person is afforded . . . hinges upon whether or not he can pay for the assistance of counsel," *Douglas* v. *California,* . . . (emphasis added). The right of appeal itself was not absolutely denied to those too poor to pay; but because of the cost of a transcript and of counsel, the appeal was a substantially less meaningful right for the poor than for the rich. It was on these terms that the Court found a denial of equal protection, and those terms clearly encompassed degrees of discrimination on the basis of wealth which do not amount to outright denial of the affected right or interest. . . .

Nor can we ignore the extent to which, in contrast to our prior decisions, the State is responsible for the wealth discrimination in this instance. *Griffin, Douglas, Williams, Tate,* and our other prior cases have dealt with discrimination on the basis of indigency which was attributable to the operation of the private sector. But we have no such simple *de facto* wealth discrimination here. The means for financing public education in Texas are selected and specified by the State. It is the State that has created local school districts, and tied educational funding to the local property tax and thereby to local district wealth. At the same time, governmentally imposed land use controls have undoubtedly encouraged and rigidified natural trends in the allocation of particular areas for residential or commercial use, and thus determined each district's amount of taxable property wealth. In short, this case, in contrast to the Court's previous wealth discrimination decisions, can only be seen as "unusual in the extent to which governmental action *is* the cause of the wealth classifications."

In the final analysis, then, the invidious characteristics of the group wealth classification present in this case merely serve to emphasize the need for careful judicial scrutiny of the State's justifications for the resulting interdistrict discrimination in the educational opportunity afforded to the schoolchildren of Texas. . . .

The Court seeks solace for its action today in the possibility of legislative reform. The Court's suggestions of legislative redress and experimentation will doubtless be of great comfort to the schoolchildren of Texas' disadvantaged districts, but considering the vested interests of wealthy school districts in the preservation of the status quo, they are worth little more. The possibility of legislative action is, in all events, no answer to this Court's duty under the Constitution to eliminate unjustified state discrimination. . . .

I would therefore affirm the judgment of the District Court.

Suggestions for Further
Reading

In addition to many of the longer works from which selections in this book have been made, and in addition to various of the works referred to in the footnotes, the following are recommended:

Aiken, William, and LaFollette, Hugh, eds. *World Hunger and Moral Obligation.* Englewood Cliffs, N.J.: Prentice-Hall, 1977.

Bell, Daniel. *The Coming of Post-Industrial Society.* New York: Basic Books, 1973.

Benn, S. I., and Peters, R. S. *The Principles of Political Thought.* New York: Free Press, 1959, Chaps. 5–7 and 13.

Braverman, Harry. *Labor and Monopoly Capitalism.* New York: Monthly Review Press, 1974.

Best, Michael, and Connolly, William E. *The Politicized Economy.* Lexington, Mass.: D. C. Heath, 1976.

Bowie, Norman E., and Simon, Robert L. *The Individual and the Political Order.* Englewood Cliffs, N.J.: Prentice-Hall, 1977, Chap. 7.

Brown, Peter, and MacLean, Douglas, eds., *Human Rights and U.S. Foreign Policy.* Lexington, Mass.: D.C. Heath, 1979, Pt. II.

Commoner, Barry. *The Poverty of Power.* New York: Bantam, 1976.

Daniels, Norman, ed. *Reading Rawls.* New York: Basic Books, 1975.

Dobb, Maurice. *Political Economy and Capitalism.* Westport, Conn.: Greenwood Press, 1972.

Dworkin, Gerald; Bermant, Gordon; and Brown, Peter G.; eds. *Markets and Morals.* Washington: Hemisphere Pub. Corp., Joh Wiley, 1977.

Ezorsky, Gertrude. "It's Mine," *Philosophy and Public Affairs* 3 (1974): 321–30.

Friedman, Milton. *Capitalism and Freedom*. Chicago: University of Chicago Press, 1956.

Galbraith, John Kenneth. *The New Industrial State*. New York: New American Library, 1967.

———. *Economics and the Public Purpose*. New York: New American Library, 1975.

Gewirth, Alan. *Reason and Morality*. Chicago: University of Chicago Press, 1978.

Harrington, Michael. *Socialism*. New York. Bantam Books, 1970.

———. *The Twilight of Capitalism*. New York: Simon & Schuster, 1976.

Heilbroner, Robert L. *The Worldly Philosophers*. New York: Simon & Schuster, 1972 (first published 1953).

———. *An Inquiry into the Human Prospect*. New York: W. W. Norton, 1975.

Held, Virginia. "John Locke on Robert Nozick," *Social Research* 43 (Spring 1976): 169–95.

———. "Men, Women, and Equal Liberty." In *Equality and Social Policy*, ed. Walter Feinberg. Urbana, Ill.: University of Illinois Press, 1978, pp. 66–81.

Henkin, Louis. "Rights, American and Human," *Columbia Law Review* 79 (April 1979): 405–25.

Hunnius, Gerry; Garson, G. David; and Case, John; eds. *Workers' Control: A Reader on Labor and Social Change*. New York: Vintage, 1973.

Lekachman, Robert. *Economists at Bay*. New York: McGraw-Hill, 1976.

Loevinsohn, Ernest. "Liberty and the Redistribution of Property," *Philosophy and Public Affairs* 6 (Spring 1977): 226–39.

Peffer, Rodney. "A Defense of Rights to Well-Being," *Philosophy and Public Affairs* 8 (Fall 1978): 65–87.

Phelphs, Edmund, ed. *Economic Justice*. Baltimore, Md.: Penguin Education, 1973.

Philosophical Forum. Special Issue: Work. Vol X, Nos. 2–4, 1978–79.

Postow, Betsy. "Coercion and the Bindingness of Contracts," *Social Theory and Practice* 4 (Fall 1976): 75–92.

Schumpeter, Joseph. *Capitalism, Socialism and Democracy*. New York: Harper & Row, 1975. First published 1942.

Schweickart, David. "Capitalism, Contribution and Sacrifice," *The Philosophical Forum* (1976): 260–76.

Sen, Amartya. *On Economic Inequality*. Oxford: Clarendon Press, 1973.

Sterba, James. "Justice as Desert," *Social Theory and Practice* 3 (Spring 1974): 101–16.

Tay, Alice Erh-Soon. "Property and Law in the Society of Mass Production, Mass Consumption and Mass Allocation," *ARSP, Equality and Freedom*. Wiesbaden: Franz Steiner Verlag, 1977, pp. 87–106.

Winch, D. M., *Analytical Welfare Economics*. Baltimore, Md.: Penguin, 1971.